Forgiveness Offers Everything I Want

ALSO BY SUSAN DUGAN

Safe Haven

Extraordinary Ordinary Forgiveness

Forgiveness Offers Everything I Want

SUSAN DUGAN

Reviews

"This is the truest practice of forgiveness *A Course in Miracles*-style you will find! Entertaining, practical, humorous, and delightful! Susan Dugan shows us through her life experiences the practical application of true forgiveness and we get to witness first-hand the peace and release that follows every time. At no point are we left stranded or wondering—Susan takes us all the way and straight into the arms of Love, and shows us how true forgiveness always leaves us embracing a much more peaceful, happy, and loving life. *Forgiveness Offers Everything I Want* is a wonderful book, written by an extremely dedicated Course teacher/student!"
—Robyn Busfield, author of *Forgiveness Is the Home of Miracles*

"Susan Dugan's writing is a joyous gift to the soul hungry for companionship on this rocky *A Course in Miracles* path Home. As recounted in *Forgiveness Offers Everything I Want*, no inner obstacle can stand against her ability to make us laugh along with her. Life, sometimes mundane, often irritating and even frightening, appears in crisp detail under her pen, and is transformed through her clear vision of forgiveness. Our inner teacher comes vividly alive through her words in a very rare, delightful way. For more than two years her regular articles at www.foraysinforgiveness.com have helped correct a major misperception of mine: we do not walk alone. In fact, the true blessing Susan shares is her absolute equality with all *A Course in Miracles* students. Allow her to take your hand in this wonderful book and remind you of your own inner teacher. He is indeed there, smiling, even as you bring him your darkest inner secrets, as Susan does."
—Bernard Groom, ACIM teacher and student, author of *Paulo and the Magician*, director of the French Centre for *A Course in Miracles*, thelighthouseinfrance@yahoo.com

"This collection of humorous and insightful vignettes highlighting the less-traveled road to true forgiveness will amuse and inform. Each brief, personal story of persevering on toward love and away from fear is both a delight and a road map for those on the path. Easy to read but laced with important truths,

Forgiveness Offers Everything I Want will leave you smiling and encouraged. Enjoy!"
—Carol Howe, author of *Never Forget to Laugh: Personal Recollections of Bill Thetford, Co-Scribe of A Course in Miracles*

"Susan Dugan has a knack for putting her readers directly in the middle of her own forgiveness experiences. I'd describe the experience of reading *Forgiveness Offers Everything I Want* and much of Susan's writings as virtual vicarious forgiveness. Or, to put it another way, it's like armchair forgiveness, which, in my experience, is the most pleasant kind. By following Susan's forgiveness thought process, the reader is led to the right mind, which is where we all should want to be. You can't go wrong letting Susan Dugan take you on a journey through her forgiveness experiences. She's certainly helped keep me on course."
—Alexander Marchand, author and artist of *The Universe Is a Dream*

"Susan Dugan is an excellent writer. She has a way with words and she has written a superb book chronicling her progress in moving into understanding, and integrating the teachings of *A Course in Miracles*. *Forgiveness Offers Everything I Want* is written in a seductive, conversational style drawing the reader into going through what Susan is going through, as she makes the Course come alive in her life."
—Jon Mundy, Ph.D., author of *Living A Course in Miracles*

"With Forgiveness Offers Everything I Want, Susan Dugan offers us poignant, sometimes very humorous, and always helpful examples of true-life forgiveness, how you can do it, and why, as *A Course in Miracles* puts it, forgiveness does indeed offer everything we want. It may not always fit our pictures of what we think we want, but through us the Holy Spirit leads us to peace, which is a prerequisite to returning home to our Source. We highly recommend it!"
—Gary Renard, best-selling author of *The Disappearance of the Universe* and Cindy Lora-Renard, MA, spiritual psychology

For Laura, who yearned

Contents

Foreword..XI

Acknowledgments XIII

A Word from the Author.. XV

The Unbearable Heaviness of Being 1

Spring Fever 4

Time-Out 9

Technological Difficulties.. 13

Hooray for Hollywood!.. 17

Faith, Hope, and Clarity 21

Pain Is a Wrong Perspective 24

There's No Place Like Home.. 28

Great Expectations.. 32

So Close to You We Cannot Fail 36

Beam Me Up, Holy Spirit—Not!...................................... 40

Let It Be.. 43

Pop Quiz... 47

Stairway to Heaven.. 51

Seek Not Outside Yourself...54

I Am So Irritated...58

My Heart Is Beating in the Peace of God 62

What Is the Christ? 66

The Sounds of Silence 70

You Like Potato, and I like Potahto 74

Something There Is That Doesn't Love a Wall................77

Where Darkness Was I Look Upon the Light 81

I Will Not Fear to Look Within Today..............................85

Happiness Runs In a Circular Motion 88

The Debt We Owe to Truth.. 93

The Impossible Dream.. 96

Everything's Coming Up Roses (Oh, Never Mind!).........100

Another Pop Quiz 104

Forgiveness Is the Key to Happiness 109

Macaroni and Cheese and the Comfort of Gracious Guidance............ 113

I Love to Laugh 117

A Hand to Clasp.. 121

This Need Not Be.. 125

The House That Guilt Built.. 129

Rocking Around the Christmas Tree.. 133

A Meaningless World Engenders Fear 137

I Want to Want the Peace of God 141

A Course in Miracles: An All-Inclusive Healing of the Heart.................. 145

A Room of My Own 150

When the Going Gets Tough, the Tough Make Red Beans and Rice.... 154

Crusader Rabbit Retires.. 159

Objects of Projection.. 163

Hooray for Hollywood Redux 169

The Runaway Bunny 174

Looking with Jesus: Now in 3-D 178

I Gotta Be Me! (Well; Maybe Not So Much) 183

Forgiveness: No Prior Understanding Required............................... 187

Wilted Lilies, Growing Up Too Soon, and a Recipe for Forgiveness..... 191

The Egg That Cracked.. 195

I Need Do Nothing 199

Just a Little Willingness 204

Choose Once Again..208

Let All Things Be Exactly As They Are 213

Objects in Mirror Are Closer Than They Appear 218

Forget This Book: Well, Maybe Tomorrow 222

Declaration of Dependence 226

Lean on Me..230

Be You In Charge..233

Shark Week..236

Should Healing Be Repeated?..240

What Is Forgiveness?..244

You Gotta Wear Shades 248

Foreword

Susan and I first crossed paths when I had the inspired idea to contact her after seeing an interview with her in *A Course in Miracles* The Movie. "There's a woman I'd like to know," I thought, without a moment's hesitation. I say "inspired" idea because I am not normally in the habit of reaching out to strangers, let alone "famous" persons of a spiritual kind! Since there is no hierarchy of famous or even infamous persons, I am so very glad I followed the inspiration to break away from a deeply entrenched distorted belief!

We bonded instantly. Though of different backgrounds, we shared a passionate commitment to the study of *A Course in Miracles* and were both drawn to the teaching approach of Kenneth Wapnick. We also shared a mutual struggle with a highly convincing ego script, a love of dark-roast coffee, the experience of motherhood, the deep vulnerability that is inherent in the writer's life, the dark probing nature of the 16/7 in our personal numerology, but, above all, a common desire, deeper than anything the ego could throw our way, for an experience of the truth of the wholeness of who we are as Children of God.

Susan's work is sheer delight for the reader. With studies in journalism and a degree in English language and literature establishing a solid foundation, the writing is rich with clever metaphors, interwoven with colorful wit and humor. At times dark, at times flippant, but all of the time right on, a delight to experience, which no doubt says something about my own twisted sense of humor, but there it is! In fact, there are segments in which she deftly describes out-of-control ego dramas that are outright hilarious. Birds of a feather … we forgive together.

As in her previous book, *Extraordinary Ordinary Forgiveness*, the backdrop for Susan's practice of diligent vigilance for her wayward thoughts is the varied activity of a very busy lifestyle. Most of us can easily relate to the daily stuff of life, dealing with the vicissitudes of parenthood, facing inner fears and self-doubt, addressing the needs and cries of a body whose reality is next to impossible to deny, or practicing forgiveness in "the trenches of intimate relationships." Of course, there is the recurring humorous take on all things in dreamland embellished through the practice of "catastrophizing" seemingly innocuous events into life-threatening crises, a practice of which I am admittedly guilty. Perhaps it's a writers' thing. But, have we not been invited to look at the tiny mad idea and laugh?

Above all, it is a treat to be invited in for an intimate glimpse of another person's inner journey. Call it voyeurism if you like; it just makes me feel less alone in my separation neurosis. But more than that, I am not alone in my sincere desire to awaken from the dream that keeps us from the full experience of our true Self. *A Course in Miracles* is a powerful spiritual tool for the intellectually sharp such as Susan, the core of its power being found in its ability to undo the mind and lead us to an experience of the truth. As Susan states, "We need to wrap our heart around this Course." Throughout this book, we follow Susan's heart as she journeys with the certainty of God's Will to the true wholeness/holiness of her Being.

Pauline Edward
Author of *Making Peace with God, Leaving the Desert,* and
Choosing the Miracle
April 2013

Acknowledgments

I would like to convey my deep appreciation to Ken Wapnick without whose brilliant teaching and consistently kind and loving presence I would have no clue at all about how to practice forgiveness *A Course in Miracles*-style. I am so grateful to my fellow Course students, especially Cher Golenda and Deb Shelly, who have walked this road with me with such grace and humor. A big thank you to my teachers in Denver, Colorado, especially Lyn Corona and Chris Dixon, whose generous sharing of their Course understanding and experience captivated me from the beginning, and whose guidance through what is now called the Course Immersion Program proved invaluable to my learning. I am also thankful to my comrades in the Course Immersion Program, the students in my regular Thursday night class in Denver, Colorado, who teach me so much, and everyone at the Rocky Mountain Miracle Center for kindly providing me the space in which to teach and learn.

Pauline Edward continues to offer invaluable support and friendship as a fellow traveler and writer driven as I am to synthesize her experience on the page. The many friends I have communicated with around the globe, including Bernard Groom, Robyn Busfield, Norman Mitchell-Babbitt, Danielle Boonstra, and Nouk Sanchez, to name but a few, continue to inspire with their unwavering dedication to healing. Finally, I remain deeply grateful to Kara and Kevin for helping me remember from moment to moment that we are one, and to everyone bravely winding their way home past fear and special interests to the all-inclusive love we never really left.

A Word from the Author

When a series of coincidences led me to *A Course in Miracles* nine years ago after exhausting all other possibilities this time around and in answer to my deep longing for a love and innocence not of this world, I had no idea learning to live by the big, blue book would become the new purpose of my life. Not my life itself, however. As premier *A Course in Miracles* scholar, teacher, and beloved guide Ken Wapnick, puts it, "The Course is not your life; it's a book. Your life is your life." Meaning the goal of our lives is not just to study the Course but to live it, to apply its unique forgiveness to everything seemingly "out there" that seems to be happening to us. By beginning to identify with the decision maker in our mind outside this dream of exile from the eternal, non-dualistic, all-inclusive, loving source we share, we learn we can choose to perceive our lives as classroom rather than prison, our relationships and experiences as our curriculum rather than the sorry, mortal hand we've been dealt.

The title of this book is borrowed from *A Course in Miracles* workbook lesson 122: "Forgiveness offers everything I want." I chose it because, despite my ambivalence toward learning, practicing the Course's forgiveness continues to dissolve my belief that the world I'm making up from moment to moment has anything real and valuable to offer me, along with the idea that there is a personal me to dissolve.

Forgiveness *A Course in Miracles*-style is the answer to the questions I've been seeking answers to all my life. It simply means learning to choose the inner teacher of love over the inner teacher of fear whenever we perceive ourselves unfairly treated or uniquely blessed. As we do, our seemingly split mind begins to heal and our identification with a false, special self begins to unravel. The guilt that drives our behavior and keeps us in conflict and competition with each other is gradually undone for us and we become kinder, gentler, and more tolerant with others and ourselves, recognizing we share the same illusory "human condition." An unconscious thought system of sin, guilt, and fear that leaves us constantly striving to exonerate ourselves by proving others guiltier than we are. Bargaining to get our needs met and positively differentiate ourselves in a futile attempt to fill the nagging lack we feel within as a result of the unconscious belief that we forever squandered eternally shared love.

We always have a choice about which inner teacher we are listening to: the ego, the part of our mind that believed the "tiny, mad idea" of separation from our source had real effects and projected the guilty thought of it into an entire universe of fragmented forms competing for survival. Or Jesus/Holy Spirit/right mind, the part of our mind that remembered to laugh at the crazy thought of it. Through day-to-day practice we learn that choosing the ego as our teacher hurts, while choosing the right mind as our teacher offers peace that defies understanding and includes everyone and everything in its warm embrace.

These essays continue to chronicle my journey practicing this extraordinary form of forgiveness in an ordinary life begun in my first collection of *A Course in Miracles* essays, *Extraordinary Ordinary Forgiveness*. Like some of the essays in the first book, these selected reflections originally appeared in my ACIM forgiveness blog at www.foraysinforgiveness.com, where I have posted weekly for several years. They begin more than three years ago, roughly where the last collection left off, recounting a period of more or less a year-and-a-half in my continuing journey home to the one, loving mind we never really left. They represent my strengthening commitment to healing my mind through forgiveness, using the contents of my life as my curriculum; learning with the help of the inner teacher of forgiveness to change my mind about all I believe. Editing them for this book helped me see this truly is a journey. My identification with the self I think I am is slowly and happily dissolving simply by choosing to change my inner teacher from moment to moment in the classroom of my life.

As you will see, my journey also involved developing and cultivating a relationship with an imaginary Jesus that has helped me learn to smile at the insanity of the ego thought system. *A Course in Miracles* uses the character of a non-dualistic Jesus (unlike the Biblical version) as a symbol of the awakened mind we can relate to and call on in the embodied condition we think we're in. Although he doesn't join with us in making our illusory experience real, he does invite us to look with him "beyond the veil" at all we believe is happening to us, to watch our lives like a movie with him beside us in the audience, thereby returning to the realization that we are not the movie's star, but its writer and director. Watching our lives from his perspective in the one mind, the ego's "evidence" of separate interests becomes proof positive that we never severed our connection with our true, non-dualistic nature.

By choosing again and again for however long it seems to take to look with the one inner teacher of truth at all we made up to defend an impossible experiment in individuality, we grow into the awareness that we are not separate from Jesus/Holy Spirit/right mind. We continue to share the memory of uninterrupted wholeness we have in truth never left and will fully embrace at the end of the seeming journey, when all our dreams of specialness return to the singular nothingness from which they sprang.

With love, gratitude, and faith that grows stronger each moment as fear subsides,

Susan Dugan

The Unbearable Heaviness of Being

The Friday before my daughter's spring break we gathered to remember a 20-year-old college student who had been heading to California on holiday when her personal story abruptly and inexplicably ended. Rain turned to snow—and back again—as we headed with hundreds of family members, friends, and acquaintances to find seating in the back of a packed Lutheran church.

Beside me my daughter's shoulders remained admirably straight as we watched the girl's family proceed to their seats in the front pew. I squeezed my daughter's hand but she did not return the pressure. She finds it difficult to accept comfort; always has. She likes to show the world just how strong she can be. I know that one. Just behind us, one of my daughter's teachers choked back tears.

We stared at an enormous photograph of a young girl with a winning smile standing on a beach, waves crashing behind her. We listened to her sister—my daughter's classmate—sing the Dolly Parton song *I Hope You'll Dance*, a heart-wrenching, courageous performance still replaying itself in my head. We listened to the girl's church youth group, high school, and college friends describe her sense of humor, her zest for life, her energy, athleticism, and kindness. We read along with prayers and watched a video celebrating her life. We dabbed at our eyes and did our best not to sob. We did not even know this girl, only her younger sister, and yet, like every human in that church, we knew her story all too well.

The minister talked about how children are a gift. But he skirted the central question weighing on everyone's mind, the question that never gets answered and rarely even asked in our experience here in this dream we call life. What kind of father would take back a gift so soon? What kind of parent would give a gift that didn't last in the first place? What kind of "gift" is this life anyway? A cruel gift which—regardless of length—always ends the same tragic way; always causes the same unbearable suffering in those left behind.

As we fought our way back to the car in the escalating snowstorm, I took my daughter's arm. She was wearing the same expression she had worn as a three-year-old listening to TV reports about Congressional efforts to cut programming for PBS children's television. Brows furrowed, eyes narrowed, fists clenched; the tasty word "bad" on her tongue.

"I want you to know that God would never do that to someone," I said, sitting in the car, staring straight ahead, longing to connect. "Not to those parents. Not to that child."

I wanted her to know what I was learning in *A Course in Miracles* and beginning at least sometimes to actually believe. I wanted her to share in the only real hope we have in this world; that its story of seeking and never finding that ends in death is not our reality but a defense against the eternal, undivided, abiding love of our true nature. That beyond this world there is a world we want, a world we have turned our backs on in our fear and selfishness but can just as easily learn to embrace right here and now in the condition we think we're in.

She broke down. "It's just not right," she sputtered. "It doesn't make any sense. I mean what kind of God? Why would …"

She didn't know a whole lot about God. Despite a couple of years during her childhood in which we intermittently attended a Unity, Divine Science, and Protestant congregational church we were not a religious family. I had rejected my Catholic upbringing and my attempts to replace it with other organized religious paths left me feeling like a serial hypocrite. Mostly I had spoken to my daughter as a child about finding the God in her heart. A God I had always sensed we existed somehow within despite all evidence to the contrary in our human experience. I urged her to remember she was part of God and could always go within to the God in her heart for comfort and guidance. I had no idea whether any of it made sense or had taken. Even so, I reached for the God in our heart now.

I held her as she cried. I don't know what I said but I know it came from a heart beyond this body—a heart without walls—because I lost track of my false self and hers, the bondage of time and space as I spoke. I could feel her relaxation in my own loosening limbs, accepting for a moment God's real "gift," the only true comfort available to us here, the memory of our one, whole mind that has never forsaken and will never forsake us. Despite our hallucination of banishment to a realm of mortality in which we obsessively reenact the original choice for individuality, casting our guilt over that alleged decision onto others to relieve ourselves of its crushing weight, continuing to push away the truth that the "tiny, mad idea" of separation from our source never happened.

For a blessedly elongated moment, face to face with the unbearable heaviness of being in this illusory world as seemingly demonstrated in a life cut brutally short, we joined our mind with the incredible lightness of our true nature and were healed. Until our secret fear came boomeranging back and we went off to wage our separate-seeming lives, once again seeking for ourselves where we can never be found.

Spring Fever

All night long I heaved my aching torso and limbs from side to side, sniffling through blocked nostrils, drenched in sweat, then wracked with chills, the dog patiently trying to reconfigure her tiny frame around the dunes and valleys of my shifting limbs and spine. Murky dreams about being discovered an imposter—visa-less in hostile territory—beating their threatening drums in my head.

For a number of reasons I've been increasingly consumed this week with bodily thoughts; once more rendered mindless by my forgotten choice to swallow the ego's dream hook, line, and sinker in my lust for specialness. After months of sub-normal cold, the weather has taken a sharp turn for the better with temperatures hovering in the 70s following a heavy, wet snow last week. Spring is busting out all over Denver, Colorado, dewy grass embroidered with violets in my front yard, the lilac branches raising their embryonic fists in solidarity, the puppy—delirious with the sensory overload of her first swipe at this season—having at the loam with contagious gusto.

But I am miserable again. I have always thought T.S. Eliot knew what he was talking about when he wrote that "April is the cruelest month ..." Every year at this time, as a frozen, dormant world gasps back to life, the trees begin to waken, and daffodils and hyacinth poke through the long-fallow ground, my eyes swell and itch, my throat closes, and my head slips into a familiar vice. As beaming neighbors in shorts and flip-flops take to the bike paths and park picnic tables, I retreat back into my lair. Barricading the windows and installing the super-micro-particle-devouring air-conditioning filters with a bitter wheeze.

No remedy known to Western medicine has thus far alleviated my severe tree pollen allergies that usually morph, as they apparently already have, into more serious sinus and sometimes bronchial infections. Expensive Chinese herbal concoctions sometimes help, and sometimes don't. Mostly I'm left mentally complaining about the irony of this world I appear to inhabit gone mad with beauty versus this body's immune system gone mad with histamine production.

This year seems especially troubling, compounded by an unrelenting lower back/hip issue perhaps a result of breaking the opposite hip the winter before last in a severe fall and over-compensating ever since. I am at times consumed with pain and fatigue, uncomfortably conscious of the burden of this frame whose presence I've long preferred to deny. Long a fit and healthy person I find this completely unacceptable. The unwelcome preview of aging it offers a kind of personal affront to my delusion that I can control what this body does or doesn't do.

Then, too, I'm apt to berate myself for taking such relatively minor, transitory physical issues so seriously when I have friends and acquaintances currently staring down life-threatening illnesses or dealing with much more dire forms of physical or psychological suffering. And then it suddenly occurs to me, staring out the window at the brave tip of a tulip poised to pop—a flower that could freeze in mid-blossoming in a matter of minutes should the arctic front predicted materialize—that a world gone mad with beauty and a body gone mad with pain are expressions of the same fundamental madness. Reflections of the "tiny, mad idea" our one mind chose to believe in the first place: the preposterous notion that we could differentiate ourselves from our wholly loving, unified source.

April is *not* the cruelest month—take that T.S. Eliot! Every month in the calendar the ego made to measure the illusion of time in this asylum meant to hide the thought of guilt over our belief in that original, mad thought is equally, insanely cruel, cleverly crafted to reinforce our belief that we attacked eternal, non-dualistic love, got away with it, and fled into a projected world. A world designed to keep the idea of that original "sin" alive while denying responsibility for it, continually projecting it on other bodies or our own to circumvent God's retaliation. Within this insane myth, God doesn't need to punish us for our crime. We punish each other and we punish ourselves throughout our lives, culminating in that greatest of all punishments: death. The ultimate proof that we indeed once lived as individuals here in a dream of separate identities waging war against each other.

A Course in Miracles workbook lesson 136, "Sickness is a defense against the truth," explains the ego dynamic fueling our attacks on our own body in the form of all kinds of physical, mental, and psychological abuse. Although we believe bodily pain and sickness attack from without via organisms, pollen, accidental forces, or the aggression or neglect of others, sickness in all its forms simply reflects, defends, and reinforces the original decision made by the one mind to take the tiny, mad idea of separation seriously. To follow the ego's plan to experience the dream of individuality by repressing our memory of that decision to defend against the truth. As paragraph 8 reminds us:

> How do you think that sickness can succeed in shielding you from truth? Because it proves the body is not separate from you, and so you must be separate from the truth. You suffer pain because the body does, and in this pain are you made one with it. Thus is your "true" identity preserved, and the strange haunting thought that you might be something beyond this little pile of dust silenced and stilled. ...

Sickness is but another effective ego ploy to keep us from returning to our right mind and remembering the separation never happened. To prevent us from taking responsibility for the belief that we could have divided the indivisible, and choosing again to smile at such absurdity. When we can do that, whether or not the body continues its apparently diseased contortions will not disturb our peace of mind. As we watch with our right mind, we recognize the ego as director of this morality play that has no meaning in the non-dualistic state in which we remain eternally complete, supported, loved, and loving.

The Course tells us over and over that the body merely reflects the choice for inner teacher—ego or Holy Spirit—we have made in the mind. When we heal our mind about the body by choosing for the memory of wholeness in our mind, the body's highs and lows no longer upset us, distract us, or bring us to our knees in pain.

When we choose to align with our right mind, we can use the body for its only right-minded purpose: to demonstrate our true invulnerability. To communicate the loving, innocent, inclusive forgiveness reflective of our true nature, thereby extending healing to all seemingly fragmented, sickened minds by refusing to make a symbol of impossible guilt real.

As we make our way home to wholeness—moving back and forth between fear and love until ready to accept our right mind's message once and for always—we can still choose to treat the body's symptoms on the level of illusory form. But as Course students committed to eventually awakening from the dream, we should try to remind ourselves that the remedy for healing the mind lies in the mind, not the imaginary body. We experience that healing by changing our mind about the body's purpose, with help from our inner teacher. Recognizing, with that loving presence beside us, just how invested we are in preserving this defense against our true, abstract nature, so that we may eventually remember we are one, invulnerable mind, not many vulnerable bodies.

> Truth has a power far beyond defense, for no illusions can remain where truth has been allowed to enter. And it comes to any mind that would lay down its arms, and cease to play with folly. It is found at any time; today, if you will choose to practice giving welcome to the truth. (paragraph 14)

I *know* this because I experienced it when I broke my hip a while back, immediately remembered "I am responsible for what I see," asked to look with Jesus, and felt the echoing pain in my head fall to silence. Leaving me pain-free from the fracture for several days before my fear of losing this special identity returned and I chose again for the ego's fearful story of suffering.

Today, as I watch that cockeyed-optimistic tulip tipping toward a weak sun about to be stuffed by a late spring snowstorm, I am choosing yet again to transcend my mistaken belief, this time disguised as allergies and back pain. To experience our invulnerability by watching once more as our loving inner teacher lifts the curtain on the ego's guilty, painful morality play. Once again smiling as the images on the stage fade to the nothingness from which they came.

Time-Out

My precocious daughter was not yet one when she threw her first tantrum. This may have been the last time in our 17-year history together in which I was actually prepared for the premature arrival of a developmental stage. She had rolled over, sat up, talked, and walked months before the books claim most children can, and so I had been reading ahead about tantrums common during "the terrible twos," the possibility of their early arrival, and how to nip them in the bud. The thinking at the time advised picking your child up, removing her from the situation (even if that meant abruptly leaving a public venue), and placing her in a quiet place for a "Time-Out," holding her, if necessary—a veritable Mommy straight jacket—until the storm of her emotional anguish over not having her needs instantly met, passed.

We were picking up takeout from our favorite Chinese Dim Sum restaurant at the time. I had already paid the bill and was attempting to interest my daughter in the tank of lobsters she normally found fascinating when she abruptly attempted a half gainer out of my arms. When I set her down she threw herself on the floor, writhing, screaming, and kicking in a meltdown so impressive and classic I secretly wondered if she'd somehow been watching some kind of secret toddler-tantrum-training video. Stepping up to the parenting plate once again months before expected, I carried her out of the restaurant as the theatrics continued, and sat holding her and talking softly as the rain drummed against the roof of my car until her cries subsided and her rigid body went slack. Sanity restored, we returned to the restaurant to pick up our food and drove home. She never threw another tantrum like that, and quickly learned to put herself, her stuffed animals, and Mama, in a Time-Out, as needed, for the greater good of all concerned.

I could use a Time-Out right now. Lately I cannot seem to keep up with apparently incoming demands on my time. The faster I work, the more work arrives for my attention via email or phone until I feel like Lucille Ball in the classic *I Love Lucy* episode where Lucy and Ethel take jobs in a candy factory to prove that working outside the home is easier than in. Pieces of candy I am expected to deal with appear to be speeding by on the conveyer belt before I can get my grubby, little hands on them. I don't remember the last time I got to the bottom of my cherished To-Do list, something the ego swears used to happen regularly. My personal life, too, seems to have spiraled out of control, with more social activities than one introvert can successfully field, leaving me breathless.

Then, too, I'm more than usually sensitized to time's passage as each new chapter in my daughter's coming-of-age story unfolds. As another school year screeches to a halt, as she begins taking her SATs and ACTs, exploring colleges and watching her best friends—mostly seniors—graduate, I'm deeply aware the coming year will likely provide a series of "lasts." Each school event we attend, each holiday we celebrate, will—fate willing—be Kara's last at home before she takes the next step in her passage through the dream and leaves for college.

There are so many things I wanted to teach her I never got around to. The many ways in which I have fallen short as a parent, have found it impossible to keep up with my daughter's meteoric trajectory through childhood and adolescence, seem, at the moment, too much in my face. But further grist for the mill of the ego's use of time, described in *A Course in Miracles* Chapter 15, I, The Two Uses of Time, paragraph 2:

> … And all the waste that time seems to bring with it is due but to your identification with the ego which uses time to support its belief in destruction. The ego, like the Holy Spirit, uses time to convince you of the inevitability of the goal and end of teaching. To the ego the goal is death, which is its end. But to the Holy Spirit the goal is life, which *has* no end.

When we listen to the ego—as I have caught myself doing once more—there is never enough time to escape the guilt over the original sin of separation acted out in the theatre of our lives. We can never project our guilt onto someone or thing "out there" fast enough to prove our relative innocence. We are Lucy and Ethel in the candy factory, attempting to trick the boss into thinking we can keep up, only to have the Lord of guilty separation accelerate the action to prove otherwise.

We can pursue our impossible dream faster and faster—as fast and earnestly as we humanly can—and even then it will never be quick enough. The dream is always just out of reach in front of us, whizzing by on a perpetual conveyer belt, forever unattainable in a fearful future, just the way the ego likes it. And even when we temporarily "realize" our dream—that magic parenting moment, a job perfectly executed—it morphs again into something bigger, better, more complex and demanding. Even the fleeting pleasure of "realizing" our dream never solves the "problem" of our past belief in a choice for separation from our eternal loving source, or our compulsion to project our unconscious guilt over that decision outside ourselves to stave off future retaliation, to hold someone or thing "out there" responsible for our internal loss of peace in an illusory world played out in an illusion of time.

The good news? We can choose again for an inner teacher that remembers that the seeming problem of separation was instantly corrected the moment the "tiny, mad idea" arose in the one child of God's mind. We can put ourselves in Time-Out by joining with our one loving inner teacher in the eternal present, "the holy instant of our release" in which we remember that no one or thing can divide us from the one and only love we never left.

We are all stuck in the same crazy candy factory when we listen to the ego. The busyness that appears to devour our days, the pivotal events that appear to measure a child's inevitable journey away from home, have nothing at all to do with the truth of our shared nature and are never the cause of the problem.

Attempting to battle the problem of guilt cast outside the mind where it never existed remains the only problem here where we believe we find ourselves in a projected world spiraling out of control. And the solution is always the same: choose again for the instant of sanity in which our wholeness resides uninterrupted through *A Course in Miracle's* radical forgiveness.

... If you are tempted to be dispirited by thinking how long it would take to change your mind so completely, ask yourself, "How long is an instant?" Could you not give so short a time to the Holy Spirit for your salvation? He asks no more. (from paragraph 11)

Technological Difficulties

I had been interacting with a website (yeah, I know) related to a recent work project when I completely lost my mind. I had received a number of email notifications asking me to respond to various site postings about the project's status but could not seem to follow the thread of the generalized requests, or interpret the messages which appeared and vanished with maniacal abandon every time I navigated away from the current page. I know I'm dating myself here because, in such cases, my teenage daughter does not take it personally. She merely pauses, mid text—iPod dangling from her elegant ear—to stab madly at the larger computer keyboard. Then she answers a few more texts before awaiting the next command. I, on the other hand, have been around long enough to recognize a threat when I see one.

As I sat at my desk wracking my brain for solutions—attempting to respond while paralyzed by the fear of revealing myself in so transparent an arena as the technological idiot I remain, despite earnest efforts to develop a meager skill base—I completely shut down. My IQ plummeted. I could no longer discern the question let alone frame an answer. Although my daughter had walked me through her best guess as to how to respond, I could not be comforted. "You've lost it all," the ego gravely whispered, all dressed up in grim reaper wear for the occasion. He was also sorry to inform me that I had made a fool of myself in the process, in infinite cyberspace, no less.

"Step away from the computer, Mom," my daughter—long wise beyond her years—entreated, before fleeing my office for a demilitarized zone. But I just sat there, clenching my teeth, waiting for someone to come and zip me into a body bag.

"Let us not fight our function," *A Course in Miracles* workbook lesson 186, "Salvation of the world depends on me," paragraph 2, advises.

Let us not fight our function. We did not establish it. It is not our idea. The means are given us by which it will be perfectly accomplished. All that we are asked to do is to accept our part in genuine humility, and not deny with self-deceiving arrogance that we are worthy. What is given us to do, we have the strength to do. Our minds are suited perfectly to take the part assigned to us by One Who knows us well.

Apparently, I had been fighting my function again. Mistaking it for meeting the obligations and upholding the reputation of Susan, rather than accepting my true and only function of forgiving the illusion of Susan, her imaginary champions and adversaries; overlooking with the right mind's help the ego's myth of individuality purchased at the price of celestial homicide.

When I stop fighting my function, stop believing I have any other function in this dream but to awaken through forgiveness, resign as my own teacher and welcome the memory of uninterrupted wholeness the right mind offers, I'm able to accept and experience my impenetrable identity as the one child of God I remain, along with everyone else seemingly "out there" cavorting on the screen of this world. As the Course reminds us repeatedly: "ideas leave not their source." I could not have left my eternal home despite my wild imaginings. My true identity has nothing to do with this dream figure invented by the ego along with all other dream figures to preserve a fantasy of separate interests designed to reinforce a mistaken notion that ideas *can* leave their source.

In every situation and without exception the ego would have the self I made up to keep this dream alive interpret the information its senses transmit as *evidence* of an unreliable, confounding, hostile world that never delivers the goods for long. When I listen to the ego I'm intoxicated with fear, convinced of my own guilt, terrified of exposure, and desperate to pin it all on an external source rather than claim responsibility for a mistaken belief in need of correction. But in every situation and without exception when I accept my true function of forgiveness by calling on the strength that remains in my mind, I'm released, no longer paralyzed by fear and frantic strivings to protect against a virtual world.

When I accept my only function of forgiveness I remember I have simply once more chosen for the ego's dire interpretation of the events transpiring on the screen. But I can choose again with help from a loving inner teacher to remember that the problem of technological difficulties has nothing to do with incomprehensible electronic demands. The problem—like all problems in a world made mad by guilt in the mind—remains my unconscious belief that I have separated from my source and must deny responsibility for it by blaming someone or thing "outside" the mind to avoid the punishment I think I deserve.

A Course in Miracles defines siding with the ego's puny concept of vulnerable individuality as the height of *arrogance*, versus the true *humility* of accepting atonement—the truth that the separation never happened and we remain awake in God, merely dreaming of exile. A dream from which we can gradually awaken by practicing forgiveness in response to every temptation to hold someone or thing "outside" responsible for our loss of inner peace.

When I relinquish the ego's arrogance and choose in true humility to forgive, I remember I have never left my indivisible, loving, eternally protected source. My only reputation lies *outside* this nightmare, beyond all possible threat. It has nothing to do with a technologically challenged writer glued to a screen rife with assaults and demands, reflective of seemingly endless individuals with seemingly endless expectations and potential judgments.

Our function has nothing to do with the *specific* forgiveness opportunities that seem to arise at warp speed on the screen of our individual lives. One is no more or less threatening, more trivial or monumental than another. The Course does not make distinctions within the "hierarchy of illusions" the ego has concocted to convince us the dream is real. Our self-worth does not hinge on an email notification. It does not depend on a romantic partner, a boss, a parent, a child, a bank account, a talent, or an award for a job well done. Our self-worth derives from our source, the source we have never left, the source that could never and has never failed us. The source we will awaken to 24/7 once we have applied forgiveness to everyone and thing we still believe can destroy or enhance our peace of mind.

We save the world by withdrawing our belief in the world of guilt in the mind. We withdraw our belief in the world of guilt in the mind by holding the person or situation we perceived responsible for our personal distress harmless. We hold them harmless by turning our mistaken projections over to the part of our mind that sees only the truth of our shared innocence. In so doing we remember: "Salvation of the world depends on you who can forgive. Such is your function here."

Hooray for Hollywood!

My husband appeared to be having words with me. He had received this nifty new coffee maker as a birthday gift. It brewed single-servings of coffee, tea, or hot chocolate from pre-made packets; the perfect solution for our on-the-go family.

I usually brew a pot of decaf each morning including one scoop of regular French roast, my caffeine quota for the day. My husband had returned from Costco with a supply of beverage packets including half-caf single servings for me.

But I didn't like them. I prefer dark roasts and hated to squander my meager caffeine ration on substandard product. When he noticed I had ignored them—in the middle of a trying work week and perhaps overdue for a stiff cup of Joe himself—he appeared to have a meltdown that quickly escalated, as ego meltdowns will, from the specific: "You don't like the coffee I bought you," to the general:

"You never like anything I buy you."

"You're impossible to please."

"You always…"

"Why can't you…?"

"Even the dog thinks you're…"

Dragging our adorable little dog into it really was the last straw, the ego pointed out.

As I charged out into the morning sunrise headed for the nearest Starbuck's to order my Venti, three-quarter-decaf, light-room Americano in retaliation, a part of my mind recognized I was at it again, attempting to momentarily relieve the buried guilt in my mind by projecting it outside myself. Once more following what the Course calls "the ego's plan for salvation" by denying responsibility for the original belief that I had separated from God in the first place. Experiencing it in the form of a secretly welcome, "unprovoked" attack by an angry husband, conveniently throwing my relative innocence into sharp relief.

This is *my* mind-on-ego, I reminded myself. How many times had I been here before? Did I really want to swallow this picture of unfair treatment I had painted over a freaking cup of coffee? To disrupt my morning with the counter-attack my mind-on-ego craved even more than caffeine?

"There has to be another way," I remembered. Silently repeating the phrase *A Course in Miracles* collaborator Bill Thetford had uttered to Course scribe and colleague Helen Schucman all those decades ago at Columbia University's College of Physicians and Surgeons. The question that had coaxed the Course's answer of unique forgiveness from our right mind into the seeming world of form.

"There has to be another way."

Bill's earnest words reverberated in my head, catapulting me into an entertaining, right-minded fantasy. I had heard an NPR story the day before about the Trust for Public Lands' efforts to rescue the Hollywood sign and surrounding acreage from encroaching development. I had always been drawn to images of that sign and, as a child, had even vowed to climb it one day, a yet unrealized dream. With Southern California still weighing heavily on my brain following our recent Spring break tour of prospective colleges with our daughter, I now imagined myself sitting atop that very sign with Jesus, peering down on the self-aggrandizing chaos of Los Angeles, discussing the seemingly more pressing case of the self-aggrandizing chaos in my own kitchen.

"That man is a saint," Jesus said.

Not exactly what I was hoping to hear.

"Sorry, you asked."

I smiled. I suppose I had. *A Course in Miracles* teaches us that what we're really asking when we cry out for help is to see (experience) all that appears to be happening *to us* differently. When we choose against the ego's drama of attack and defense that appears to have hijacked our peace of mind, we automatically become right-minded, taking the seeming external problem back to its internal cause and correction in the mind.

We see with Christ's (that *symbol* of the embodied awakened mind used in *A Course in Miracles*) "vision." A way of seeing that has nothing to do with the body's senses made to reinforce a dualistic world invented to defend against the whole, uninterrupted, eternal love we believe we pushed away. We see the error of our guilt projected onto another body; recognize it as our own mistaken call for the real love we believe we squandered, and answer by holding the other harmless, allowing us to re-experience our own shared innocence.

I sighed. "I suppose he has put up with a lot over the years," I said, thinking of my husband. How my penchant for strongly brewed dark roast coffee was really just the tip of the proverbial iceberg. I had been born opinionated, after all, still had a lot of opinions, and still tended in one way or another to make them known.

"Right?" Jesus said. "And that girl of yours."

"Wait a minute."

"You were just thinking about her."

My mind had in fact been wandering, reviewing my daughter's most recent lack of regard for my delicate feelings. That tone in her voice, that roll of her eyes, that toss of her beautiful hair.

"She's been a good sport from the day she came in," Jesus said.

Easy for you to say, I thought. I mean, colic, the complete inability to nap. Rolling off the bed at a week old—infants were not supposed to be able to do that—and nearly scaring me to death. Getting kicked out of day care at six months, I mean. And that was just the first year. I could go on.

"You could."

"But I don't really want to, do I?"

"Not so much."

I smiled. The Course tells us Jesus doesn't know about this world. That asking him for specific advice is akin to asking him to make the error of our perception of competing interests real. And yet in answer to Bill and Helen's cry for help with a troubled relationship in a conflicted environment, he spoke. And he continues to meet us where we think we are in the condition we think we're in, if we let him. On this particular day, I needed to picture him in the flesh, speaking to the individual I had again mistaken for my real self, even as I reminded myself this could not be.

When we catch ourselves feeling unfairly treated by what the Course calls our "special relationships," those people we have chosen to meet our expectations for special love and special hate—to ultimately fail us as all partners do—we can always choose again to look with Jesus. When we do we figuratively rise "above the battleground"—as the Course puts it—where nothing seems quite so serious anymore. Where we can look beyond the movie of unrelenting special interests playing out in the smoggy valley we call life to the reality of our true nature, where we remain eternally awake, supported, and complete, merely dreaming of fragmented exile.

"That man really is a saint," I said.

"Right?"

"And she's a good kid."

"You're not so bad yourself," he said.

"Yeah, but, God knows, you say that to everybody."

Jesus smiled. "Pass the popcorn, please," he said.

Faith, Hope, and Clarity

Hope may be "the thing with feathers" but—no offense Emily Dickinson—things with feathers fly away. And die. I learned this lesson early. As a little girl, I built a hospital for wounded creatures in the woods, ministering to abandoned baby birds and wounded butterflies with generally tragic results the adjacent makeshift graveyard served to accommodate. While I buried most of my patients, one small robin with a wing issue actually recovered. One day it leapt from my hand and circled away. I watched it rise in the sky with self-righteous elation until I realized it wasn't coming back. When it disappeared into a cloud, I rushed home, locked myself in my room, and sobbed.

I have been thinking about the word hope, defined by Webster's as: "a wish or desire accompanied by confident expectation of its fulfillment," and asking for help from my right mind to accept that no one or thing in this world has ever or can ever completely fulfill my expectations. Especially not those people I hold *especially* responsible for preserving my peace of mind by meeting my expectations; what *A Course in Miracles* calls our "special relationships," those closest "others" with whom we forge unspoken bargains for meeting our needs. People like my daughter, who I learned over the weekend had betrayed my trust, as teenagers will.

I have the personality of an oldest child, intent on following rules, comingled with a generational urge to topple every symbol of authority that appears to thwart my treasured autonomy. I came of age in the 70s after all, and still sometimes find myself waxing nostalgic for phrases like "hell no, we won't go!" whenever I feel somehow herded by the prevailing culture into conformity. And so I'm forever at war with myself. Except when it comes to *my* daughter, where the oldest, rule-abiding, law-enforcing child within me always prevails.

Without going into the gory details, suffice it to say I discovered she had lied about her whereabouts and what she was up to. Although nothing horrible ensued as a result, it could have, my ego fretted, happily enumerating various graphic scenarios. I was outraged, even though I recalled having done something similar at her age, and might have shown a glimmer of compassion. Instead I chose to guilt trip, reviewing all the sacrifices I had made for her, all the earnest parenting I had done. Feeling more and more guilty, I began to berate myself. How had I failed her? I wondered aloud. What had I done to deserve this, I did not have to say. My message was clear. Look what you have done to me despite all I've done for you.

"This is not about you, Mom," she said. And she was right. Even as I spoke, a part of me recognized nothing I had said had any bearing whatsoever on the real problem or solution. I begged for help from my right mind. I held her as she cried. I stopped talking, and started listening. She hated high school, she said; hated being dependent, hated not being able to make all her own decisions. She just wanted to fast-forward and be in college where everything would be OK—that unreliable thing with feathers again.

I told her I had felt exactly the same way at her age. But you can't fast-forward through life. You have to look at and deal with what's in your face, even when it takes on the sickening, slow-motion quality of an accident. You have to make decisions and, when you make poor ones, self-correct. I said all the things a mother is supposed to say, including that there would be consequences, even as a part of my mind watched gently, compassionately, fully aware it was all a bunch of hooey.

Later, still vacillating between the ego's fearful litany of "what ifs?" and "how could she?" and right-minded awareness that she had not betrayed my love because there was really no me apart from her—no love apart from us—to betray, I opened *A Course in Miracles* to Chapter 17, VII. The Call for Faith, and read:

…you did not believe the situation and the problem were in the same place. The problem was the lack of faith, and it is this you demonstrate when you remove it from its source and place it elsewhere. As a result, you do not see the problem. Had you not lacked faith that it could be solved, the problem would be gone. (from paragraph 1)

I had identified the situation with my daughter as the cause of my distress. Even though the Course tells us again and again that the real problem is always the same: my belief that I actually separated from the one, eternal love I am, and exist as an individual dependent on an outside environment for my physical, emotional, and psychological wellbeing. My attempt to deny responsibility for my existence by projecting my guilt outside myself—and experiencing it as an incoming affront, disappointment, broken promise, betrayed confidence, breach of trust—was keeping me in hell. My faith in my daughter's body and faulty adolescent logic had been misplaced. But what had that ultimately to do with her or me? How could it possibly affect the truth we share, or the one, enduring love we remain?

Through practicing the Course's forgiveness in which I recognize with my right mind that the only thing I need to forgive is my belief in separation, I am learning that placing my faith in any body including my own is always misplaced. But placing my faith in forgiveness is always justified. Turning my error in perception over to the truth of my right mind is always rewarded. I am relieved and released when I remember with help from my loving inner teacher that all calls for love—my daughter's, my husband's, my clients', my neighbors', my fellow Course students'—are my own. And that answering them will never fail to release me from the enervating burden of that thing with feathers.

Pain Is a Wrong Perspective

I woke up the same way I had gone to bed: in pain. I had recovered nicely from a hip fracture a year-and-a-half earlier, what doctors like to label "a traumatic injury" involving a severe fall on ice during a family vacation. But unconsciously compensating for my compromised left side ever since had thrown the rest of my body out of alignment, resulting in unrelenting pain in my right hip and lower back, as well as my left shoulder; home to several decades-old injuries. I finally sought help from a chiropractor who snapped multiple bones throughout my neck, shoulders, ribs, pelvis, and hips back into place, explaining that it might take a few sessions to convince my muscles to stop protecting an area of my body no longer in need of their services.

As I lay in bed registering a déjà vu of twinges and throbs, I asked for help from my right mind to recognize them for what they are: but another ego ploy to keep me distracted from returning to the one mind and choosing again for peace. It was Monday morning, a fresh start. Today, I vowed not to be deceived, not to make a go of navigating this minefield of a world alone. Today I would call on the Holy (Whole) Spirit in my mind—the part of our one mind that holds the memory of our invulnerability and innocence intact—for help with interpreting every illusion that pesky magician of an ego would tempt me to take seriously. I would scoff at the ego's shadowy projections. They would not interrupt my peace today.

In the bathroom I learned from NPR that the oil spill in the Gulf had already invaded fragile wetlands and contaminated wildlife, and heard more about the horrific fate of the men killed and injured in the explosion that caused it. Obama had nominated his pick for Supreme Court, sure to trigger another feeding frenzy among Republicans, and financial markets were still reeling from a possible contagion caused by the potential bankruptcy of Greece.

In the hallway my husband informed me that a local teen-age girl had narrowly escaped causing her own death and the death of several others when she rolled her SUV while texting at a busy intersection near our daughter's school. He had copied the newspaper article and was trying to convince our daughter to read it. Our daughter was attempting to convey her dismay over a neighbor's Labrador retriever once more dashing across the street and into our yard while our daughter took our Maltipoo out for her morning constitutional. This had happened several times, and we were naturally concerned that one of these days we would not grab Kayleigh in time to prevent the Lab from delivering a killer bite to her tiny jugular. After all, another wayward Lab had nearly killed our next-door neighbor's dog only a few weeks earlier.

In the kitchen, as I did the dishes my family had neglected from the night before, I made the mistake of asking my daugh-ter—overwhelmed with end-of-the-year academic and extracur-ricular responsibilities—if she would be home for dinner, and got *the look*. I made the mistake of asking my husband—consumed by unpredictable work and extracurricular demands—the same question, and got the middle-aged male version of *the look*. Once they had gone, I reached down for my dog—unhinged by a week-end of undisciplined frolicking with my husband and daughter—and got the young canine version of *the look*.

I carried the dog nestled like the filling of a burrito in her little bed into my office, set her down on the floor, took a swig of coffee, and opened the big, blue book to the day's *A Course in Miracles* workbook lesson 190.

The ego sat bouncing away on my bad shoulder.

"You're invisible," I said.

It rolled its eyes in a perfect imitation of my daughter.

" 'I could choose the joy of God instead of pain,' " I read.

"Are you freaking kidding me?" the ego said.

"I can't hear you."

"Really? And when's the last time you were joyful?"

Against my better judgment, I tried to think. Certainly practicing the Course had made me calmer, more peaceful, less apt to judge and attack, more likely to catch myself when I did, and generally more willing to let others off the hook. I did not sit in front of the television renouncing political figures as I once had. I did not lose it navigating recorded phone hell with large organizations, waiting in endless lines, or stalled in city traffic. I did not take it personally when my family neglected their dirty dishes as they once again had this very morning, seemed to sabotage my efforts to train our puppy, or gave me *the look*. But joyful? Not so much.

"My sentiments, exactly," the ego said.

"Bye, bye," I told it, and delved into the lesson instead.

Pain is a wrong perspective. When it is experienced in any form, it is proof of self-deception. It is not a fact at all. There is no form it takes that will not disappear if seen aright. For pain proclaims God cruel. How could it be real in any form? It witnesses to God the Father's hatred of His Son, the sinfulness He sees in him, and His insane desire for revenge and death.

My morning vow to allow only my right mind's perspective had galvanized a threatened ego to present me with an array of painful problems seemingly out of my control. But studying *A Course in Miracles* and practicing its forgiveness—looking with my right mind at what thankfully could never be—had helped me learn to identify my mind-on-ego. It had taught me that pain in any form—from my hip to my government to my environment to the eye-rolling in my kitchen to my identification with the word *my*—shared one purpose: to convince me I had indeed pulled off the crime of separating from eternal, loving oneness.

... Peace to such foolishness! The time has come to laugh at such insane ideas. There is no need to think of them as savage crimes or secret sins with weighty consequence.

… It is your thoughts alone that cause you pain. (from paragraphs 4 and 5)

And what determines my thoughts? My choice of inner teacher. When I (the decision maker in the one mind that has never left its source) choose to listen to the ego I am convinced the world outside and inside this apparent body has gone to hell. But when I choose and actually allow the light of my right mind to shine away the shadows of the ego's ugly magic show, I remember that a sleight of hand means nothing, unless I believe in it.

The ego would even have me question the true joyfulness that returns to my mind when I choose the Holy Spirit's unified perspective of only common interests. A joy unrelated to this false self preoccupied with a body of pain. It would have me measure that gentle, loving, *knowing* against the fleeting, adrenaline-fueled passions of a physical and psychological body addicted to a roller-coaster ride of pleasure and pain that keeps it constantly searching outside the mind where real peace and joy can never be found.

And so again we make the only choice that ever can be made; we choose between illusions and the truth, or pain and joy, or hell and Heaven. Let our gratitude onto our Teacher fill our hearts as we are free to choose our joy instead of pain, our holiness in place of sin, the peace of God instead of conflict, and the light of Heaven for the darkness of the world. (paragraph 11)

The many varieties of pain I had embraced so far that morning receded. I shut the book and went about my day.

There's No Place Like Home

Last week I worked my daughter's high school's traditional breakfast for graduating seniors and their families, held on the last day of regular classes before final exams. The PTO had asked parents of juniors to handle the festivities and I found myself stumbling into the cafeteria at 6 a.m. along with a handful of other bleary-eyed volunteers to set tables, fill vases with sprays of lilacs pilfered from neighbors' yards, set out fruit and pastry, and pour orange juice.

At 6:30, as senior students and their parents descended on the buffet tables and a sentimental feeding frenzy ensued, I hastened to replenish supplies and remove rapidly accumulating debris. As I greeted several of my daughter's dearest friends, among the group scheduled to graduate two weeks later, I struggled to conceal unexpected waves of emotion. This was not even my daughter's class, and yet.

I have not always been such a crybaby. In childhood I cultivated what I came to refer to as my *stone face*—modeled after a photograph of a statue in a book of Greek mythology I read in fourth grade—at the many wakes and funerals I was forced to attend as a result of my large, extended tribe's alarming and frequent tendency to perish without warning. The stone face also came in particularly handy during adolescence when dealing with a variety of authority figures, from those in my kitchen and classrooms to those in uniform fanning out at anti-war rallies other authority figures insisted I was too young to attend. But last week in that cafeteria, the mask that had served me so well all those years ago appeared to have mysteriously vanished.

As I watched dazed-looking parents photographing their soon-to-be-headed-for-greener-pastures spawn, I saw only my daughter grinning up at the camera with her bagel, only my daughter clasping the cap and gown she had picked up that morning to her chest and clowning around with pals, only my daughter

28

wondering aloud how it had all passed so quickly—the whole year a blur, really—how she had waited so long for this moment, and yet. Only my daughter who had confessed but weeks earlier that she just couldn't wait to go off to college, free at last to make her own decisions, to find her people, free at last to mine the treasure of the true self she had been seeking all along, a self whose excavation the world so far had seemed so hell-bent on preventing.

I downed water and pulled myself together. I did my best to act normal—always a stretch—smiling and hugging and snapping family pictures. I helped clean up and take out trash. Back at home I considered *A Course in Miracles* workbook lesson 182: "I will be still an instant and go home," a breathtaking description of the largely unconscious albeit universal sense of loss we carry over the belief that we have forever forfeited our eternal childhood home, the home of our one, true, and only self beyond the ego's shameful dream of separate interests.

> … We speak today for everyone who walks this world, for he is not at home. He goes uncertainly about in endless search, seeking in darkness what he cannot find; not recognizing what it is he seeks. A thousand homes he makes, yet none contents his restless mind. (from paragraph 3)

The lesson goes on to describe the "hero" of the ego's dream journey to find fulfillment in a meaningless venue designed to make real the ultimately impossible idea of individuality triumphing over indivisible, inclusive, everlasting love. The nagging self-doubt we experience as a result and attempt to repress by donning our masks of stone, while secretly blaming the authority figures of our earthly childhood for imprisoning us far too long.

> … Yet some try to put by their suffering in games they play to occupy their time, and keep their sadness from them. Others will deny that they are sad and do not recognize their tears at all. Still others will maintain that what we speak of is illusion, not to be considered more than but a

dream. Yet who, in simple honesty, without defensiveness and self-deception, would deny he understands the words we speak? (from paragraph 2)

That would be my mind-on-ego, again, of course. As I watched my daughter's friends that morning on the threshold of reen-acting the ego's story of striking off on its own, considered my daughter's approaching senior year and, with any luck, gradua-tion, I asked for help from the eternal child in our one mind—that *symbol* of our enduring, invulnerable defenselessness we carried into the dream—to see clearly. To observe the feelings of loss already flooding my mind-on-ego, feelings generated by the belief that the eternal love we share could be somehow compromised. Somehow diminished by a child heading off to begin her own journey in discovering that we will never find the forever-loving self we think we lack in a world imagined to prevent us from accessing the part of our mind that remembers we have a choice outside the confines of linear time in which to experience our true and only self.

When you are still an instant, when the world recedes from you, when valueless ideas cease to have value in your rest-less mind, then will you hear His Voice. So poignantly He calls to you that you will not resist Him longer. (from paragraph 8)

No one is literally *calling* to us, of course. It is merely the song of our true and only self we hear when we stop listening to the ego's 24/7-spin of separate interests purchased at the expense of enduring unity. I need only call on the strength that lingers in my mind for help in observing my choice to believe I am losing a part of myself along with my daughter's impending departure. When I do so, loving awareness of our unalterable connection returns and all fear and guilt vanish. A connection that has nothing to do with the war of independence waged within every parent-child relationship here in a world that reveres the impossible idea of independence.

Gazing through the whole spirit's lens, I see a photograph replete with shadowy images of "special" love developing backwards into the brilliant light of our true, non-dualistic source. And I remember I am already home along with my daughter despite the dream's apparent story arc; always have been. Even as I observe the ego strengthening in her as she prepares to seek her worldly fortune outside the mind, and begin, at last—through practicing the Course's forgiveness day in and day out—to weaken in me. So that there are elongated moments these days in which I find myself reaching for the muscle of judgment, control, and autonomy only to find it—like a mask I once wore in childhood for protection from imagined pain—happily missing.

> ... In that instant He will take you to his home, and you will stay with Him in perfect stillness, silent and at peace beyond all words, untouched by fear and doubt, sublimely certain that you are home.

Great Expectations

About four years ago I came to a place in my then two-year study of *A Course in Miracles* where I recognized I didn't have a clue what the Course meant by forgiveness. I had been reading the big, blue book—diligently practicing the lessons in the first part of the workbook designed to begin to undo the ego thought system—but still thought there was a me at the center of it all. That earnest, Susan-of-Arc self of my childhood, that justice-seeking, spiritually inclined missile of a me, who had decided to take the high road in my closest, most challenging relationships. A me within whom the peace of God could shine, a me that could cajole the divine into intervening on my behalf, a me entrusted with the salvation of the world.

But since my identification with all things me was what had gotten me into this mess of seeking and never finding—this hell of special, constantly competing and opposing interests—in the first place, I was stuck. The Course was not working for me. My relationships had become more trying than ever. My professional life seemed fraught with constant rejection and disappointment. The world around me seemed headed for certain annihilation, just like the doomsday nut cases constantly proclaimed.

I was facing another birthday but I really had nothing to celebrate. The deep longing for something unknown and unnamed that had plagued me all my life seemed deeper and more futile than ever. And so I prayed to a God I still—cockeyed optimist that I remain—hoped to somehow find outside me somewhere peeking down through the constellations. A God I had not found in the church of my childhood or in the many wacky venues in which I had sought him since. A God I suppose I had hoped to find in the big, blue book but so far had not. I felt that I had come to the end of the proverbial road. I would either find what I was looking for in this book, or I would quit looking, give up, throw the book out the window, run over it with my car. Defect to the dark side.

And so I prayed to really understand what the Course meant by forgiveness. I prayed to learn how to practice it in my life. And I prayed to experience the title of my favorite workbook lesson 189: "I feel the love of God within me now," because I at least recognized and was willing to finally admit that I did not feel the love of God within me, not even close. I did not even know what the hell the love of God was supposed to mean. I only knew I wanted to feel love, real love, love that would stay. I wanted to feel forever loved and loving, to reach beyond the rainbow of my needs, to finally find a better way of living in this world.

Over the next year, my birthday prayer was answered in surprising ways. I suppose I had expected some kind of Hollywood transformation, a sanitized mystical experience complete with a sound track and angels from central casting. I had expected my vision to go all Disney on me, pastel clouds and song birds, heartfelt confessions from those who had wronged me. The kind of thing that would make most grownups want to puke. Instead I learned to step away from the cartoon, to really look with our inner teacher at the selfishness of the ego thought system at work in my so-called life. At the glaring differences I constantly tracked and measured between myself and others, the comparisons I made that always left one of us feeling slimed. Instead I experienced the burden of carrying this heavy pack of lies based on the original lie that we could have differentiated ourselves from our indivisible, loving source, and the incredible relief and release available when I finally chose—from moment to moment, delusion to delusion—to just put the baggage down.

I learned in sharp contrast that when I was willing to resign as my own teacher I could finally feel the love I never left within me still. I experienced a self outside the hallucination of me, a self without agendas of any kind. I learned that the you the author of *A Course in Miracles* addresses is not the ego self we think we are when we first pick up the book but the decision maker in our one mind, the part of our mind that first chose in selfishness to push its creator's love away but can learn to choose again for selflessness. The part of our one mind that can learn to recognize that no one or thing outside the mind can destroy or enhance its everlasting peace in any way, thereby experiencing the extraordinary, transformative power of no me.

I learned we are mind, in ways we totally do not understand here where we think we reside in the condition we think we're in. Mind: a word whose closest translation on the level of form would be heart. The truth of *A Course in Miracles'* message of forgiveness does not reside in its gossamer pages. The power of no me does not stem from trying to wrap our heads around this Course. We need to wrap our heart around this Course. Not the heart of our ephemeral bodies but our one, enduring heart that has nothing to do with illusory bodies. When we do we return to the eternal present we have never left, the only place in which we can feel the love of God within us now. As workbook lesson 189 tells us:

> Simply do this: Be still, and lay aside all thoughts of what you are and what God is; all concepts you have learned about the world; all images you hold about yourself. Empty your mind of everything it thinks is either true or false, or good or bad, of every thought it judges worthy, and all the ideas of which it is ashamed. Hold onto nothing. Do not bring with you one thought the past has taught, nor one belief you ever learned before from anything. Forget this world, forget this course, and come with wholly empty hands unto your God. (paragraph 7)

In this season of great expectations, of final exams, graduations, weddings and anniversaries, failures and triumphs, chapters coming to a close and held up to the darkness of the ego mind for critical review. This season of glorifying personal differences, measuring current accomplishments and achievements against unspoken lists of ego goals, I have once again forgotten what I am, what I could possibly be without my relationship with someone or thing outside myself. I have found myself merely flirting with my right mind before diving back into the ego's mosh pit of specialness for another excruciating romp. Once more blasting lyrics set to a vicious base lamenting the many ways in which others (including the ego self I think I am) have fallen short of my great expectations.

I keep trying to force the self I think I am to once more replay the ego's tune of dueling interests. But in the moment when I have actually done what the Course asks, the whole instant of forgiveness in which I have held another harmless for my distress, heard the gentle call of our one healed mind, and known what the Course means when it tells us "Not one note in Heaven's song was missed," I remember that this is the only music I really want to hear. When I turn away from all the illusions I have concocted to hurt me, I see the peace of God shining in everyone and feel God's love within us all. This is the gift of forgiveness *A Course in Miracles*-style, the answer to the only real prayer we could ever truly utter, the power and glory of no me.

And so I remind myself today that I got my birthday wish. I have felt the love I have never left within me, the all-inclusive love that returns to our mind when we forgive our illusions of specialness with help from our inner teacher. And having heard that call, I cannot bear to listen to this horrid static much longer because I know I can choose again for the song of forgiveness instead. And so I do.

So Close to You We Cannot Fail

In the dream I am accompanying my daughter on a college tour. We are descending difficult-to-navigate metal stairs in some kind of towering outdoor stadium as high as a skyscraper, with each step almost as tall as we are. The whole apparatus shifts—more like scaffolding than a permanent structure—groaning and creaking with our every move. The metal stairs are pebbled with tiny holes. A thin, wrought-iron railing to our right is all that stands between us and plunging to our death thousands of feet below. People keep pushing past us on the left, practically bolting down the swaying stairs. My daughter's high heel catches in one of the holes on the step below and she stumbles. (I told her not to wear those ridiculously inappropriate shoes!) Her teammates on her soccer team call her Bambi for her tendency to trip on those long, lean legs of hers; *Bambi*, after the classic Disney film in which a little fawn loses its mother—I suppose that would be me—to a hunter.

The heel is stuck. The apparatus pitches and I can't reach her to help. Somehow, my daughter extricates the heel and continues down the stairs. But I remain paralyzed with fear, simultaneously aghast at my inability to sacrifice myself to protect her. Suddenly the scene shifts as scenes in dreams inexplicably do. I am still on the same stair, but the other people have disappeared and so have the stairs below me, replaced by a kind of hammock of fragile webbed netting like the bags lemons come in at the supermarket. I cannot see what supports the netting on the other side. I know I am expected to crawl across it but I am *so* not *Survivor* material; there is just no way in hell I am going to risk it. Instead I turn and go back up the suddenly carpeted and indoor stairs. And I wake up; desperate to find the daughter I have once again somehow failed.

Things have been a little tense around here lately. My husband and daughter have not been seeing eye-to-eye. My days have been seemingly punctuated by their outraged outbursts. He feels she does not appreciate all he does for her. In his mind she is not stepping up to the many looming college, financial aid, and scholarship application tasks confronting us this summer, not adequately preparing for her ACTs and SATs, not taking the steps necessary to complete her required IB and college application essays. She feels victimized, persecuted, and misunderstood. Both of them are very talented at sharing their feelings with me.

When not listening to their complaints, I, on the other hand, have been further amusing our right mind by secretly trying to resurrect a recurring little fantasy in which my daughter and I—this last, nostalgic summer before her senior year in high school—get to do all those mother-daughter things we've been largely putting off since her adolescence hit so freaking early and hard. We will drive to Boulder, take a little morning hike around the Flatirons, indulge in a fabulous exotic lunch, and spend the afternoon window shopping on the mall, trying on nutty hats and glasses the way we used to and watching street performers fold themselves up and stuff themselves into little plastic cubes. We will get our nails done, see all those indie movies we never had time to, hit the public pool and read the same novels we will later discuss over the chocolate chip cookies and banana bread we will bake. *I know.*

Yesterday, the last day of a long weekend dedicated to honoring those who sacrificed dearly to protect our American way of life, launching a summer of sentimental cravings for what *A Course in Miracles* calls our "special relationships" to comply with our fantasies; it all came to a head. My husband had had it with her. My daughter had had it with him. They both had had it with my disinclination to try to jump in and fix it for them as I once would only to have both of them turn on me.

There were slamming doors, raised voices, tears. My daughter stormed out the front door. My husband stormed out the side. Our little dog ran around in frantic circles, licking my ankles. I sat in my office, the innocent bystander, reaching for the muscle of indignation only to find it disabled. What did these theatrics really have to do with me, I wondered? I could feel my husband's fear that our daughter would somehow not make it to adulthood, somehow fail to take her place as a responsible, independent citizen in a world filled with irresponsible citizens; masking the real fear: that he had failed her. I could feel my daughter's fear that whatever she did would never be enough to live up to her parents' expectations. That she might not make it in this world—might not become the independent, responsible citizen we expected—masking the real fear: that she had failed him. And all at once I could claim the fear playing out in the characters in my dream—the sleeping and the waking one—as my own.

A deeply comforting line I had read in the introduction to Part II of *A Course in Miracles'* workbook came back to me then like a phrase of welcome music:

I am so close to you we cannot fail.

We have not failed each other, have not failed our creator; have not failed our one and only self. A self that remains seamlessly bound to its source. The notion that we have somehow failed our perpetual wholeness by selfishly declaring our independence is a bunch of hooey despite the ego's elaborate reenactments of individuals vying for control in a hallucinated world of dueling interests.

We had a wish that God would fail to have the Son whom He created for Himself. We wanted God to change Himself, and be what we would make of Him. And we believed that our insane desires were the truth. Now we are glad that this is all undone and we no longer think illusions true. The memory of God is shimmering across the wide horizons of our minds. A moment more, and it will rise again. A moment more, and we who are God's Sons are safely home, where He would have us be. (paragraph 9)

We cannot fail to return to God, the shared eternal peace and wholeness with which we are seamlessly fused, because, as the Course tells us again and again, ideas leave not their source. Despite our impossible desire to experience ourselves as "other," we remain one, resting in eternal, united love, dreaming our trippy dreams of exile. Despite the repressed guilt we carry over the belief that we have pulled off the impossible and must create a world of other bodies on which to pin the crime, the idea of guilt has never left its source in the mind. Our attempts to get rid of it by projecting it on someone "out there" will always fail us. But the moment in which we recognize a dream figure's call for love as the same miserable call of the dream figure we identify with, the dream vanishes, the credits roll, and we find ourselves transported with a gentle, compassionate smile to our right mind. A mind that sees only common interests and knows without question that our true, unified nature has never—and could never—fail us.

When my daughter came home the ego attack had passed. We sat down together and reviewed the many daunting tasks she needed to complete. She admitted she had been feeling a little overwhelmed. I couldn't blame her. I helped her break the tasks into doable pieces and set up a calendar. My husband drifted in from the backyard and we calmly reviewed the information we needed to collect to fill out the financial aid and scholarship applications. With a relieved sigh, the dog curled up and took a well-deserved nap at our feet.

Beam Me Up, Holy Spirit—*Not!*

Beam me up, Holy Spirit, I thought.

I was sitting in my office contemplating the day's *A Course in Miracles* workbook lesson 230: "Now will I seek and find the peace of God." We had just started the second half of the workbook (in the Thursday night class I lead here in Denver) wherein we begin to embrace the light that returns to our mind when we recognize and then turn away from the ego's grim fairy tale of sin, guilt, and fear. But as I read this message of hope and truth uttered from beyond this dreamy dream we call living, I found my mind once again drifting into the kind of blissed-out mindlessness I often slip into as I consider these revelatory passages. Once again believing (or at least wishing I could still believe) I could awaken from this guilty dream simply by closing my eyes and repeating a mantra like some kind of *A Course in Miracles* robot. Beam me up, Holy Spirit; I caught my mind-on-ego thinking. *Not!*

From my understanding this is so *not* a course about clicking my heels together and leaping to perfect love. I mean—duh—if we could do that, we would have. Don't get me wrong, if it works for you; by all means go for it! It's just that—in all honesty—it rarely works for me. As Chapter 16, IV. The Illusion and the Reality of Love suggests:

> Your task is not to seek for love, but merely to seek and find all the barriers within yourself that you have built against it. It is not necessary to seek for what is true, but it is necessary to seek for what is false. Every illusion is one of fear, whatever form it takes. And the attempt to escape from one illusion into another must fail. (from paragraph 6)

I am at a place with this Course where I am beginning to clearly recognize my attempts to escape into an airbrushed version of a world in which I feel the love of God pulsing in this bogus physical body for what they are: ego-driven defenses against returning to our one mind and really looking at the ego's sneaky ways. This time around, the lessons in the second part of the workbook are revealing to me once more that this is a course in opening my eyes on the ego's thought system, the secret guilt I have tried to distance myself from all my life by perceiving it in you. A course in witnessing and preserving my "shameful" hatred and terror and thereby inviting the part of our one mind that knows better to gently reassure me this cannot be. Once again I have caught myself thinking, I just need to close my eyes, make all kissy face, breathe deeply, and poof! I'm walking the earth like Jesus, in it and not of it, without even having ingested any mind-altering substances.

I am *so* not there yet. This dream quite often seems all too real to me—from the hole in the Gulf continuing to contaminate our waters, wetlands, and wildlife to the brutal physical attacks being acted out around the planet in the name of God to our attempts to protect our borders and punish undocumented workers to the ways in which we all play the blame game in our special relationships. Again and again holding those we claim to love most responsible for our compromised peace of mind. Most of the time, I still cannot shift my perception of the hatred I still see outside myself by simply reminding myself we are one and all we need is love. Although I can sit at my desk in meditation and sometimes hear the voice of love's message that it's all an illusion, only rarely can I carry that message onto the pavement of my life for any extended period of time. Often, I can't even read the lessons in the second half of the workbook without completely spacing out.

But here's what I can do, and it is helping me heal my one mind about all I believe and everything I think I experience "out there." I *can* count the many ways I do not love you as they appear to arise from moment to moment, and recognize in each—with help from my right mind—my own projected fear and guilt over the thought of separation I secretly take seriously. I *can* see the underlying fear and hatred feeding the painful images I believe I am attacking and defending against with the part of my mind that does not take them seriously and, as I do, remember to smile at their nothingness.

As I once again recognize my call for love in the relentless scenarios reported each evening on the news as the same call for love in my daughter's fearful meltdown over failing to meet all the demands on her this summer, including my own unspoken expectations, as I once again recognize my impulse to distance myself from what my mind-on-ego perceives to be a fellow Course student's "mistaken" interpretation, I can recognize my own call for love. And learn to answer with kindness to all.

I do that by returning to our one seemingly split mind and choosing again for the part of our mind that clearly speaks the only message I really want to hear—*nothing happened*—in response to every seeming expression of the ego thought system I have chosen to make real. Despite its elaborate and ingenious disguises, the ego's theatrics always reflect the same mistaken belief in the impossibility of separation from our source while the Holy (Whole) Spirit/right mind always provides the same comforting remedy. Our shared, invulnerable, eternal innocence prevails unscathed by a mind made mad on ego. Despite our trippy dreams of exile we remain forever resting in the boundless, loving creativity of our source.

Here's what works for me more and more on this journey home: seeking and finding the peace of our true nature by changing my mind about the relationship I think I am having with you that seems so messy and troubling. When I return to the alleged scene of the crime and seek *there* to recognize my mistaken belief in our guilt I am literally dying to pin on you, the transformative memory of our collective innocence and the peace it always brings returns to my mind. No beaming up required.

Susan Dugan

Let It Be

Last week I attended an outdoor concert featuring one of those Beatles impersonator groups that have become so popular in recent years with my husband and a good friend. It was one of those perfect, rare June evenings in Denver, the purple mountain majesties still capped with snow. The heat relieved by a light breeze, the blazing sun partially obscured by towering, anvil-shaped clouds on their way to battering the plains to our east with hail rather than once again wiping out our newly transplanted tomatoes. Giddy with the sense of having dodged the torrent these concerts too often morph into and transported by the rhythms and lyrics of our youth we sang, danced, ate, and drank, and—during intermission—even managed to converse.

My friend who is not on this path but nonetheless faithfully reads my blog and had just generously recommended it to a mutual friend also not on this path observed that she considered herself an agnostic, and didn't think she would ever enjoy my "certainty." By that I suppose she meant that she considers me a believer in our source: God/wholeness/eternal oneness, whatever you want to call it. I don't think I have ever been called a believer before. Frankly, it left me a little flabbergasted. Feeling a little like an imposter, not unlike the way I began to feel growing up as a child, attending a mass whose exclusive message seemed so at odds with all I felt to be true despite colossal evidence to the contrary.

It didn't occur to me then, but it occurs to me now, that I am not really a believer in the sense I think my friend meant, however enthusiastically I have embraced *A Course in Miracles*. I am not so much a believer in the divine as I am someone who has exhausted her belief in the brutality of the earthly dream I believe I have navigated for so long. A fellow doubter for whom the pain of seeking for myself in the world has simply become too much to bear. Someone who—by practicing forgiveness *A*

Course in Miracles-style day in and day out—has begun to experience moments of yearning for a better way interrupted, elongated instants in which I feel absolutely completed; beyond all need, and happily wrong about everything I once believed.

> And I am free because I was mistaken, and did not affect my own reality at all by my illusions. Now I give them up, and lay them down before the feet of truth, to be removed forever from my mind. (from workbook lesson 227, paragraph 1)

I am not so much certain as I am finally growing into the welcome doubt that anything here will work, with help from a part of my mind I only recently discovered. By learning to look with that part of my mind on all I once thought I wanted and believed, I am starving my faith that anyone or thing can fulfill me, as well as my belief in a separate self in need of fulfillment. Learning once and for always that there is *absolutely nothing* certain in this world, but that beyond this world of form there is a non-dualistic mind restored to wholeness I can always count on.

In a Course class I am teaching we have just begun Part II of the workbook that invites us to allow God—the symbol for perfect oneness the Course uses to ultimately undo our belief in symbols—to reveal itself. To suspend our belief, set aside our defenses as one of my favorite Beatles tunes—*Let It Be*—also entreats us to do. This shouldn't be that difficult since my defenses have never worked very well for me. I have always been too in touch with the emotional pain in myself and others (as if there were a difference). And yet I am very resistant as I begin these revelatory lessons in the second half of the workbook to allow the "Love of God" to shine in me when I still equate the G word with the God we humans crafted, the God of most organized religions created in the ego's image to reinforce the original myth of separation from perfect love, and our creator's inevitable punishment.

Even though I am learning through attempting to live *A Course in Miracles* that the abstract, all-inclusive "God" the Course would invite us to join our minds with has nothing to do with the ego's insane, worldly God, I am still, on some level beyond my understanding, too intimidated by that unconditional light; still too dependent on a false identity—however painful— for sustenance. Still too afraid of being obliterated by that light because of my belief in the selfish crime of coveting individuality over perfect oneness I can't even remember. But despite my fear, the Course offers a gentle, practical path home that provides us with gradual glimpses of wholeness as we practice forgiveness and learn to choose love over fear. Heavily supported by the right mind that returns to our awareness when we turn away from the ego's threats, thereby figuratively "calling on Him." As we are reminded in Chapter 16, VI. The Bridge to the Real World:

> … He needs only your willingness to share His perspective to give it to you completely. And your willingness need not be complete because His is perfect. It is his task to atone for your unwillingness by His perfect faith, and it is His faith you share with Him there. Out of your recognition of your unwillingness for your release; His perfect willingness is given you. Call upon Him, for Heaven is at His Call. And let Him call on Heaven for you. (from paragraph 12)

This is my growing certainty: the world I think I find myself in, along with the self I think I find myself in, offers only pain, despite its ingenious, occasionally thrilling, always ephemeral disguises. The Course readily acknowledges that there are many paths home, and that we are all heading there, regardless of our chosen transportation. It claims only to be a shortcut for those of us engaged in the world. After all, it came to two renowned psychologists (at Columbia University's College of Physicians and Surgeons) who were *so* not religious people—*so* not believers—and very engaged in the world. It uses the specifics of our lives in form—primarily our relationships with others—to undo our belief that specifics and others can in any way affect our peace of mind. It employs Christian terminology because it is so embedded in our Western culture, so entwined with our mistaken beliefs about what we are, so in need of undoing. As Course scholar Ken Wapnick often points out; we should read it like we read a great epic poem teeming with metaphor, rather than taking most of it literally.

Ultimately I suppose this is not a Course for people delighted with what they experience in the world and body. Despite its many breathtaking passages pointing to a reality beyond this dream, this is a Course for people whose faith in the dream world's promises has waned, for people who have absolutely had it with the world. Who have been clobbered over the head and clobbered others over the head at the ego's bidding once too often. This is a Course for those of us willing to embrace the idea of trading the seemingly endless substitutions we have made for eternal, inclusive, universal love for the real thing. I am almost certain I am one of those people.

And so when the dream seems clouded by fearful guilt, I continue to choose again to be happily wrong, to forgive what cannot be; certain only that I can no longer be certain about anything I used to believe, including what I am. And in *that certainty* in all I am learning I am not, I begin to allow the healing light that shines on me, and you, and all— yesterday, today, and tomorrow—to return to our mind.

Pop Quiz

I was heading to Washington, DC, where my daughter had been attending a youth leadership conference at the end of which we planned to visit several prospective colleges. A half hour into the flight, pale-faced attendants abruptly aborted the beverage service, offering me an up-close-and-personal look at just how far I have come with undoing my belief in the reality of this individual, physical existence.

Pop quiz, I thought. In a class I'm teaching we had just been joking about the way in which *A Course in Miracles* invites us to regard our lives as a classroom in which we learn the lessons of fear or love, depending on which inner teacher we have chosen to interpret figures and situations that appear to arise in this dreamy dream of exile from our source. I had just been talking about the random tests the ego thought system likes to throw in an effort to strengthen its position, scaring us mindless with situations seemingly arising out of the blue, completely beyond our control. Pop quizzes we can use to recognize we have chosen the ego as our teacher but can experience peace if we but choose again to learn from the inner teacher that knows it's all just a dream. Situations such as finding ourselves in a metal canister buffeted about by turbulent winds at 36,000 feet without so much as a Diet Sprite to cling to.

Without further ado I found myself uttering that most primal of prayers that at least had kept me placing one foot in front of the other in this world before finding *A Course in Miracles*: *help me, help me, help me*—whoever or whatever you are—*please, please help me!*

I had risen at four in the morning to catch this plane and did not feel up to tackling another forgiveness lesson. Could we just postpone this quiz, I pleaded? I know I'm supposed to turn this around by using the very specifics of the ego's drama to undo my belief in a story of fearful specifics but, as you may recall, flying scares the crap out of me. Surrounded by these towering, IMAX clouds, I just can't possibly withdraw my belief in this body. I need you to rescue me, Holy Spirit, swoop down here this minute, wrap your loving superhero arms around this plane, and get us the hell out of this mess.

Pitiful eyes shut, pressing into the left side of my left wrist with the fingers of my right hand as my Chinese Medicine doctor recommended to stave off anxiety and motion sickness; I sat, conscious of watching my own fear. Trying to turn over its cause as the Course would have us do rather than the fear itself; always no more than a symptom of the guilt in our one mind over believing we successfully separated from eternal, loving, oneness. Challenged by each terrifying rock, roll, and rattle of the overhead bin doors to remind myself this is only an illusion, only my mind-on-ego again.

Pressing on the acupressure point, grasping at what the Course calls "magic," I indulged a little fantasy of Jesus himself materializing in the flesh—strolling down the aisle like a politician working a reception handing out his grace—even as I apologized for doing so. And yet, in truth, I began to notice that the familiar physical reactions of terror—pounding heart, sweaty palms, rapid breath, burning desire to scream at the top of my lungs—seemed much less severe than they had in similar situations in the past. On our way back from Ireland, for example, on the last flight to land before they closed DIA for deadly wind shear, during my brief albeit hopeful "calling all angels" phase in which Archangel Michael and I teamed up to muscle that plane safely to the ground.

But it wasn't over yet. The weather channel my mind-on-ego found it nearly impossible to resist consulting on my little TV had dubbed it "the busiest nationwide severe storm warning to date." Each time the flight attendant announced that the seatbelt sign remained fastened and repeated the word "turbulence" her voice seemed to speed up, and rise an octave. The pilot wasn't even speaking, as if the situation was simply too dire to convey, as if he could not possibly sacrifice a single neuron to keeping us updated when keeping this 747 aloft required every micro unit of his gray matter. There were dueling polar bears painted on the plane's tail, I recalled. Polar bears? How much do those things weigh? What were these people thinking?

"Ladies and gentlemen, a reminder that the captain has turned on the seatbelt sign because of *turbulence*," the flight attendant panted, before barricading herself back in her seat. I dug my nails into my wrist and prayed. Ironically, the day's workbook lesson—the content of the pop quiz I appeared to be failing—contained a very clear and comforting message should I ever manage to actually read it and remember that the single answer to all the multiple choice questions posed in every pop quiz remained the same. "Fear is not justified in any form," lesson 240 in the second half of the workbook maintains. "Not one thing in this world is true," it tells us. "It does not matter what the form in which it may appear. It witnesses but to your own illusions of yourself."

Illusions such as finding the self I still think I am hurtling through the sky among strangers completely unprepared to meet its maker. "Fear is not justified in any form," I silently repeated, reminding myself as I often remind students that we are all afraid here, perpetually threatened by malevolent forces engendered to keep our illusory body identification intact. Most of the time I go about my days pushing my belief that I could perish at any moment and forfeit all I think I have and am away. Thank God for pop quizzes allowing me to look at the depth and power of this belief with the part of our one mind that can truly see.

The Course is not asking us to deny our fear; merely to recognize it and remember its purpose: supporting separate over common interests. Convincing us we are bodies instead of one mind. We are not asked to stop digging our fingers into our wrists to calm our bodies down, merely to stop justifying our belief that we need to do so. As Ken Wapnick thankfully reminds us, we don't need to have mastered this Course to practice it. We need only choose again for right-mindedness by turning away from the ego's fearful rant, thereby allowing the quiet center of reason—the endless, gentle eye inside the storm—to prevail.

The weather ended in Pennsylvania. As we prepared to land in DC, circling low over white monuments lined up like pieces on a Monopoly game board luminous in a pink summer haze—flags flapping a message of liberation from our source—I had to smile. Happy to have once again passed a pop quiz designed to expose the depth of my attraction to a body of guilt and a world of fear, and thereby awarded a gold star for the day from our right mind.

Stairway to Heaven

Over the long Fourth of July weekend we drove up to Mount Evans, a very accessible "fourteener" (local speak for mountains higher than14,000 feet) backed up against the foothills of Denver like a stairway to heaven. Our friends who have two adorable girls—eleven and six—joined us, along with their Chesapeake puppy, Poppy, and our Maltipoo, Kayleigh. Even my seventeen-year-old daughter—intent on acclimatizing herself to climb Mount Kenya with a school group later this summer—made a winning appearance. As we tumbled out of our vehicles on a windswept ridge and started down the trail, the party quickly split into predictable camps: Anne, Poppy, and I—the "responsible" ones—winding down the trail as the signs entreated, and the rest of our brood breaking free to scramble up the rocks, followed by a tiny dog with big ambitions.

My family's tendency to defy rules and tackle what I consider much more dangerous terrain has long rankled. This time, however, watching them with a different teacher, I recognized in their efforts to summit and my impulse to control only our common ego at work again, enticing me once more to differentiate myself from the pack as the "innocent" victim. To relieve myself of the secret burden of guilt in the one mind we all carry over the repressed belief that we have separated from our one loving source and ventured out into a world of differentiated selves competing for both survival and salvation.

When a European woman stopped to remind us that the rest of our party might be jeopardizing fragile vegetation; I found myself reaching once more for the muscle of anger at my family only to find it again happily disabled. While on the level of form I certainly agreed with her, I also knew from experience where efforts to rein the pack in would lead. They were not deliberately trying to destroy anything, my right mind knew, and would probably do a good job staying on the rocks as usual. They just wanted to climb for the sake of climbing, I thought—as we stood making polite small talk, attempting to ignore the children's elated cries—to proclaim their independence on a long weekend commemorating that universal ego impulse. They just wanted to make it to heaven like the rest of us while preserving their sweet individuality, here in this world created to make that preposterous desire real.

The ongoing practice of forgiveness *A Course in Miracles* style—the habit of watching the ego with the right mind we all share whether we're aware of it or not—is beginning to help me recognize on a regular basis the truth behind the myth the Course uses to explain the underlying cause of our constant state of turmoil in this world. As we learn in Chapter 27, VIII. The "Hero" of the Dream:

> ...Into eternity, where all is one, there crept a tiny, mad idea, at which the Son of God remembered not to laugh. In his forgetting did the thought become a serious idea, and possible of both accomplishment and real effects. Together we can laugh them both away, and understand that time cannot intrude upon eternity. ... (from paragraph 6)

Despite the ego's efforts to keep me forgetting, to convince me I am the hero of the dream—an alternating victim and victimizer intent on a singular journey away from my source—I remain fused to my eternal home, seamlessly connected with infinite creation and unfettered by adventures played out in an illusory theatre of linear time. A screen onto which I project my seemingly sinister delusions in an ultimately futile effort to distance myself from the crushing responsibility of having jeopardized eternal wholeness by instead seeing it acted "out there" by you.

> The body's serial adventures, from the time of birth to dying are the theme of every dream the world has ever had. The "hero" of this dream will never change, nor will its purpose. (from paragraph 3)

The dream's purpose always remains keeping me focused outside myself, mindlessly projecting shadows of my own denied guilt on an imaginary screen, attacking other shadowy dream figures and defending the shadowy dream figure I call me. There is no way out of this insane dream from within it. Only when I return to the mind we share *outside* the dream and choose again to view the dream figures and the theatre itself informed by the memory of my true, uninterrupted, non-dualistic nature can I smile gently at the dream hero's journey, that fairy tale of running away from home we all share playing 24/7 in the theatre of our mind-on-ego.

Like the Von Trapp family, our children of all ages towered above us on a formation resembling a dinosaur's jagged back, poised to burst into song, our little, loyal dog facing them, oblivious to the sweeping panorama at her back. And I recalled climbing a real fourteener years earlier, my then two-year old daughter thumping in her pack between my shoulder blades. "Slow ones!" she'd called down to my husband and his friend below; the giddy pleasure of it all.

"Losers!" the girls chanted down at us now, giggling, intoxicated with their accomplishment. And I had to laugh with my right mind at the preposterous idea of a world of winners and losers, valleys and summits. A tiny, mad idea I all too often take so seriously but on this beautiful morning at 14,000 plus feet could finally—for a little while, anyway—see clearly.

Seek Not Outside Yourself

Driving home in "the heat of the day" as my mother used to call it I noticed that the little plastic Buddha on my dashboard had developed melanoma, his bald bobble head a Rorschach of darkened, malevolent, sun-damaged lesions. I had purchased him in California years earlier and even after having identified *A Course in Miracles* as my chosen path home, had no desire to remove him from his place of honor. His permanent smile—unfettered by the motion of my vehicle's acceleration that had him banging against the windshield—continued to inspire me, a reminder of the right mind always available to us all, completely independent of "external" circumstances. Even Buddhas get melanoma in this world, I thought, reminding myself again that we can count on nothing here except change. That seeking for ourselves in an ephemeral, illusory world designed to reinforce a thought of guilt in the mind—pinning our inner peace on outer symbols—will never work.

I came of age in the late 1970s, an era in which young people and even the wannabe young—disillusioned by the failed idealism of the '60s and leaking brain cells from years of hallucinogenic experimentation—were flocking to cults, becoming born again in droves. They wore midi skirts and thumped Bibles. They joined the Moonies. They shaved their heads, strapped bells on their ankles, and took up panhandling on city sidewalks and outside suburban shopping malls. They followed cult leader Jim Jones of the People's Temple to Guyana to create the agricultural commune Jonestown. They drank cyanide-laced Kool-Aid en masse to meet their heavenly maker to prevent a Congressional team from shutting them down.

Fresh out of college, working in Washington, DC, at the time, all I wanted to do was get as far away as fast as possible from every symbol of misguided divinity that flashed across the screen, showed up on my doorstep, or attempted to wave me down to exchange a blessing or a wilted rose for a quick buck. For reasons that currently evade me I decided to move to San Francisco to make a fresh start. Having renounced the unpredictable God of my childhood years earlier, I embraced agnosticism, philosophy, and psychology and turned my attention once more to the many social justice causes in need of another able-bodied hand.

But something was always missing. When I finally decided to quit smoking I came face to face with the nameless anxiety that had plagued me all my life, and, against my better judgment, began taking meditation classes at a nearby New Age Center in an effort to calm my endlessly restless mind. Like a gateway drug, the classes triggered an insatiable desire for all things energy-healing, quantum-leaping, and law-of-attracting I could wrap my proverbial head around. Despite the self-aggrandized pride I had taken in my once reasonable tendencies, I found myself swept away in a current of metaphysical phenomenon.

It wasn't until I'd moved to Denver, married, and become a mother that I allowed myself to entertain the secret, nagging possibility that none of these supposedly healing modalities had in any way come near repairing the hidden part of me I feared forever maimed. I continued to search outside myself for answers, paying psychics, energy healers, and past-life regression special-ists hard-earned cash for their take on what ailed me. I enrolled in a week-long training at the Zen Center in which we sat in hours of painful Zazen watching our thoughts commit hara-kiri, and were patiently taught how to correctly don our robes, enter, navigate, and exit a temple, bow, and chant.

Although there were moments in prolonged meditation when my thoughts actually stopped and I experienced a hallucination in which a kind of theatre curtain rose before me to expose a comforting screen of silent white light, I never really got the hang of Zen. Although I sensed its wisdom and could see the joy its practice brought those with whom it did completely resonate, rising nearly crippled from my pillows for breaks of walking meditation, I always turned the wrong way, inevitably knocking into something sacred. I never tied the robes right, could never remember which way to enter the temple, bowed in all the wrong places, and, during lunch breaks of brown rice and vegetables on the deck, inevitably found myself squashing mosquitoes having once again forgotten my oneness with all sentient beings. A dear friend and kindred seeker I had dragged along had the same issues and we still fondly refer to the episode as "Lucy and Ethel Visit the Zen Center."

Suffice it to say the process of getting over myself has been a long and—when I listen to the ego's opinion that I am giving up something of value along with my judgments and mad notions of differences—painful one. But the process of finding my true, shared self is always short and indescribably rewarding. It doesn't require a guru, a center, a healer, a magician, an external teacher, or a Holy Spirit swooping down in superhero garb. It requires only that I change my mind about all I think is happening to me in a world made mad by guilt over the thought of separation from eternal love. When I do that, all thoughts of differences, all comparisons, all cravings for someone or thing to rescue or complete me disappear in the light of our collective, inalterable, loving truth and I am once more complete and completely relieved of the wacky thought of "me."

As we are gently reminded in *A Course in Miracles* Chapter 29, VII. Seek Not Outside Yourself:

> ... Seek not outside yourself. For all your pain comes simply from a futile search for what you want, insisting where it must be found. What if it is not there? Do you prefer that you be right or happy? Be you glad that you are told where happiness abides, and seek no longer elsewhere. You will fail. But it is given you to know the truth, and not to seek for it outside yourself. (from paragraph 1)

Even Bhuddas get melanoma in this world but it doesn't matter one bit to the Buddha. He continues to smile gently, wildly thumping against the window as I press on an accelerator still hoping to get somewhere but finally willing to entertain the possibility that I would rather be happy than right. Rather look for myself where I eternally am and can always be found.

It doesn't matter to the Buddha and it doesn't have to matter to me when I remember that the only center I need to visit exists in our one mind, a mind that still abides in peace—and in which I still abide—*outside* this dream we call living, and dying. In that quiet center I am healed and whole, eternally safe from all that would appear to hurt me "out there," and reunited in innocence with you.

I Am *So* Irritated

I could not even remotely remember the Course workbook lesson for the day. It had not even crossed my mind since first reading it that morning in the milky light of dawn after rising to take our poor little doggy to the vet to have her baby teeth—which refused to leave their sockets unassisted—removed. What had started as a worsening of my chronic sinus infection had overnight morphed into a full-blown respiratory assault. The day had passed in a blur of breathlessness, searing throat pain, and twinges of fear. What if this goes into pneumonia? What if I permanently lose my voice like those people with some strange new disease they were serendipitously talking about that very morning on NPR? I assuaged my fears with *Desperate Housewife* reruns, the reality TV program *The Next Food Network Star*, and the 1996 movie *Independence Day*. I quaffed copious amounts of herbal teas, nibbled cheese pizza and chicken pot stickers—my teenage daughter's sworn remedies for just about anything the world might dish out—I found hard to swallow.

I never get sick, I mentally whined. Not true, of course. I get sick like everyone else and always for the same reason that has nothing to do with stressed-out immune systems, malevolent pathogens, or communicable disease outbreaks. Like everyone else I get sick whenever the memory of unified, all-inclusive love flashes across the screen of our one, split mind, reminding us of the denied guilt we feel over believing we destroyed it. The resulting déjà vu causes us to automatically attack another body—mine or yours, it really doesn't matter. Either way I keep that love where the ego thinks it belongs; *outside* the dream of special interests it believes it exchanged for reality. While the "I" I still think I am keeps right on dreaming.

Between dry coughs, shallow sighs, and aborted attempts to answer the phone and return emails, I found myself once more immersed in the saga of special relationships run amuck on

Wisteria Lane. Creepy George's infamous plan to off Bree's husband Rex by switching out his heart medication, Lynette's obsession with Tom's colleague and former girlfriend and relentless plot to separate them, Gabby's cheeky affair with the underage gardener, and Carlo's ill-fated revenge. I could feel my IQ plummeting in deeply satisfying ways as I dove in for another dab of soy sauce.

"I am *so* irritated," Bobby Flay, one of the celebrity chef judges in the latest installment of the Food Network's search for another culinary mega personality muttered, commenting on the audacity of one of the contestants substituting a bottled version of a pickled condiment for homemade in the latest challenge. If I could have chortled, I would have. My daughter and I adopted it as the mantra for the remains of the wasted afternoon. "I am *so* irritated," she chanted and I whispered, navigating an obstacle course of construction zones as we headed out to pick up the puppy in a haze of summer ozone.

"I am *so* irritated," I thought, later, collapsed among listing towers of dirty dishes, watching the puppy chase her tail in mad circles as the pain medication wore off. Watching fighter pilot Will Smith punch an alien—intent on destroying civilization as we know it and passed out in a crash-landed spaceship—in the face. "Welcome to earth," he said, before lighting up a cigar and inhaling. And I had to smile, like Will Smith and poor President Bill Pullman, secretly grateful to be defending myself and the bodies I identify with against all those other whack job aliens "out there" hell-bent on destroying us.

Prior to the onset of my debilitating condition I had been reading the latest of *A Course in Miracles*' definitions in the second half of the workbook, descriptions of the ego thought system nestled within the revelatory passages evocative of our true nature outside the dream. Under "What is the Body?" we learn:

The body is a fence the Son of God imagines he has built; to separate parts of his Self from other parts. It is within this fence he thinks he lives, to die as it decays and crumbles. For within this fence he thinks that he is safe from love.

Don't let the G word fool you. The "Son of God" the Course refers to is merely symbolic of the indivisible, eternally loving oneness in which we remain, dreaming our dreamy dream of exile from love; the truth, the whole truth, and nothing but the truth; the memory of which scares the living crap out of us. There is only *one*. A oneness fused in oneness with our creator in ways beyond our current understanding here in the frail, fragmented, deeply irritated condition in which we seem to find ourselves. Here in a dream engendered to keep us from remembering that the puny, preposterous idea of running away from home to inhabit separate bodies in a world of competing interests never happened. Our eternal, all-inclusive innocence remains unfettered by our mass psychosis.

Prior to the full-blown onset of my condition I had also been once more indulging the ego's judgments designed to deny responsibility for the resurfacing, free-floating guilt in my mind by pinning it on you. Complaining to other selves as well as the self I still think I am about yet "other" selves and their less than loving ways. Thank the G word as reflected in *A Course in Miracles* I can't get away with that for very long anymore. It hurts when I use the body's voice to further separation rather than for its right-minded purpose: as a communication device to heal our one mind. So much so—in this case—that I could no longer speak for the pain. Not that that stopped me from projecting.

Now, not quite even twilight, I lay in bed with the blinds drawn thinking about how much my throat hurts. About the unrelenting tightness in my chest and burning in my eyes, counting the many ways in which the ego strives to render me mindless with its secret whispered fears which have, these last couple days, appeared to have literally scared me speechless.

And yet, I can choose again to forgive right here and now. When I do the form of the day's forgotten workbook lesson may or may not reemerge, but its content will. I will remember that when I choose the ego I am just *so* physically, mentally, and psychologically irritated. But when I choose the right mind, I can smile at the ego's sneaky ways, again aware I am not the ego and certain this current episode in the wrong mind's hallucinated journey of separation, too, will pass, if I but watch.

P.S. The workbook lesson for the day I couldn't remember? Lesson 257: "Let me remember what my purpose is." Ha! In which we learn: "No one can serve contradictory goals and serve them well." Another of the Course's colossal understatements about the ego thought system we all share in either indulging or undoing that helps me remember to smile.

My Heart Is Beating in the Peace of God

"My heart is beating in the peace of God," I read. I was sitting at my desk, the big, blue book open to Lesson 267, a deft description of the happy dream available when we have completed all our forgiveness lessons within our individual curriculum arising in the classroom of our daily lives. When we no longer hold anyone or anything responsible in any way for our peace of mind, that lofty state the ego would convince us must remain forever elusive, as perpetually beyond our permanent grasp as our one right mind.

Earlier that morning we had risen along with twelve other sets of bleary-eyed parents to drop our 17-year-old daughter off at the airport at 3 a.m. She was on her way to a three-week sojourn in rural Kenya, an adventure planned for many months I still found myself unable to fully process. The words of that day's *A Course in Miracles* workbook lesson seemed equally obscure. "My heart is beating in the peace of God," I read. But my heart—just like that pesky God of my childhood—seemed once again to have forsaken me.

It had been a difficult week. I was not bouncing back from the respiratory infection that had so well served the ego's agenda of distracting me from watching my impulse to project as quickly as usual. The more I pushed myself to catch up with work projects the further behind I seemed to fall. My calendar presented a tangled web of conflicting commitments I could not even wrap my head around. And with every item we laid out on the bed of the guest room and eventually crammed into my daughter's duffel I felt a little less stable—her possessions like withdrawn ballast—oddly unmoored and in danger of vanishing. Having just celebrated her first birthday, the dog appeared to have taken the impending defection of a fellow pack member as a personal affront. She raced around in frantic circles, now and then pausing to consider the scene with plaintive eyes, and made her own feelings of abandonment known in no uncertain terms more than once on the carpet.

As I considered the day's lesson—the dog licking every atom of my bare feet and toes in an effort to reinforce our continuing bond—I once again marveled at how real this dream of exile from our source can seem. How intimately identified with this body I call myself, and other bodies I call *my* family and *my* pet, I continue to be despite having chosen *A Course in Miracles* as the tool to help me undo the ego thought system I must stop taking seriously along with the idea of individuality if I ever hope to actually awaken from this dream.

In short, I caught myself judging myself again, and, in so doing, instantly remembered that judging me serves the same purpose as judging others: reinforcing the seeming reality of the original error of separation in our one mind. A mind that—despite its woeful tale of rejection at the hands of an unreliable God—remains eternally complete within our singular, indivisible source, its guilty fantasy of running away from home forever unrealized. Our source continues to recognize only the truth of our perfect wholeness; completely unaware of our hallucinated "defection" and its continuing reenactments within our seeming relationships.

Once again I had forgotten that although the Course uses the ego's language to meet us where we think we are and help us transcend the ego it is merely offering us an interpreter—that memory of our true nature that always looks without judgment—in the dream. A sane translator that enables us (when we choose its translation) to see that "nothing real can be threatened" because "nothing unreal exists" as the Course's Preface boldly states. Allowing us to smile gently at all the conditions we have chosen to limit and control boundless and eternally liberated love, the only real love there is.

Our one gentle translator meets us where we think we are—apparently stranded in bodies designed to arm ourselves against unwavering wholeness—with words like:

> Surrounding me is all the life that God created in his Love. It calls to me in every heartbeat and in every breath; in every action and in every thought. Peace fills my heart, and floods my body with the purpose of forgiveness. ...

And there it is again; that one whole word: forgiveness; defined in *A Course in Miracles* as looking without judgment with my right mind at my wrong-minded compulsion to deny responsibility for my state of mind by blaming it on others. When I choose the right mind we all share as my internal guide I observe the many mad ways I choose to defend my position that God has forsaken me. I am able to see the problem as it is, as the Course puts it in Chapter 27, VII. The Dreamer of the Dream, "and not the way that you have set it up." When I do so I remember there is never a problem in truth. We could not have abandoned, diminished, or divided oneness. The body's heart will one day cease to beat and I and every perceived "other" dreamer of the dream will continue to rest in the loving arms of our source as we always have until my fear completely subsides and I awaken to the one love I have never left once and for always.

I do that gradually, gently through practicing forgiveness; looking with my right mind's kind vision at all I think could hurt me and recognizing in every instance the same illusory defense against the truth engendered only by a mistaken guilty belief. When I remember to look at the ego with my right mind, I also remember that my heart does not beat to the rhythm of a different drummer (no offense Thoreau), but to the song of wholeness in our one heart where not one note in heaven's song has ever been missed.

> Let me attend Your Answer, not my own. Father, my heart is beating in the peace the Heart of Love created. It is there

and only there that I can be at home. (from lesson 257, paragraph 2)

Bon Voyage, Kara, my daughter, my heart!

What Is the Christ?

Last week, I came face to face with my resistance to where practicing *A Course in Miracles* is really leading. After putting my teenage daughter on a plane to Kenya and seeking additional medicine—referred to in the Course as "magic"—for my lingering respiratory infection, I headed to a yoga retreat in the mountains outside Denver with a good friend. Anxious to indulge in another kind of magic I hoped might cure my continuing physical distress while offering my overly taxed nervous system what my ego considered a well-deserved break.

I have visited this working ashram and yoga teacher training center for many years, usually near my birthday to celebrate a kind of personal New Year's. Participating in the daily yoga classes, meditating in the Ma shrine devoted to female Hindu deities, hiking the pristine hills, ingesting delicious vegetarian fare, and partaking of various Ayurvedic body treatments always offers just the respite I am seeking. The retreat also appears to enable me to more easily suspend my preoccupation with the past and future and enter the quiet center the Course refers to wherein we remain right-minded, observing the ebb and flow of thoughts, forms, and judgments with gentle kindheartedness.

As I experienced that kindheartedness reflected back to me in the serene faces of the ashram residents, I realized how much I still didn't want to allow that vision to permeate everyone and everything in my life. It was one thing to experience it with strangers on a secluded mountaintop to the rhythm of our joint breath but quite another to sustain it in the trenches of our intimate relationships. I still had trouble generalizing the Course's all-inclusive message all the time as we are ultimately challenged to do, especially when it came to those with whom I had the longest and most personal history. What the Course calls our "special" relationships, those particular dream figures we choose to love and—when they fail to meet our expectations as they inevitably do—hate.

It occurred to me as my sinuses and lungs began to clear, as I drank in pure water and thin mountain air, soaked up the pink light of dawn, and opened the big, blue book to "What is the Christ?" in the second half of the workbook, that, try as I might, I could not seem to count myself among the seeming fragments of God's post-thought-of-separation son the Course addresses. At that moment, to the tune of an indifferent wind whistling down the canyon, I also really saw in my secret compulsion to push the love of those closest "others" away both my fear of awakening to unalterable love and my continuing investment in this individual self I still must on some level believe offers something of value. If only the quaint idea of protection from the punishment I still must think I deserve for the original, imagined "crime" of separation at the root of the ego's thought system.

I was sitting outdoors at the time, watching a hummingbird madly circling a feeder of sugar water dangled above an ancient-looking golden retriever apparently trying to muster the energy to interact. An understanding that I shared the dog's reluctance to completely engage—to truly open myself to those I love once and for always—arose in me. And I saw that although I am not actively condemning my special relationships, too often I continue to distance myself from them, confusing a talent for dodging conflict with actually healing my mind of the belief in separate interests that always leads to conflict.

In the hummingbird, I recognized the part of my mind still frantically searching outside the self I still think I am for a magical cure to my unloving thoughts and unworthy feelings. The part of me that still believes embracing my oneness with you will obliterate the self I still think I am. But I also recognized—turning back in growing faith and longing to the big, blue book and what it had to say about our one, Christ self—that I truly wanted to find myself again within that circle of our common light. And

I remembered I could do this through forgiveness, looking with my right mind without judgment from moment to moment at all the illusions of suffering I still cling to, all my judgments of you and the self I still think I am, at all I would use to douse our common light.

> … For when forgiveness rests upon the world and peace has come to every Son of God, what could there be to keep things separate, for what remains to see except Christ's face? (Workbook 6. What Is the Christ? paragraph 4)

I still do not see Christ's "face" (that symbol of the enlightened mind) when I look in the mirror, and I still do not see it in you *except* when I catch myself judging myself, judging you, and pushing your love away. That's my signal I need to choose a different inner teacher, to turn my dark thoughts over to the bright Christ light—that memory of our true, eternally united nature that has never forsaken us—that still shines in our mind. Then I can gently accept how much my false judgments have cost me, and how much better I feel when I exchange them for simple kindness.

Apparently I am still afraid of awakening but at least when I choose my right mind, kindness flows. I see your call for love as my own. I am less guarded with you, less afraid to express affection for fear of rejection. The heaviness in my heart begins to lift. This journey without distance is helping me gradually awaken but I recognize I am not yet fully ready to open my eyes. For right now, practicing forgiveness *A Course in Miracles*-style helps me find the kindness and affection I keep misplacing in my heart. I am not at the end of this seeming journey without distance but somewhere in the murky middle; ready at least to remember that the real magic I seek lies in changing my mind once more about what I really want in my relationship with you.

Wake up? I'll think about that tomorrow when I have healed my mind through forgiveness about this theatre of time. Until then, I will continue to try to look with my right mind at all I still believe I can hurt and be hurt by right here and now, and, in so doing, embrace the possibility that I will one day make it to the end of this long and winding road. Wherein the journeyer I still think I am returns to the one, loving fold. Wherein all my seeming illusions dissolve, instantly corrected at the moment that first illusion of separation arose in the one mind we have never left.

The Sounds of Silence

Lately I have been thinking a lot about silence. The hollow thrum of a baby's breath I can still feel against my neck after all these years, the hush of my little dog asleep in my arms, the ocean I thankfully no longer need a conch shell tipped to my ear or an actual body of water flirting with sand to recall. I have been thinking about the way I still nonetheless hunt for that blessed white noise of completion *outside* but not so much inside myself where my thoughts continue to spin out to the rhythm of the perpetual soundtrack in my head.

I became somewhat obsessed with the elusive nature of silence last weekend on a camping trip with my husband and another couple to the remote Flat Tops Wilderness nestled in the mountains about 30 miles southwest of Steamboat Springs, Colorado. We pitched our tents within a forest licked largely clean by a raging fire so hot it killed off seeds of the future along with all possibility of spontaneous regeneration as it roared down the canyon on a parched summer wind, leaving a purple haze of almost unbearably beautiful fireweed in its wake these eight years later.

The state in general and the mountains in particular had succumbed the past couple weeks to a continuing deluge of thunderstorms, the result of a predictable monsoonal flow from the South Pacific that seemed particularly pronounced and prolonged this year, fueling dinner party speculation about the dire reality of climate change and the malevolent feeble-mindedness of those who continued to deny it.

The projected unstable weather conditions—combined with our groups' intention to climb the many trails snaking off of Trappers Lake toward the sheer summits, and a body that continued to rebel against perceived overload—made my decision to spend Saturday at the campsite by myself a no-brainer. I have never been a fan of risking lightning at altitude having come far too close to its consequences the first time I hiked a fourteener after relocating to Colorado. Besides, I had a novel to finish reading, a Course class to prep, and a stack of accumulated cooking magazines to peruse. More importantly, the call of silence that had left its seeds when I fell asleep so long ago was—like the fireweed—in full bloom. I longed to unplug, in every sense of the word, and once again mistakenly believed I could do so better alone than in company; that my outer circumstances had anything at all to do with my inner condition.

After my husband and friends set off—our little dog casting a furtive glance over her shoulder at me before disappearing at their heels into the skunkweed—I tidied up and battened-down the camp beneath the popup canopy for the onslaught that seemed inevitable given thunderheads already organizing into pyramids along the horizon like drunken cheerleaders. I finished my Course reading and scribbled a few notes for the next class, rummaged in the cooler for a Vitamin Water, saturated my legs and arms with highly toxic bug spray, propped up my feet on one of our camp chairs and leaned back in the other. Breathing in through the third eye and out through my heart as my inner yoga teacher instructed to quiet my mental chatter, I turned my attention to the day's workbook lesson 275: "God's healing Voice protects all things today."

> … Join me in hearing. For the Voice for God tells us of things we cannot understand alone, nor learn apart. It is in this that all things are protected. And in this the healing of the Voice for God is found. (paragraph 1)

I called on the "Voice for God," what the Course calls the Holy (Whole) Spirit or right mind we all share, that memory of eternal, benevolent oneness that followed us into the ego's nightmare of competing interests into which we seemingly plunged the moment we believed our wish to experience individuality had real effects. I tried to open to that sane part of our seemingly severed mind that remembers our true nature and quietly waits for us to join with its uninterrupted, silent knowing.

A single, engorged mosquito circled my head, now and then dive-bombing my closed eyes. I longed to squash it. The small tarp I had used to blanket our firewood flapped beneath the saw and shovel I'd anchored it with. Suddenly shifting, the wind carried the acrid smoke from our nearly doused breakfast fire to my nostrils. Eyes still stubbornly closed and watering, I began to cough as faraway thunder grumbled, praying no one would die out there.

A spontaneous slideshow of apparently less than forgiven faces in my special dream launched itself against the screen inside my head complete with little sound bites designed to rekindle the embers of my annoyance, even though I am learning through practicing *A Course in Miracles* the faceless nature of the truth behind the ego's lies. And then my mind-on-ego decided to up the ante. My teenage daughter's image—propelled by the fearful thought that we had driven far beyond cell-phone range—arose phantom-like, leaving me to wonder again what would happen should something run amuck during this second week of her work project in Kenya.

My fears and judgments chiming like church bells I called out again for the voice of reason, once more marveling at the way in which the ego mind generates judgmental and fearful thoughts to keep us essentially mindless. Captivated by our own projected illusions designed to prevent us from remembering we chose to suffer in the first place through a story of our own making but can choose again for the silent certainty of truth.

Eyes still closed, I continued to watch my thoughts reveal themselves like the nonsensical centers of fortune cookies or the buried-treasure proverbs in the Cracker Jacks boxes of back in the day. "Things about to get much worse," I imagined unfurling a tiny white flag with my fingers, and had to smile. The reel of my thoughts continued to spin but my reactions came to a screeching halt. And I found myself above the battleground again, looking down light-heartedly with Jesus, that embodied *symbol* of our mind healed of the tiny, mad idea of it all.

"Cracker Jack?" I asked, and could finally hear the silence I'd been seeking.

You Like Potato, and I like Potahto

"You're an introvert," the ego said, with that smug little smile of his that could really tick me off, if I let it.

"And you, sir, are merely a figment of my tortured imagination."

"I know you are, but what am I?"

"I can't hear you."

"An introvert," he repeated. "Always have been, always will be, and that, my friend, is that."

"Friend," I said. "Seriously?"

"I am nothing, if not serious."

Ha! I couldn't have said it better myself.

He had been eavesdropping again on my thoughts. Blatantly exploiting my secret desire to join him again in recounting the many ways in which I differ from those I profess to love. Reflective of that original selfish impulse to differentiate and then take the tiny, mad idea that had started this whole ball of projection rolling in the first place seriously. How do I love thee? Let me count the ways I would, if it weren't for all these glaring differences. *My* introversion versus *their* extraversion. *My* lark over *their* owl tendencies. *My* acute sensitivity over *their* legendary cluelessness. *My* need for order and organization versus *their*—how to put this right-mindedly?—more lax approach to the state of our household possessions in particular and this so-called life, in general. In short, "You like potato and I like potahto," I thought, the lines from a song in one of my favorite Fred Astaire movies, *Shall We Dance*, boomeranging back into my so-called consciousness to bolster my mind-on-ego's argument.

I am a big fan of all things Fred Astaire; the realization that I did not have the chops for anything remotely approaching a career in dance one of the earliest of the many personal disappointments I have cherished to this day but am learning through practicing forgiveness *A Course in Miracles*-style I really feel a hell of a lot better about when I relinquish. In the Gershwin duet

Let's Call the Whole Thing Off, Fred and Ginger—cornered into a pretend marriage/publicity stunt—vocally tally their many differences in an effort to dodge the inevitability of a special relationship. My brother and I used to sing this to each other after watching the movie on TV. Like most of our attempts at collaboration, it usually ended in a fist fight followed by banishment to our respective corners.

And yet, it is, of course, these very differences—these very doomed attempts at collaboration at the core of our relationships with those with whom we have the longest and most intimate history—that keep the heart of the ego thought system beating its guilty, fearful dirge of competing interests. The problem does not rest in the differences—our unique preferences and personality traits—but in the hefty meaning we assign them. The seriousness with which we regard them with our little frowny faces that leads us to defend our position and attack those we consider different and thereby threatening.

In my 20s I had to take a Myers Briggs personality test for an employer and discovered I was an INFJ (accounting for only one percent of the population, the rarest of the 16 types). No wonder nobody got me, my mind-on-ego triumphantly whined—how special is that? Our mind-on-ego delights in differences, the body of evidence it perpetuates to build the case that I exist at your expense, a reenactment of that original hallucinated separation from eternal wholeness that—taken seriously—seemingly gave rise to a gazillion bodies of evidence.

And yet, practicing *A Course in Miracles'* forgiveness—learning to watch the ego's daily arguments in defense of mindlessness over mindfulness with the part of my mind that has never abandoned the latter approach, I am beginning to recognize that traits such as introversion and extraversion are merely two sides of the same ego coin—the former an effort to extract one's juice from outside and the latter an effort to distance oneself from others perceived as draining one's juice—both equally futile self-delusions perpetuated to keep the mind seemingly split and at war with itself.

The love of our true nature may make no comparisons but the ego relentlessly chalks up differences to justify calling the whole thing off. But when we choose the help of what the Course calls the Holy (Whole) Spirit or right mind we all share—that correction for the ego's endless projection of special, guilty differentiation that remains in our dreaming mind—we can see the differences our mind-on-ego takes so seriously for what they are: attempts to defend against the one, eternal love we have in truth never left. A love that—recognizing only its infinite, all-inclusive completeness—refuses to acknowledge illusory comparisons.

We need to learn to really look with our loving inner teacher at our investment in our personal differences, and recognize what taking them seriously has cost us: the very love we perceive lacking in our lives. So you say tomato and I say tomahto; so no one seems to get me—what in hell has that to do with true peace of mind?

My mind-on-ego is always cooking up another publicity stunt on its behalf that always seeks to justify calling the whole thing off, distancing ourselves from those we love, sanctifying our impulse to exclude others and ourselves just as we believe we excluded the one love we are at the seeming beginning. But when I choose to see its motives with my right mind, I remember that differences have nothing to do with the one loving mind we truly share and remain. You can say tomato and I can say tomahto until we are blue in the face but my right mind just continues to smile gently at the screwball comedy of special relationships run amuck in a movie of my own making.

Something There Is That Doesn't Love a Wall

I did not grow up in a family or community that embraced poetry—I mean, how many American families or communities do? And yet I secretly wrote it as a child, and remain a closet poet to this day. My clandestine incantations at best affirmations from beyond this individual self of a truth that—while not exactly ego-free—often conjures ego freedom with its neutral acknowledgement of the predicament in which we self-banished fugitives from real love often find ourselves. Seemingly stranded here in bodies and lamenting an absence of any true connection while actively building and maintaining fortresses that render our longing's fulfillment impossible.

I grew up among hard-working people who, for the most part, had far more serious matters on their minds than poetry. And yet I devoured what I could get my hands on at the library in stealth mode, sitting in a tree in the woods behind our development or under the covers with a flashlight at night, as if perusing pornography. Those days seem long ago and yet, the lines of favorite poems I once cherished in solitude all those years ago have lately resurfaced in my mind like long-delayed answers to questions posed to a Magic 8 Ball.

"Something there is that doesn't love a wall," for example.

So begins the poem *Mending Wall*, by Robert Frost, the exception to the rule, the anointed one who endeared himself to our family forever by speaking at John Kennedy's presidential inauguration of a simple life, and simple ways.

Something there is that doesn't love a wall.
That sends the frozen-ground-swell under it.
And spills the upper boulders in the sun.

The split rail fence bordered by forsythia bushes that separated the house I grew up in from a lonely, old woman next door did little to prevent our footballs, kick balls, and soft balls from sailing over the fence into her tomato patch. She would stab the former with a kitchen knife and confiscate the latter, leaving my father apoplectic. "Good fences make good neighbors," I would read, opening my Robert Frost and wondering why we couldn't just spring for a stronger, higher, better fence to keep the balls in, our neighbor's vengeance and my father's wrath out.

I didn't understand that poem at the time, could only vaguely grasp the poet's confusion over his neighbor's stubborn insistence on constantly rebuilding stone walls marking boundaries that seemed superfluous in a rural New England where land loomed expansive and generous without livestock or children or balls to protect. But I *could* sense the disturbing implication of a deeper malaise at work in the impulse to fence, even without recognizing it as reflective of the ego's mindless reenactment of that original desire to wall out love, our "individual" special selves "in." Even without readiness to claim it as my own.

I live in a Denver neighborhood that borders on a walled community complete with fancy wrought-iron security gates. I mean, this is a nice neighborhood in Denver for crying out loud. Not Afghanistan. Not Juarez. We are not dealing with the threat of suicide bombers or random insurgent uprisings. No drug cartels that I know of, and yet. What exactly are we fencing out, or in; literally, and figuratively?

What Is the Body? in the second half of *A Course in Miracles'* workbook, profoundly answers that question:

The body is a fence the Son of God imagines he has built; to separate parts of his Self from other parts. It is within this fence he thinks he lives, to die as it decays and crumbles. For within this fence he thinks that he is safe from love. (from paragraph 1)

According to the mythology underlying the Course's two thought systems, when the "tiny, mad idea" of wishing to separate from whole, all-inclusive, eternal love arose in our mind and we took it *seriously*, we found ourselves figuratively cast into darkness, the light of our true nature no longer visible. In our fear and self-loathing and still curious about the possible benefits of individuality, we followed the ego into an entire projected universe of fenced in "others" and fell asleep, plunged into a dualistic dream in which we interact from behind our fences. Lobbing missiles of the hidden guilt in our mind over the belief that we destroyed our oneness over the fence, only to perceive it as an incoming assault perpetuated by another in an effort to prove our greater innocence and avoid God's punishment.

I am not making this up. This is the script we wrote and forgot, the preposterous, repressed story that nonetheless drives us. We have attempted to parcel infinity into little plots of DNA we identify with as our own, inside which we believe we attack and defend, wage love and war, age, sicken, and die. But despite our vast hallucination, the common ground beneath our imagined feet remains completely unaffected by our continually-rising-only-to-crumble-again fences.

Bodies of ego evidence to the contrary, there is no way out of this guilty, fearful script from inside. Only by learning to choose the part of our mind that observes our dream but remains lucid within it can we see the fences for the silly *defenses* against invulnerable truth they truly are, watch them crumble, and recover our abiding common ground. By recognizing the pain our fences actually bring us and thereby choosing to change our inner teacher from the ego to the Holy (Whole) Spirit, the illusion of walls designed to block our awareness of love's uninterrupted, eternal presence falls away. And we experience our all-inclusive innocence reflected back at us from our neighbors' eyes.

How do we break free of our self-imposed prisons? By changing the purpose we have assigned them.

The body is the means by which God's Son returns to sanity. Though it was made to fence him into hell without escape, yet has the goal of Heaven been exchanged for the pursuit of hell. The Son of God extends his hand to reach his brother and to help him walk along the road to him. Now is the body holy. Now it serves to heal the mind that it was made to kill. (paragraph 4)

As I write these words, my little dog sits at the gate to our backyard hoping to justify her low growl with a whiff of or peek at that big, bad yellow neighbor cat that continues to gleefully torment her from the other side of our fence. And I recall Robert Frost's words, ready—at least for the moment—to side with the "something there is that doesn't love a wall," and, in so doing, healing my mind of the childish notion that gave rise to our mindless habit of erecting and preserving fences.

Where Darkness Was I Look Upon the Light

Early in this dream we call life, at maybe three years old, I was walking with my parents in a large shopping mall—the old fashioned, outdoor type recently once more in vogue—on a winter night in northern New Jersey. I had stopped on the sidewalk to check out a tiny toy train chugging away inside a faux snow-crusted store window before glancing up to fasten my gaze on a woman I mistook for my mother from behind. I hurried toward her, and took her hand. Preoccupied with the shuffle of passersby and Christmas scenes beckoning from other store windows, I have no idea how long we walked like this before the woman looked down at me and gasped. I looked up. She was carrying another younger child, I noticed, and it was not my little brother. And she didn't look anything like my mother.

I don't recall the details. I imagine she called to her real daughter, the owner of the hand she assumed she'd been holding, a year or two my elder, who'd been walking on her other side. I suppose she bent down to take in my face, question me about my parents' whereabouts, and ask my name. I remember standing with her and her two children for a long time in a cold little office with cement floors and cinder-block walls, chatting with a man in uniform while they paged my parents. The woman gave me graham crackers, I think. I don't recall being frightened. But it scares the crap out of me all these years later. Now that I've been a parent quite a while and can all too fully entertain the possible ramifications of grasping the wrong hand.

So here's the thing: that's exactly what I've been doing lately, befriending the ego again while turning my back on the only friend who can actually lead me out of this nightmare of special-ness I claim I want to flee. How do I know this? Because I have once more felt deliciously attacked in what the Course calls our "special relationships," those "others" we have selected to deliver the love and attention we crave. The ones who inevitably fail to measure up; unconsciously set up from the beginning to prove the ego's mantra of "seek but do not find" that keeps this lie of separate interests at God's expense going.

As an *A Course in Miracles* student, I am learning that the missiles of anger and guilt I perceive coming from outside are actually an inside job, unconsciously fired by the part of my mind that wants to see them "out there." The part of my mind that wants to distance itself from the original, guilty thought of it all, to prove that I exist but it's not my fault. The part of my mind that chose for the ego in an effort to deny responsibility for the original impulse to separate and then take it seriously that started this whole Big Bang of a projected universe in the first place. Apparently landing me here where I think I find myself, a perpetual fugitive from real love.

"Look at all the work you've done with this Course, all the forgiveness you've been offering in your mind," the ego—always ready, willing, and able to join the journey—entreated, as I sat wallowing. "And, I mean, here it goes again. Isn't the definition of madness doing the same thing over and over again and expecting different results? Listen up, girlfriend. You will never be able to break the habit of projection. This Course is so not working for you."

He sighed his Academy Award-winning sigh.

"Let's face it; this Course is ruining your life by setting an impossible goal that can never be reached. You are not going to wake up because there's nothing to wake up from or to— got it? That was all finished a long time ago, and—trust me—you *really* don't want to go there. Anyway, you're just trashing everything you've worked so hard for. There are ways to find peace right here, and now; you just need to focus. You just need to back away from the ones that are hurting you for no reason. You need therapy, maybe, a warm bath, Reiki meditation, chakra balancing, a slab of chocolate (solid milk, not that healthy dark crap) washed down with a glass of that divine Pinot Gris you tried the other night, perhaps? You need a silent retreat, another workout, maybe a massage even."

He snapped his fingers. "Or, I've got it, the extended hand of just one other person on this freaking planet that actually *gets* you. Because—how do I put this—these nut cases just never will."

He almost had me. After all, I *had* put so much time and effort into understanding and practicing *A Course in Miracles*. It didn't seem fair that I still had to find myself in this rawest of places, humming along right-mindedly only to find myself inexplicably sideswiped by an apparently unprovoked attack.

But as I sat listening to the ego's rant, once again seemingly unable to hear another voice, I began to pray. I prayed to want to offer everything I had accused myself and everyone else of—from the beginning of seeming time to the seeming present and out into the seeming future—to my right mind. I prayed to know true forgiveness *A Course in Miracles*-style once and for always; to remember that what I think another did to me cannot be if we are one in truth, despite these vivid images to the contrary. I prayed to remember I am the dreamer of the dream, and that the dream figure I keep thinking I am—whose innocence I constantly attempt to preserve at another's expense—is no more real than any of the other figures I would love to throttle if I wasn't such a spiritual person. I prayed to want to offer every dark corner of my mind-on-ego to the light of the Holy (Whole) Spirit that I might be healed and learn to be an instrument of healing. I turned to workbook lesson 302: "Where darkness was I look upon the light"—fully cognizant at least that I could not tell the difference—and prayed with every fiber of my being to open to the part of my mind that could.

"… We thought we suffered," I read. "But we had forgot the Son whom You created. Now we see that darkness is our own imagining, and light is there for us to look upon." (from paragraph 1)

I prayed to grasp the hand of Jesus (that kind *symbol* of our one, awakened mind that holds the light for us within the dream) and walk with him until the pain passed. Until I could remember I am not here to maximize pleasure and minimize suffering; I have done that too long and it has not brought me any lasting joy or solace. I am here to awaken to my true, non-dualistic nature wherein the thought of opposition vanishes, the credits roll, the screen fades to white, and I can once more rest in real, all-inclusive, never-ending love, my mind forgiven of all fearful judgments of others and myself.

> Our Love awaits us as we go to Him, and walks beside us showing us the way. He fails in nothing. He the End we seek and He the Means by which we go to Him. (paragraph 2)

I give you my hand today because I want to learn what you would teach. I give you my hand to discover the love I still think belongs exclusively to you, and to see my innocence lurking behind the many masks I would have it wear. I give you my hand because I want to drop the ego's forever. I have lost myself again following him, but in the light of your love, recall our collective wholeness and remember I am found.

I Will Not Fear to Look Within Today

I was sitting on the sidelines during the second half of my seventeen-year-old daughter's soccer game last weekend, a refugee from the scorching aluminum bleachers in the 95-degree heat, sharing the shade with the mother of one of the girls on the opposing team. We had positioned ourselves in our little camp chairs a few feet away from each other to accentuate our divided loyalties, in case they somehow slipped our minds. My little dog panted away in my lap as I listened to the other Mom speaking loudly into her cell phone about the fact that her daughter's team was finally going down in a close game because they had no subs. Our girls had been in the same position the day before, the ego longed to point out, and nonetheless triumphed. Besides, only their formidable goalie had kept our girls from crushing this other team.

Of course, I said nothing of the sort out loud, contenting myself with indulging the ego's running commentary as I continued watching the game, pretending not to overhear the other Mom's conversation. But as my judgments continued to surface in the theatre of my mind like subtitles in a foreign film, it dawned on me that I was nearing the denouement in yet another chapter in the story of Susan. This was my final year in a more than decade-long role as soccer Mom. Next year at this time I would—with any luck and barring catastrophe—be helping my high school graduate move into a dorm somewhere, my in-house parenting days behind me, another big chunk of what I long considered my identity dissolved.

A little jolt of grief passed through me. Despite what I am learning in *A Course in Miracles* about the real capital "I" Identity we share *outside* this dreamy dream of exile from real, eternal, capital "L" Love, I continue to resist and at times lament the dissolution of specialness the Course's forgiveness offers. Even as I watch the many ways in which I try to differentiate myself from others—positively and negatively. Even as I feel the full pain of that decision designed to prove the original decision to separate from God really happened; that I exist autonomously within a real world of other autonomous beings capable of enhancing or jeopardizing my identity. That I exist at all, at God's expense.

A Course in Miracles tells us again and again that the initial separation from our one, perpetually loving source that gave rise to the guilt and fear of the ego thought system and a projected universe of bodies designed to defend that thought system does not exist, even though it unconsciously runs us. We can grasp this intellectually while still experiencing terror at the very thought of relinquishing the roles of parent, child, spouse, employer, employee, and *A Course in Miracles* student we believe *define* us. Even as we eventually relinquish the very body we believe we inhabit as we play out our roles.

Only by admitting once more that I do not know the thing I am—and metaphorically grasping the loving hand of an internal teacher that does know—can I watch my identification with the roles I play and gently forgive my urge to cling to the meaning and protection I still believe they offer me, understanding at last that in trying to protect myself from the one love I am in truth, I prevent myself from ever experiencing the wonder of our invulnerable innocence. I find that innocence by first honestly recognizing just how addicted I am to the idea of a personal self with special roles, how I use them in the same way I use what I consider "my" body, as both armor and weapon. But I can learn to use them for the purpose of forgiveness by watching the ego with my right mind and accepting without judgment all my addiction to specialness has cost me.

As workbook lesson 309, "I will not fear to look within today," reassures us:

> Within me is eternal innocence, because it is God's Will
> that it be there forever and forever. I, His Son, whose will
> is limitless as is His Own, can will no change in this. For

to deny my Father's Will is to deny my own. To look within is but to find my will as God created it, and as it is. I fear to look within because I think I made another will that is not true, and made it real. Yet it has no effects. Within me is the Holiness of God. Within me is the memory of Him. (paragraph 1)

Without asking for help from my right mind I can't possibly grasp what in hell a passage like this means because I still think looking within means scanning the mind of the body we call a brain. I still believe in a person named Susan reading this big, blue book and trying to apply what it says in a real life. And I unconsciously believe the ego's lie that returning to the scene of the crime in our one mind equals certain annihilation.

But when I turn to the part of my mind that knows that when the Course uses the word "within" it means within the one mind *outside* this dream of specialness, the one mind that knows itself completely and endlessly shares its loving knowing, I experience the innocence and completion of the one mind I have never really left. My mind is healed of the idea of separate interests and identification with roles that ultimately mean nothing and have only brought me fleeting pleasure.

As the referee blew the whistle marking the game's end and our team's victory—my dog squirming in my lap—I turned to the other mother. I told her (and actually meant it) what a fine team her daughter had, and how much I sympathized with them having to play in the blazing heat without subs. Then I folded up my chair, put the dog back on her leash, and waited to congratulate my daughter. Reassured at least for the moment by the part of my mind that favors sanity that, the ego's shifting roles notwithstanding, the love we share could never be divided.

Happiness Runs In a Circular Motion

"Welcome home, Jim Dugan," said the Irishman at the Customs' desk in Dublin, appropriately ruddy-cheeked and blarney-tongued, stamping my father's passport and causing Dad to pinken to his very toes with glee, stepping foot at last onto the sacred soil of the motherland. His moment of perfect bliss expanded generously to engulf us all, until we overheard the same phrase uttered to a gentleman not far behind us and realized it was standard fare for greeting Americans of a certain age with Irish surnames. Still, on the ego's scale of one-to-ten the trip was a ten, marred only by my then four-year-old daughter's car-sickness in the back seat of what passed for a van in the Republic of Ireland at the time. Into which we stereotypical Americans had crammed four adults, one child, and an embarrassing abundance of luggage, some of which the owners of our guest house in Dublin had mercifully offered to store as we hit the road for more rural pastures in Killarney and Cork, hot on the trail of leprechauns and dead Dugans; the details of my father's lineage largely unknown despite fanciful conjecture over a pint or four.

Our first trip to the emerald isle with my parents when our daughter was little looms in my memory as one of the happiest, most present times of my life. Immersed in a seemingly infinite variety of shades of my favorite color, glimpsing faces in doorways that resembled my own, touring ancient Druid stone circles and romantically ruined abbeys, a deep sense of belonging welled up in me. I reveled in stories of long-term victimization at the hands of the English often celebrated in exuberant, irresistible song by day, cooking mussels and root vegetables for my family by night on a stove in our own rental cottage where we burned real peat for warmth, just like our ancestors. Everyone got along. Our daughter learned to skip on that trip, play the tin whistle and a mean game of poker. I bent over backwards and kissed the

Blarney Stone, convinced despite the hype that I would find my muse at last.

We have been talking a lot about happiness in the weekly *A Course in Miracles* class I lead. As Course students, it often seems much easier to identify the denied guilt in our mind over our belief that we separated from our one, loving source with our *negative* projections, plentiful as they are. The attacks we perceive as coming from outside the seemingly separate body we have chosen to "inhabit," defend, and justify that are actually coming from within the one ego mind constantly intent on establishing its greater innocence relative to another's greater guilt.

As we begin to embrace the Course's forgiveness it often seems easier to learn that all our negative emotions are red flags that we have chosen the ego as our inner teacher and need to choose again for the Holy (Whole) Spirit/right mind if we hope to experience inner peace. It may seem much more difficult to also accept that the pleasurable experiences we cling to in this world and credit with making us happy are likewise defenses against the truth. Both are intentionally (although unconsciously) manufactured by the ego to keep us from returning to our right mind and recognizing that what passes for pleasure and pain in this world is an illusion, a literal projection of a mind made mad by its belief in guilt, hell-bent on proving its existence at God's expense while denying responsibility for it.

The more we blame someone or thing outside the mind for our problems, the more innocent we seem. Most Course students can grasp that, at least intellectually. More challenging is the notion that the more we hold something external responsible for our happiness, the more real we make this illusory world and the less motivated we are to choose again for the unwavering, all-inclusive, eternal solace that awaits us in our right mind. Immersed in our exclusive, ephemeral pleasure, our split mind once again appears to seamlessly fuse with the ego and we forget all about the decision-making mind that can choose again for something real outside the dream. We even buy the ego's argument that something exclusive such as the heady identification with our cultural heritage has greater value than something eternally all-inclusive and loving. And that something fleeting—like all pleasures in this mortal world in short supply—is all the more precious in that weepy, poignant way our mind-on-ego can't get enough of.

The movement to generate, celebrate, attract, and sustain earthly happiness advanced in self-help books and workshops over the last several decades often invites us to vividly recall a time when we were supremely happy, and focus on our sensory memories to recreate it. Where were you? What did it look like, sound like, smell and taste like? What were you doing? Who were you with? How did it make you *feel*? The idea is to both identify the components so you can pursue and invite more of those into your life, and identify the feeling, so you can resurrect it when the less-than-happy developments of day-to-day existence rear their ugly heads in your otherwise essentially idyllic state. This technique can help us accentuate our positive and minimize our negative feelings, but it will do nothing to help us awaken to the truth of our invulnerable, endlessly peaceful nature *outside* this dream of opposing interests created by a terrified split mind to defend itself against a truth it believes would annihilate it.

The problem with peak experiences here in this dream of exile from perfect, loving oneness is the way in which—like all special relationships—we grant them power to limit love through exclusivity. Our needs temporarily satisfied by others chosen to justify and defend our story and with no memory of the magnificence we believe we have forfeited, we have no desire to choose again for the part of our mind that allows us to experience the real grandeur of our loving wholeness. During that trip to Ireland, I did not once muse as Bill Thetford (original Course collaborator) famously did, that there must be another (better) way of relating in this world, inviting the scribing of *A Course in Miracles*. I mean, what could be better than this?

The problem with peak experiences is the inevitable valleys. Nothing here lasts. Not the idyllic trip to Ireland. Not the little girl skipping beside me playing a tin whistle, not the way I feel when I'm meditating, not this strong, healthy body or the bodies of people I love. Peak experiences offer at best shabby substitutions for the real loving state that awaits us when we choose to forgive our investment in differences designed to prove the lie of separation with our right mind that has never taken our fantasy seriously.

A Course in Miracles does not implore us to judge or avoid worldly pleasure. But it does invite us to question its purpose and begin to observe with help from our right mind how its pursuit seduces us into mindlessness in the same way our pursuit of proving our innocence at another's expense does. The Course does not ask us to "sacrifice" our pleasures, only to see their purpose clearly with the part of our mind that can clearly see. We must learn to observe with our loving inner teacher just how addicted we are to attributing our internal state of mind to external factors if we ever hope to find guilt-free happiness that blames no one, excludes no one, lasts forever, and will never fail us.

As workbook lesson 66: "My happiness and my function are one," reminds us:

> … Think also about the many forms the illusion of your function has taken in your mind, and the many ways in which you tried to find salvation under the ego's guidance. Did you find it? Were you happy? Did they bring you peace? We need great honesty today. Remember the outcomes fairly, and consider also whether it was ever reasonable to expect happiness from anything the ego ever proposed. Yet the ego is the only alternative to the Holy Spirit's Voice. (from paragraph 9)

We all know how to find pleasure in this world and there's nothing wrong with doing so. The problem comes with mistaking fleeting, sensory, emotional pleasure with the eternal, stable happiness we believe we traded for this unique individual, finite, existence. The problem comes with expending our energy on maximizing pleasure and minimizing pain and deluding ourselves that playing in the illusion, fixing up the dream, can ever satisfy the deep longing to return to our awareness of our loving home we all share. I still enjoy travel but more and more recognize it for the escape/distraction from healing my mind it can be if I don't embrace it mindfully as merely another expression of the illusion offering opportunities to forgive. It is not and will never be a substitute for what I really want.

As we learn to look honestly with the part of our mind that followed us into the dream and remains capable of honesty at all we think can hurt or help us, we begin to realize a peace of mind completely independent from the ups and downs of this world and the need to mask our guilt over a crime that never happened. We begin to taste a peace that—as we continue to practice forgiveness—expands to include everyone and everything. Complete, infinite peace that—when we have completed all our forgiveness lessons in the classroom of our lives—invites us to step onto the soil of the one motherland we have in truth never left and welcomes everyone home.

The Debt We Owe to Truth

In her last year of high school, my daughter—already glimpsing emancipation from the yoke of the parental unit—has been flexing the muscles of her independence while struggling to meet the daunting requirements of an IB (international baccalaureate) diploma and keep up with the responsibilities of Student Council, Key Club, competitive soccer, college essay and application deadlines, and a job as a part-time nanny. My efforts to communicate with her around these responsibilities—some of which require my direct involvement—have been, at times, classically strained.

I spent a lot of time last week engaging with the ego about this, even as I earnestly summoned the right mind and—finding that line busy—called on Jesus himself to make his presence known. As if he were an embodied entity separate from this embodied entity I think I am; which *A Course in Miracles* is teaching me the good news of remembering I am not. As if he changed in phone booths of yore into tights and a cape. an action figure endowed with superpowers. Faster than a speeding bullet, more powerful than a locomotive, and capable of leaping tall buildings in a single bound. You get the picture.

Suffice it to say I exhausted myself again trying to forgive while still entertaining the ego's sneaky arguments that I was forgiving something real, despite the Course's frequent assertion that the two seemingly distinct thought systems—ego/wrong mind versus Holy (Whole) Spirit/right mind—cannot speak over one another. That I—the decision maker that chose to listen to the ego's preposterous fantasy of separation from loving wholeness in the first place—must first back away from that 24/7 rant of specialness before inviting the voice for truth, innocence, and the way of common interests if I have any hope at all of experiencing inner peace.

Of course, it wasn't my fault; the ego pointed out. I had once more—for no apparent reason whatsoever, void of any provocation on my part, and with only the kindest of intentions—found myself unfairly treated by my family, discounted, attacked, and hopelessly misunderstood. The scapegoat of an all-too-familiar triangle wherein I tried to negotiate and collaborate with opposing forces—in this case my daughter and husband—only to find myself the object of scorn on both sides. Reliving a deliciously painful childhood pattern wherein I attempted to keep the peace among two younger siblings with largely unjust and devastating consequences for my finely tuned, highly sensitive nervous system.

I squandered the good portion of a day in full Lois Lane mode, tallying up the tragic details of it all in my imaginary girl reporter notebook, the ego's blow-by-blow commentary a welcome score for the film-noir tale of my discontent. I had tried everything in my cavernous handbag of tricks to help solve and salve the situation. I had consulted friends and articles, memorized and rehearsed my lines, and bowed my head in prayer. *Please, please, please,* I begged Jesus, help me see through your lens. Help me answer my call for love in these bodies that seem so hell-bent on pushing my love and help away (having completely lost track once again of who was really doing the pushing).

But the relief and release I have learned forgiveness always brings (sooner or later) continued to elude me.

"Don't be so hard on yourself," the ego said. "You've tried everything. I mean, how much more can one person be expected to do? This is not your problem anymore. Time to let the pieces fall where they may, girlfriend; you are just so done with this."

Yes, I thought, *exactly.* Done.

I am sorry to say I have been here before; unwittingly reduced to accepting comfort from the ego, seemingly paralyzed in darkness in my attempts to approach the threshold of our common light with a mind that would really like to have its ego and forgiveness, too. Unloved and unloving, staggering beneath the full weight of my crushing resistance to learning this Course which asks us but to acknowledge our judgments with the part of our mind that would never judge. But that is exactly the part of our mind that apparently scares the living crap out of me. The part of our mind that I have allowed my mind-on-ego to convince me will return me to the scene of the original crime of separating from our source and the punishment I secretly believe I have had coming ever since. The punishment I secretly enjoy experiencing as coming from *outside* this innocent form, rather than as the external projection of an internal condition it actually is.

Oddly enough, as I went about my day, my mind a war zone, continuing to ask for help from anyone "up there" in any form that might actually have my best interests at heart—at least mindful that I did not—something strange appeared to occur in my special relationships. My husband opened up a calm, rational, non-judgmental conversation in which I felt secure enough to convey my frustration and sense of isolation without expecting a resolution of any kind. Later, my daughter—the seeming "cause" of it all—snuck up and threw her arms around me from behind as I stood at the sink, lay her head on my shoulder, and asked for a hug; a shockingly welcome development I literally embraced with awe.

And so here I find myself again at last unwittingly released, inhaling a whiff of my own innocence on the heels of yours; looking with Jesus (that *symbol* of the mind restored to wholeness we share) at the nothingness of the ego's seemingly endless, imaginary defenses against the truth. My mind still and, for the moment at least, healed in the infinite absence of all judgment.

And as we pay the debt we owe to truth—a debt that merely is the letting go of self-deceptions and of images we worshipped falsely—truth returns to us in wholeness and in joy. We are deceived no longer. Love has now returned to our awareness. And we are at peace again, for fear has gone and only love remains. (from workbook lesson 323, paragraph 2)

The Impossible Dream

Shhhhh. I'm going to tell you something but I'd like you to keep it to yourself. I have been having a lot of bad dreams lately. In one, a friend—completely out of the blue—made an unkind remark, leaving me scouring the cavernous recesses of my scant gray matter for evidence of provocation. In another, I am struggling to find a way to sugarcoat a conversation I need to have with a family member in an effort to overt a typical defensive response. In the next, I find myself cast as the mother of a—dare I say it?—*teenager.* I am obsessing about a seemingly insoluble dilemma facing an organization with which I am affiliated in another. Later, I am on stage, about to deliver a talk to a crowded auditorium, feeling like an abused Sissy Spacek in that old horror flick *Carrie*, humiliated beyond all redemption and waiting for my telekinetic powers to kick in.

But here's the really creepy thing. It is 9 a.m. I have been "awake" the whole time; alone for the past hour, sitting in my office staring at the computer screen, robotically opening and answering emails all the while indulging these trippy little nightmares involving past, current, and future events. They would lock me up if they knew. Please don't tell anyone.

OK, maybe I should explain that I have once again caught myself completely lost in the serial episodes of Susan, the colossal dream of a separate self I am continually scripting, acting, critiquing, revising and in one way or another selling. All to keep me preoccupied with seemingly "out there" people and situations rather than returning to our one mind and choosing again to see with the Holy (Whole) Spirit's vision rather than the ego's seemingly embodied eyes. To see beyond the endless, detailed, illusory drama of the ego thought system to the abstract simplicity of truth, wherein the credits roll and an empty screen fades to the nothingness from which it arose.

It has become more apparent to me as I practice *A Course in Miracles'* forgiveness day in and day out here in the condition I still think I'm in most of the time that I do not even need another "actor" present to perform my script. When it comes to projection, I am—like everyone else here in dreamland—able to fantasize and dredge up the most dire situations interspersed with just the right amount of hard-won triumph over seemingly formidable adversaries to keep me diving back in for more all without interaction with a single other human being.

The Course compares all our experience in this world to the universal human experience of dreaming, in which we find ourselves lost in an illusory habitat we have unconsciously crafted to live out our fears and wishes. An experience in which—having mistaken ourselves for the "hero of the dream" rather than the dreamer—we interact with other imaginary dream figures; completely unaware that we're only dreaming. However bizarre; our dreams seem real as we sleep. We don't question their logic but merely react to the circumstances we find ourselves facing, only at times vaguely aware of a nagging sense of disorientation and loss.

Suffering is an emphasis upon all that the world has done to injure you. Here is the world's demented version of salvation clearly shown. Like to a dream of punishment, in which the dreamer is unconscious of what brought on the attack against himself, he sees himself attacked unjustly and by something not himself. He is the victim of this 'something else,' a thing outside himself, for which he has no reason to be held responsible. He must be innocent because he knows not what he does, but what is done to him. Yet is his own attack upon himself apparent still, for it is he who bears the suffering. And he cannot escape because its source is outside himself. (Chapter 27, VII. The Dreamer of the Dream, paragraph 1)

A Course in Miracles teaches us that our sleeping dreams are no different whatsoever from our waking ones. When "the tiny, mad idea" of separation from our source arose in the one Son of God's mind and we took it seriously our one mind appeared to split into the ego/wrong mind and the Holy (Whole) Spirit/right mind. The part of our mind drunk on the prospect of individuality that believed it had pulled off the impossible and deserved punishment for its crime versus the part that remembered we remain whole, but dreaming an impossible dream of exile from our source while continuing to rest in indivisible, loving wholeness.

We could have listened to the Holy Spirit, of course, at the seeming beginning. But equally intoxicated by the possibility of experiencing uniqueness and simultaneously terrified by the prospect of our creator's retaliation, we listened to the ego's plan for our salvation instead. It entailed ridding the mind of our guilt over the belief we separated from God by projecting it outward into an entire universe of fragmented forms. Its plan offered us a dualistic illusion to hide out in. We assumed separate bodies and fell asleep to prevent us from remembering we had a mind that chose for the ego in the first place but can always choose again for the part of our mind that knows we are only dreaming.

Here in the dream, we continue to interact with other figments of our selfish, frightened imagination in an effort to prove our existence as discrete identities vying for relative innocence. Seeking to blame the repressed yet constantly resurfacing guilt in our mind over the denied belief in separation on equally illusory "others" to reinforce the idea of our existence and relative innocence versus their greater guilt in hopes of somehow exonerating ourselves with God. But it never works to relieve the nagging guilt in our mind for long and we soon enough find ourselves fending off perceived "incoming" assaults, forgetting they are merely disguised projections of the guilt that lingers in our mind over a crime that never happened.

As we practice choosing again to look with our right mind at the ego's sneaky ways and claim responsibility for our attraction to victimhood, the "incoming" dark threats dissolve in the light of right-mindedness. And we experience a more and more welcome state: the absence of sin, guilt, and fear in which we breathe a figurative sigh of relief; our eternal, invulnerable, collective innocence seemingly restored. With help from our right mind, we see through the eyes of truth beyond all we would use to hurt us, until all our fearful ego adventures in dreamland have been exposed for the nothingness they remain. Until we awaken to find ourselves within the one, infinite love we never really left.

... All that is needed is you look upon the problem as it is, and not the way that you have set it up. (from paragraph 2)

Amen to that.

Everything's Coming Up Roses
(Oh, Never Mind!)

So, I have this book coming out which may require me to actually venture out from the relative comfort of my little writing den into the wild blue yonder where I may have to actually open my mouth in front of a group of complete strangers, a terrifying possibility I have been denying for a long time. In an ego-fueled effort to self-medicate I had taken this class on overcoming the fear of public speaking that offered some really helpful exercises for getting out of our fearful ego heads and engaging more in the childlike Zen of the moment. Techniques like beating your chest and howling like Tarzan to release fear and empower (my personal favorite) and dancing like a snake to get rid of nervous body tension. This one stumped me because I couldn't quite figure out whether to lie down or stand up. The quandary left me experiencing that all too familiar shallow breathing—precursor to a full-blown panic attack—the fear of which had gotten me into trouble with the prospect of this whole public speaking debacle in the first place. I moved down the list.

The next suggestion involved identifying your "power song," the kind of tune capable of firing long dormant optimistic neurons and sending you twirling around the house a la Mitzi Gaynor. A song robustly cheerful enough to brainwash you into thinking you had the audience in the palm of your God-like hand. I racked my brain. In a sudden chilling epiphany I realized I did not know a single happy tune by heart except for *Polly Wolly Doodle,* memorized from a children's tape someone had given me during my daughter's colic phase. Although sung to my screaming infant with earnest exuberance, the tune only served to ratchet the wailing up a notch, deepening the shade of her already purple face, her fists beating my chest in a most un-Tarzan-like manner.

As I contemplated my inability to retrieve motivational music from my personal archives, this latest attempt to conquer another ego-cooked-up phobia ground to a painful halt. Why had I not committed the lyrics of a single happy song to my memory in my entire (not so short anymore) life? Why was my psyche instead rife with the lines of deliciously mournful ballads crafted by the likes of Leonard Cohen and Joan Baez?

I had been thinking a lot about blissninnies, Ken Wapnick's term for people who perceive the world as a perfect place, those capable of attracting happiness while denying its illusory, ephemeral nature and thereby circumventing the motivation to choose against the ego thought system and its unspoken tale of sin, guilt, and fear. People who float around in protective force fields of their own making seemingly immune to the roller-coaster ride of what we refer to as the human condition. I suppose I had been listening to the ego, congratulating myself on some level that—despite my many *A Course in Miracles* student flaws—at least I was not a blissninny.

Quite the contrary, I seemed to have come in this time around a few defenses short. This world of suffering had largely horrified me from the get go, an observation I learned early to keep to myself so as not to alarm my keepers. A conviction that only grew more acute as my accumulated experiences on crazy planet reinforced in my own life what I had initially detected in the lives of so many around me, those I knew intimately, and those I only read about or watched on TV. It seemed to me that everyone here suffered in one way or another, and even those who didn't seem to be doing so at the moment could be struck down by disease, injury, abandonment, ridicule, criticism, or even sudden death at any time. Although Catholics talked as if hell were a place bad people went to after death, it seemed all too clear to me we had already arrived.

As I sat at my desk worrying the nuances of this topic like beads on a rosary, I suddenly realized it ultimately made no difference whether we tended to view the world through a lens rubbed with Vaseline that made everyone look like starlets or a crystal clear one that revealed every little flaw. Both were what *A Course in Miracles* calls "defenses against the truth," efforts to render an ego-concocted illusion real. To keep us invested in a dream of exile from eternal, perfect oneness; defending our optimistic versus pessimistic viewpoints through our projections; bolstering the idea of discrete selves with unique personalities in need of preserving.

Whether we stand on a stage belting out *Everything's Coming Up Roses* like Ethel Merman (now there's a scary thought!) or cowering in our little office indulging in another heartbreaking Leonard Cohen ballad, we believe we exist individually complete with our preferences and styles of denial. While we must first "see" the nature of the ego thought system, designed to keep our guilt over taking the impossible thought of separation seriously alive by experiencing it outside the selves we think we are, we can only do so with help from our right mind. The part of our mind that knows it never happened and does not take the dire consequences—the suffering we observe in others and experience within our own lives—seriously. The part of our mind that sees past shadows crafted to seduce and deceive to the one, whole, all-inclusive love we remain. An unalterable state we remember as we join with our right mind to look at all our mind-on-ego would use to scare the living crap out of us. To the point that we will sometimes do anything to convince ourselves this is really a happy dream despite ever-accumulating evidence to the contrary.

The happy dream happens when we forgive from moment to moment our impulse to blame others for the guilt we deny in our mind whenever those less than happy emotions surface and we seek to pin them on someone or thing seemingly outside ourselves. The happy dream happens when I rediscover (with help from my right mind) your innocence and in so doing, remember that nothing here—not a speech before strangers, an unkind thought or word, a seemingly broken body or relationship—can in any way jeopardize our loving union. We need do nothing to enhance the impersonal joy we remain except resign as our own teacher and allow a better way.

> … What must I do to know all this is mine? I must accept Atonement for myself, and nothing more. God has already done all things that need be done. And I must learn I need do nothing of myself, for I need but accept my Self, my sinlessness, created for me, now already mine, to feel God's Love protecting me from harm, to understand my Father loves His Son; to know I am the Son my father loves. (From workbook lesson 337: "My sinlessness protects me from all harm." paragraph 1)

Another Pop Quiz

The X-Ray technician had a mouth like a closed zipper. Still, she managed to deliver a somber little speech after leading me to the dressing room. Something to the effect of "Understand that after looking at these mammograms the doctor may call you back if he or she needs more information. That may or may not mean anything but you should be prepared in case you get a call."

The quality of her words seemed as surreal as her funeral home demeanor. I had been diligently coming in for routine annual mammograms for years but did not recall this protocol. It caught my attention. Suddenly, the reason I was really there—to detect possible breast cancer—seemed a little too much in my face. A little more plausible than I liked to admit. The procedure seemed more uncomfortable than usual, too, and I drove home wondering about the change in the clinic's practice.

I'd forgotten about the whole thing nearly two weeks later when I received a cryptic call from the HMO advising me I needed to return for another mammogram and possible sonogram. Could I make it a week from today? Sure, I said, fingers of fear creeping up the back of my neck. Could they tell me what the doctor had seen that seemed suspicious? They were not allowed. But if they'd actually seen something really threatening, they wouldn't make me wait a week, would they? Probably not, said the disembodied voice, without audible conviction. I would just have to wait and see.

As I set down the phone, I realized I was facing yet another pop quiz in the classroom of my lessons in forgiveness, challenged this time to review what *A Course in Miracles* has to say about the body. Things like: "Sickness is a defense against the truth" and "The body is a wholly neutral thing." But reviewing workbook lesson titles didn't help. While we are ultimately asked to understand and accept the Course's contention that the world of bodies is an illusion—a literal projection of the thought of guilt that arose in the one mind when it took the idea of separation from its source seriously—in practice it is not so easy.

In practice, I thought—stubbing my toe as I rose from my desk to refill my coffee and hopped around like an idiot causing my little dog to race around in mad circles with a cloth lamb hanging out of her mouth—the physical fragility we deny in our haste to project our guilt and fear on others remains. In this nightmare of guilt in which we identify ourselves as dream figures rather than dreamers, bodies are subject to all kinds of painful assaults designed to prove the ego's agenda of the serious sin of separation realized. Only checking in with the part of our mind that remembers that nothing real can be threatened—we remain awake in God, merely dreaming of exile—can release us from the physical and emotional pain and terror of the ego thought system.

But, adrenaline coursing through my veins, I forgot to do so, reveling instead in the ego's fantasy of doom. I have several friends who are breast cancer survivors, and am acutely aware of the frightening challenges they have bravely faced in the last few years. Although I have had a handful of similar health scares before, my reaction to this one seemed way out of proportion to the actual circumstances.

The ego mind reviewed them in excruciating detail. What if, what if, what if … Then it dragged my daughter into it. In ways I couldn't understand my fear of losing my own body seemed hopelessly entwined with losing her. After all, she would be heading off to college next year. Consumed with keeping up with all the requirements of senior year and college application tours, forms, and deadlines, I tended not to dwell on my feelings of loss. Now, they too, loomed. The thought of the death of this physical and psychological body I still obviously valued did its little slasher movie dance around the screen in my head, interrupted by commercials advertising my daughter's imminent defection. (As if love required the presence of a body to express itself.) I closed my eyes and breathed, begging for a consult from my right mind.

The line seemed busy at first as I resisted releasing my belief in an individual self needful and worthy of protection. But eventually I felt the familiar return of sanity and completeness, a deep, universal, abstract comfort replacing the specific, current form of my mind-on-ego's suffering. I went about my business for a couple of days largely unperturbed by the impending re-test. Until I received a form letter reiterating that my mammogram had been recalled and they needed further tests to rule out the possibility of cancer. Although only 5-10 percent of all mammograms are recalled, I should be reassured to learn the vast majority of these cases turn out benign. If I had any further questions, I should contact my primary care physician.

Suffice it to say I was not reassured. Instead, the ego leapt to action, grabbing the phone and navigating the various recordings necessary to actually speak to another human being. I was finally informed that a nurse would call me back to go over the original mammograms that afternoon. The information she later conveyed was sketchy at best, and difficult to hear over the ego's diatribe that practicing the Course had somehow brought this on. Did I really want to push this to the limit? Sacrifice my very body and relationships with my loved ones just to prove I am not a body?

That's when a line from the Course came boomeranging back to me and I turned to the big, blue book once more. As we are reminded in Chapter 16: VI. The Bridge to the Real World: "Fear not that you will be abruptly lifted up and hurled into reality. Time is kind, and if you use it on behalf of reality, it will keep gentle pace with you in your transition."

Jesus—that kind symbol of the awakened mind that brought us *A Course in Miracles*—knows the ego will try to scare us away from a practice that is actually working to change our mind about our belief in separate interests. For most of us, this is a gradual journey home. It does not require crucifixion from its students. It merely asks us to pay attention to our reactions to what we perceive as external assaults. To bring those reactions to the part of our mind that knows there is nothing "out there" in other bodies or forms that can hurt us. Just as there is nothing "inside" the bodily form we have chosen to identify with out to get us. All are shadows within a dream of our own making designed to protect us from the wrath of our creator over a crime that never happened.

A Course in Miracles calls with compassion to us from beyond the dream, meeting us where we think we are in the condition we think we're in until our fear subsides enough to open our eyes. As the Manual for Teachers, 9. Are Changes Required in the Life Situation of God's Teachers? paragraph 1, reminds us:

> Changes are required in the *minds* of God's teachers … There are those who are called upon to change their life situation almost immediately, but these are generally special cases. By far the majority are given a slowly evolving training program, in which as many previous mistakes as possible are corrected. Relationships in particular must be properly perceived, and all dark cornerstones of unforgiveness removed. Otherwise the old thought system still has a basis for return.

I sighed. Resting on the floor in her bed, my little dog sighed, too. My shift to right-mindedness remained until the day of the next exams when I started listening to the ego's rant again. But it didn't seem quite as scary this time. Whatever happened next, I knew my right mind would see me through. Although enormously relieved to learn the second round of tests detected nothing, I was also grateful to realize just how invested I still am in the body.

Despite having chosen *A Course in Miracles* as my path home and committed to practicing its unique forgiveness in my daily life. I was humbled to have fully experienced the real fear of annihilation at the core of all the seeming "threats" to my existence my mind-on-ego has projected to prove I exist at God's expense. Back to the work of forgiveness, I thought. Maybe next time, I'll catch myself a little sooner imagining a self capable of destruction, maybe not. In the meantime, I continue to choose again to follow the inner teacher of love instead of fear.

Forgiveness Is the Key to Happiness

It reminded me of a whiteout I got caught in once; having minutes earlier exited the Silver Queen Chairlift in Crested Butte, Colorado. Standing at the summit, tightening down ski boots and adjusting poles and goggles in preparation for our descent, my friends and I found ourselves suddenly enveloped in a blizzard that left us completely disoriented as to up and down, right and left, forward and backward. We stood motionless within the stillness of a cloud, staving off vertigo. Laughing nervously and adjusting to the acute sensory deprivation in predicable ways.

The Warren Miller movie wannabes waxed all macho about taking off blind. Certain expressive females delivered admirably restrained meltdowns. I stood wracking my brain to remember Lamaze breathing techniques that—although useless during the delivery of my daughter—might prove helpful in controlling impending hyperventilation. Time ticked haltingly by, rapid breath by breath, until the Ski Patrol arrived equipped with special lanterns to lead us down a catwalk to safety.

But in the dream I had last week, instead of a whiteout I found myself swaddled in darkness so profound it had a similar effect, disabling my senses. And this time I stood in the void alone, with nothing to distract me from an all-too-familiar-seeming terror. I was about to begin teaching a new class and had been revisiting a chart I had drawn to depict *A Course in Miracles'* version of the creation myth explaining the Son of God's choice to believe it could separate from eternal, seamless unity. The belief that appeared to plunge him into darkness, convinced he had somehow destroyed the light. The crushing guilt over which appeared to split the mind into an ego thought system that reinforced the preposterous idea of separation and the Holy (Whole) Spirit's that remembered the truth of our uninterrupted invulnerability.

In the dream I stood immersed in the horror of the chart I had made to depict the horror of a choice I could not remember making, overwhelmed with loneliness. A sense of loss and long-ing I at first mistook for fear over something dreadful having felled my daughter and husband who seemed to have gone miss-ing washed over me in waves that left me struggling for balance like real ones. I silently called out as I have learned to do to a part of my mind the Course is teaching me to trust, a part without hidden agendas or special interests; a part that retains the light of our shared wholeness and never goes missing.

A few moments later I could distinguish an initially vague impression of light surrounding the simple silhouette of what appeared to be a woman. As I stood marveling, the golden glow outlining her form grew brighter, burning a familiar outline in the darkness of someone I recognized within the waking dream. Someone I believed had recently wronged me for no apparent reason. Whose call for love I had trouble in the last few days rec-ognizing as my own as the Course teaches us we ultimately must if we wish to heal our minds of the burden of guilt we carry over the denied belief we separated from our source.

Even though the nature of this person's seeming "attack" within what the Course calls the ego's "hierarchy of illusions" would be considered by most egos quite trivial, the ego I at times still forget I am not considered her apparent defection especially hurtful for a host of invented reasons that in retrospect make no sense whatsoever. As the light around her strengthened, I watched in awe as if taking in a sunrise for the first time, embraced and then liberated by the rays of her certain innocence and the long lost recognition of my own.

I opened my eyes and sat up in bed, wishing I could render to canvas the singular beauty of this image, haunted for days by ways I might depict it artistically despite my meager talents in that direction. I had been calling to my right mind as the Course invites us to do to help me see this person and situation differ-ently, even as I resisted. Now I had my answer. In the following days, the vision lingered—backlit along the horizon of my mind, the visual version of a song stuck in your head—in a good way. It eventually expanded to include other forms etched in light, people from my past, present, and future I once had judged or soon would. People I no longer could. I staggered around in a daze—a deliriously grateful visitor to an internal gallery I had been trying to locate forever—endlessly absolving and absolved.

A Course in Miracles workbook lesson 121, "Forgiveness is the key to happiness," delivers the very marrow of this practice that—when approached with growing willingness to understand I know nothing—undoes the ego's impulse to project its guilt outside the mind while denying responsibility for it in an effort to exonerate ourselves with an imaginary, punitive God. It offers us a practical, symbolic exercise to reverse our projections by observing our seeming enemies with help from our right mind, thereby reclaiming the "light" we believe we extinguished within by first identifying it without. It prompts us to consider someone we have an issue with and:

> … Try to perceive some light in him somewhere; a little gleam which you had never noticed. Try to find some little spark of brightness shining through the ugly picture that you hold of him. Look at this picture till you see a light somewhere within it, and then try to let this light extend until it covers him, and makes the picture beautiful and good. (from paragraph 11)

The lesson instructs us to embrace our changed perception and then envision transferring the light of innocence we discovered within our former enemy to the image of someone we consider a friend.

> Then let him offer you the light you see in him, and let your 'enemy' and friend unite in blessing you with what you gave. Now are you one with them, and they with you. (from paragraph 13)

A Course in Miracles is not a direct path to the light. There is no beaming up involved. Our fear over the unconscious guilty thought of separation is far too great to simply open our eyes on a beautiful morning of oneness. Instead, the Course leads us gently through each dreamed up relationship and situation in which we find ourselves in judgment to a better way.

We remember the brilliant, enduring innocence of our true nature by changing our minds about what's really happening in our relationships, choosing a different inner teacher whenever we catch ourselves again believing in the reality of an illusion of victimization at another's hands. A teacher who illuminates the ego's lie designed to keep us so preoccupied defending ourselves from "incoming" attacks that we forget we *chose* the teacher of darkness. A teacher who teaches me again and again until the need for learning has passed, how to find the sunrise of my eternal wholeness rising from the darkness I once saw in you.

Macaroni and Cheese and the Comfort of Gracious Guidance

Although we had been languishing in a state of suspended animation these last few weeks of summer refusing to vacate to fall, the nights had finally cooled enough to don sweaters. A devoted fan of bare feet, I found myself resenting the imminent requirement for socks and shoes combined with the beckoning chores of an expiring garden. Then, too, I had not slept well, silently griping about a host of trivial annoyances, leading me to once more pronounce myself unloved and unloving, an all too familiar state *A Course in Miracles* has helped me identify as just another symptom of the constantly resurfacing guilt in my mind over the fantasy of running away from our eternal home and slamming the door behind me. I was downright homesick, bereft over autumn's fading palette and my seemingly unrequited love for God, and craving comfort. It was time to make macaroni and cheese.

I still have the *Betty Crocker's Cookbook for Boys and Girls* given to me around age seven that includes the first recipe for this ultimate of American comfort foods I ever made. It calls for eggs, I think, and a block of that fluorescent substance revered in the 60s and 70s for its apparently infinite shelf life, supreme melt ability, and complete lack of potentially offensive sharp cheddar character. Back then I was thinking about mushroom clouds and our proximity to the probable commie target of New York City should the cold war further escalate as I struggled to chop that squishy faux cheese into cubes. Coupled with the alarming propensity for close relatives and the President of the United States to abruptly meet their maker, an entity I found myself compulsively doubting despite my efforts to impersonate a virtuous—on good days possibly even convent-bound—Catholic girl.

By the time I parted with the church and what I considered its God's at best conditional love in high school, I had perfected my macaroni and cheese to the point that even my father—a cook in his own right as well as our family's most critical diner—could not resist seconds. Stirring crumbly white cheddar we bought in bulk on visits to the Adirondacks where the rest of our tribe continued to reside, I weighed the chances of actually ending the Vietnam War. Experimenting with the fragile ratio of crunchy top to creamy middle in my casserole, I considered the forsaken morality of an electorate capable of returning a criminal like Richard Nixon to office despite *The Washington Post's* persistent, detailed disclosures about Watergate.

Over the years, my recipe for macaroni and cheese has morphed to keep up with my developing taste for bolder flavors and an inherited cholesterol count that has forced me to find lower-fat alternatives to whole milk, and full-fat cheese. But the impetus for making the dish in the first place—my desire to find respite from a world of unrelenting conflict while filling a nagging feeling of emptiness sometimes referred to as the human condition—remains. When I listen to the ego, I seek to distance myself from the world of hatred I see, identifying and condemning it "out there" in an effort to redeem an inner state of relative innocence. But it never works for long. Soon enough I find myself feeling unloved and unloving anew, grabbing my keys and heading out the door to purchase the ingredients for cheesy goodness I know will provide at best fleeting relief.

And so, I choose again, as the Course is teaching me to do. I choose a different inner teacher as I stand at the counter whisking béchamel and cooking pasta. A teacher who continues to assert that it is not the boxes of Halloween decorations still strewn about the dining room from yesterday's decorating blitz or the recent political poll that showed a homophobic candidate neck in neck with someone who more closely mirrors my personal views. It is not a stubborn recession that continues to devour our retirement accounts and worry over how to pay for my daughter's college education or seemingly endless email demands that has forced me to the stove but my fear that I have slammed that door on

God for good and will never be welcomed home again. But my fear is based on a lie the teacher capable of providing the only real comfort I really want will expose if I but look with him.

We are nearing the end of the workbook lessons in a Course class I am teaching, a year of learning to rely on the internal teacher of inner peace always available to help us correctly identify all problems as reflections of the only problem: believing we could differentiate ourselves from eternal, unified love. And the one solution: looking with our inner teacher at our projected guilt in all its costumes and seeing beyond the ego's illusions to the eternally open door of our one and only home. As the Introduction to the workbook's final lessons eloquently reminds us:

> His is the only way to find the peace that God has given us.
> It is His way that everyone must travel in the end, because
> it is this ending God Himself appointed. In the dream of
> time it seems far off. And yet, in truth, it is already here;
> already serving us as gracious guidance in the way to go.
> (from paragraph 2)

The tiny, mad idea that we could separate from our source and squander our creator's love was instantly corrected, even though we seemed to follow our tortured mind into a nightmare of competing interests and tenuous, hard-won, and always temporary survival. Our loving inner teacher retains the memory of our shared, eternal truth, a truth we gradually awaken to by learning to choose his gracious guidance whenever we find ourselves holding something external responsible for our internal distress.

We reclaim our innocence, the enduring memory of our creator's love as we learn to hold the maker of the bomb, the sender of the email, the condemning politician, the sloppy one among us harmless for our loss of peace. As we learn from our gracious guide to recognize and answer our own call for love in every seeming fragment of the ego thought system cast and perceived outside the eternally united mind.

When we choose our true and only comforter, we gently smile at our preposterous mistake, see the door to our father's love as it is rather than the way we dreamed it up, and are redeemed of a crime that never occurred. I'll eat to that!

Macaroni and Cheese:

1 14.5-ounce package macaroni (preferably whole grain)
2 T unsalted butter
2 T all-purpose flour
2 C skim or 1% warmed milk
2 ½ C grated low-fat sharp cheddar
½ C grated Romano cheese
2 heaping T Dijon mustard
¼- ½ t cayenne pepper
coarsely ground black pepper to taste
freshly ground or Panko breadcrumbs

Preheat oven to 350 degrees. Spray 9 x 12 inch glass pan with cooking spray. In saucepan, cook macaroni according to package directions. In another pan, melt butter and whisk in flour until incorporated, then whisk a little longer. Add small amount of milk to form a paste (resembling cake frosting) and allow to briefly bubble. Very gradually add remaining milk, whisking constantly. Cook for a minute or so at a low bubble. Turn off heat and gradually whisk in cheeses and remaining ingredients. Drain pasta and mix with sauce, spoon into glass pan, and top with bread crumbs and additional pepper. Bake for 30 minutes until top is slightly browned and crisp.

Enjoy with your gracious guide.

I Love to Laugh

"I think definitely this one," I say, and hand him the photo.

He holds it up to his eyes a moment and pretends to study it, even though we both know he is just being polite—can't help it, really.

In the picture my daughter sits on the stairs of our former home, the 1890 Victorian short on space and long on charm my husband bought in graduate school and we finished renovating together. She clutches an unidentifiable white stuffed animal to her heart, tiny bare toes digging into the mauve carpet, a color I had inexplicably favored during my pregnancy and have loathed ever since. Her odd little outfit is velour and studded with pink roses. A matching headband anchors her blonde bangs. She stares at the camera with an expression we referred to even back then as "the look," a cross between a pout, a plea, and a rebuke for which she remains justly famous. 95-12-28, the digits in the corner read, and I wrack my memory for what might have precipitated this adorable gaze of recrimination in a newly turned three-year-old so soon after Christmas.

He waits patiently as I set it aside and pick up another—Easter this time—and nods as I hand it to him.

In this photo, my friends Peggy and Beth had flown in to join us bearing the world's most fetching, life-size solid chocolate duck from an exclusive confectionary shop in San Francisco. My daughter has obviously already partaken of an edible beak or wing and popped out of her chair Jack-in-the-Box-style, eyes shut, hair flying, and beaming with what could only be described as maniacal rapture. A little golden halo undulates around her head, a trick of our dining room lighting perhaps, who knows? I point it out to him.

He hands me a tissue. That's just the kind of guy he is.

I am sitting with my imaginary Jesus over tea—organic chamomile lavender to be precise because who couldn't use a little calming down these days—engaging in a one-sided conversation involving the selection of childhood photos for the traditional ads parents of high school seniors are expected to purchase for their children's final yearbook. It has been a week of such activities in a year that at times feels like a kind of elongated final parenting exam. Needless to say I am, at times, a little anxious about my grades.

My daughter has but one of the arduous college applications left to finalize and submit. We attended her final club soccer game over the weekend, an event that brought tears to my eyes along with blurry visions of her and several teammates swarming across the field like a tiny beehive that first couple of years. This weekend, I will work our final silent auction benefit for the high school sports program where she will play her final Varsity season this spring. In hot pursuit of emancipation for such a long time, these recent harbingers of actual independence seem to have shifted her, too, into a temporary stage of largesse. She has been staying home more than usual, happily accompanying me as she once did on errands, and last night, my husband out of town, even climbed into bed with me for the night, a literal dream come true for our little dog sprawled out between us.

I take down the photo I keep on the bulletin board in my office of her taken at five years old, sitting on a bench in the garden outside the Rodin Museum in Paris looking oh so bohemian in black leggings and turtleneck, scribbling into the journal I bought her to chronicle our trip, and, you know, just in case she wanted to be a writer when she grew up. On that same holiday, I carried her on my shoulders in the Luxembourg Gardens and was asked for directions in French by a woman who knew how to tie scarves, if you know what I'm saying.

Je ne sais quoi, I had responded helplessly, nonetheless feeling that we had somehow finally arrived on the planet, no longer mistaken for ugly Americans.

He throws back his head and chuckles at that. His laugh is contagious. Buoyed by its lightness, I can feel myself rising along with my desk, our chairs, the computer, the pot of tea, the pile of photographs, and the blank page on which I am supposed to come up with a sentimental caption. Something that captures the specialness of the last 18 years I have spent attempting to nurture and guide this divine creature to this very threshold of striking off on her own that has left me dabbing at my eyes and counting the many ways in which I have failed to rise—no pun intended—to the occasion.

C'est la guerre, I say, and we laugh some more, giddy in our shared stance above the battleground of my illusions, clinking our tea cups together in the theatre of my imagination, transported by healing mirth like Uncle Albert and the children in the *Mary Poppins* movie, deaf to the nanny's dissenting opinion.

As *A Course in Miracles* Chapter 23, IV, Above the Battleground, reminds me when I choose to be reminded:

> Be lifted up, and from a higher place look down upon it. From there will your perspective be quite different. Here in the midst of it, it does seem real. Here you have chosen to be part of it. Here murder is your choice. Yet from above, the choice is miracles instead of murder. And the perspective coming from this choice shows you the battle is not real and easily escaped. (from paragraph 5)

I have worked with *A Course in Miracles* long enough not to be put off by this reference to murder in response to my ambivalence over my daughter's looming independence. Whether in touch with it or not, everyone shares the same unconscious belief that we have chosen to separate and thereby destroy our source, leaving us to fend for ourselves, seeming fugitives from eternal wholeness in a projected world of dualistic, competing forces. Every relationship in this so-called world thereby becomes a battleground in which we attempt to reenact our impossible defection from perfect wholeness, convinced our identity rides on the outcome of our war to prove ourselves guilty of hard-won autonomy at true love's expense. Is there any more perfect venue than the parent-child relationship in which to perpetuate from both seeming sides a story of misunderstanding, self-incrimination, disappointment, and ultimate abandonment?

And yet I am learning there is no difference in the regrets I may find myself clinging to as I prepare for this final exam before moving on to the continuing parenting education I hope will follow me to the grave and the annoyance I feel with a client, the knee-jerk condemnation the very image of certain politicians can arouse, or the tribal fear I can easily embrace in the guise of another terrorist plot or natural disaster. *A Course in Miracles* has taught me that we are in the battleground—blindly obeying the ego's orders to attack and defend our projections through a smoky haze—or we are above it, having chosen the inner teacher that remembered to gently laugh at the tiny, mad idea of it all from the very beginning, patiently waiting out our inevitable return to sanity.

When I choose to turn away from the ego and join with Jesus (that *symbol* of our one, eternally lucid mind that followed us into this illusory experiment in fragmentation), I can view the pictures of my life with my daughter kindly and clearly without any need to step back into the frame. I can smile and even learn to laugh at the tearful idea that her inevitable launch into adulthood will somehow diminish me. As I rise above the battleground with Jesus in my mind, gently laughing my head off, I begin to share his vision. These negative and positive images dissolve as if developing backwards into the ether of illusion from which they emerged. And the loving caption for our life together flows easily and unimportantly through my hand and onto the page.

Susan Dugan

A Hand to Clasp

I was "working"—read staggering through tunnels of long tables in high heels wearing an official volunteer nametag—the annual silent auction to benefit the sports program at my daughter's high school the other night, another final, official, obligatory appearance in this parenting gig before she graduates in May. We had "choiced" into this school in a nearby suburb three-and-a-half years earlier to enable her to attend its respected International Baccalaureate (IB) program. I had admittedly felt something of the outsider ever since, a self-imposed exile seemingly exacerbated now by my daughter's senior status.

As I perused the offerings of restaurant gift certificates, baskets of gourmet treats and wine, sports, theatre, and hotel vouchers, hand-made crafts and health and beauty services struggling to fend off tears, I couldn't help but recall the first year I had volunteered for this event. The hopes I had for my daughter's basketball and soccer participation. My little closeted theatre Mom fantasies arising from her inclusion in the selective concert choir; worries over her spending time in all these unknown homes among all these unknown suburban children of unknown suburban parents—instant replays from *Desperate Housewives* spinning in my head—my uncertainty over whether we had chosen the right program.

We had come a long way together since. With help from *A Course in Miracles'* forgiveness practice I had learned to change my mind early and often about the fears and control issues parenting a teenager inevitably arouse, and trust in the greater love we have never left that envelops, satisfies, and protects us all. And yet, my daughter is turning eighteen next weekend and I can no longer ignore the handwriting on the wall when I listen to the ego. It delights in pointing out that after all we have been through and just when the conflicts that once loomed so irreconcilable have dissolved leaving only our shared interests and laughter, she will soon be striking out on her own. A given for which I thought I had prepared myself, but recently discovered I have not.

I have been thinking a lot about relationships—parent and child to be specific, as well as all the special relationships we use to try to fill our insatiable need for a love we think we squandered—and the development of the only real relationship that can lead us home. Our relationship with the part of our mind that remembers where we truly reside and what we truly are. The part of our mind that followed us into this self-imposed, hallucinated banishment from perfect love we conjured when we took the tiny, mad idea that we could separate from eternal unity seriously.

A Course in Miracles offers us a symbol of the lucid dreamer—the awakened mind that knows itself as one beyond the prison of the body—in Jesus, who speaks to us (the decision maker that once chose in its fear and selfishness for the ego thought system but can learn to choose again for wholeness) directly through the Course's symbolic words. He meets us where we think we are here in the dream in the embodied, unstable condition we think we're in, and teaches us a kinder way of living in this world if we but choose to learn our lessons of forgiveness with him.

He offers us an endlessly patient ear with which he invites us to share all our doubts and delusions. He asks us to exchange the combative, tortured images our bodies' eyes generate to reinforce our sense of isolation and victimization for his perfect vision of all-inclusive, forever-invulnerable peace. He holds out his proverbial hand to us on our proverbial journey home, a journey illuminated by his light in our mind to which he would have us bring the darkness of the guilt we continually project onto others in an effort to prove someone else responsible for the imaginary "sin" of choosing individuality over perfect wholeness.

As the Manual for Teachers, 23. Does Jesus Have a Special Place in Healing? reminds us:

> What does this mean for you? It means that in remembering Jesus you are remembering God. The whole relationship

of the Son to the Father lies in him. His part in the Sonship is also yours, and his completed learning guarantees your own success. Is he still available for help? What did he say about this? Remember his promises, and ask yourself honestly whether it is likely that he will fail to keep them. … from paragraph 3)

It took me a long time to begin to believe the Course's Jesus' promises, to begin to replace the terrifying image of his crucifixion branded in my brain as I stared up at a porcelain cross over the altar of the Immaculate Conception in the parish of my childhood and listened to sermons about a Jesus seemingly as unpredictable and unstable as I secretly was. Sure, he had many positive traits, but he also grew weary and angry and impatient. He played favorites and denounced his enemies but nonetheless died for our sins, a sacrifice a frightening God apparently exacted. For all my complicit pretending, I couldn't trust either of them.

But once I really began to practice the Course's forgiveness by catching myself holding people and situations responsible for an inner condition and asking for help from a kinder and gentler Jesus I wasn't even sure I believed in, I began to experience the complete comfort and release that comes from recognizing my essential innocence by seeing it first in another. The uninterrupted experience the true Christ with whom we remain in truth seamlessly fused has been demonstrating since the beginning of seeming time, correcting an error that could never be.

When I find myself once again engrossed in the ego's story of abandonment and loss playing out in the guise of my daughter's coming of age in the dream, I remember I have and always have had a relationship that will never fail me, the same relationship that will never fail her or you. Sometimes, I offer him my illusions to shine away in his light, conscious that he is really but the presence of light within my mind that never could be doused. Sometimes, having deluded myself into thinking my relationship with a little girl whose divinity I have had the challenge and pleasure of shepherding through this dream for eighteen years is somehow about to be compromised, I believe I need a concrete version of that quiet, forever-loved and loving presence in my mind. And so I have learned to imagine reaching for his hand. He never fails to clasp it.

I am learning through practicing forgiveness that the only place we're going when we choose to be happily wrong is home, the place we never truly left and the only place we really want to be. And we never walk without a hand to clasp along the way. Not even in the suburbs.

Susan Dugan

This Need Not Be

I don't remember most of the dream but the sudden appearance of George Bush in its finale certainly grabbed my attention. We were in a spacious, old mansion somewhere on the East Coast overlooking the shore. For unknown reasons I was expected to lead him up the broad staircase and show him around. *Seriously,* I thought? As we ascended, he turned to me and drawled: "I just think there has to be a better way."

I am not making this up. (Well, never mind.) Suffice it to say I awoke startled; the all too familiar jab of pain in my ribs a recurring reminder that I am still a body, not yet free. The possibility of an all-inclusive forgiveness that sees *only* common interests and could even expand to heal my mind about our former president loomed just out of reach on the horizon of my perception, an ocean bathed in sunlight conjured in the ego's desert.

And yet I was thankful, as my little dog assumed the position on her back inviting me to our morning ritual that involved my stroking her chest and generally adoring her. I had been asking for days to once more hear the steady voice of our right mind with which I seemed to have lost all contact. Our former president of all people had suddenly catapulted me back to the source of the original split. Where the decision maker who first chose to take the tiny, mad idea of separation from our source seriously and follow the ego into a projected universe of guilt over that failure to smile can always choose again for truth. Once it remembers it is not the victimized/victimizing ego but the dreamer of the dream in which a person named Susan cracks her ribs and recalls an imagined president with whom she once took issue.

For a variety of seeming reasons too boringly self-absorbed to enumerate, I had been once more entertaining the ego's 24/7 rant of competing interests. Judging myself and others (the former inevitably resulting in the latter through the "magic" of ego projection), and consumed with self-hatred and physical pain resulting from said rib cracking in a fall while walking the dog on an uneven bit of pavement the weekend before Thanksgiving. Every excruciating breath I drew as we headed home recalled my attachment to the story of my personal suffering at the hands of a galaxy of insensitive forces. But now, as I rose to take the dog out and face another embodied day, I heard quite clearly the ultimately soothing message I'd been refusing to acknowledge:

> If you cannot hear the Voice for God, it is because you do not choose to listen. (*A Course in Miracles* Chapter 4, IV. This Need Not Be, from paragraph 1)

I do not choose to listen to the Holy (Whole) Spirit, that correction for the ego's belief in separation realized that continues to shine in our one mind, because I still on some level—in my fear and selfishness—buy the ego's empty threats and promises. My mind, after all, is split. I want the Voice for God, but only on my terms. Terms that involve preserving this body and this life with which it identifies, however tumultuous. I want to have my Course and my special identity, too. Yet, when I listen to the ego, I am in constant danger of losing this life in one way or another, the final "proof" bolstered by sensory data that I exist at God's expense. Competing for my very survival and seeking for love, attention, success, and solace in all the wrong places; endlessly thirsting after a mirage that remains forever just out of reach.

But as we learn in This Need Not Be:

> I have said that you cannot change your mind by changing your behavior. But I have also said and many times, that you *can* change your mind. When your mood tells you that you have chosen wrongly, and this is so whenever you are not joyous, then know *this need not be*. In every case you have thought wrongly about some brother God created, and are perceiving images your ego makes in a darkened glass. (from paragraph 2)

The more I practice forgiveness *A Course in Miracles*-style, the more apparent the relationship between my negative feelings and my projected guilt becomes. Even when I seem to be grappling with physical pain resulting from an "accidental" fall, I am beginning to see that I can always trace the perceived incoming attack back to my own harsh judgments of myself and others. The day I cracked my ribs for example, I was walking way too fast, hoping to dispel the tension building within over my burgeoning Thanksgiving To-Do list combined with a variety of mounting external obligations I secretly resented. The injury served to up the ante in my ego's story of holiday martyrdom.

"How in hell are you going to lift a 22-pound turkey?" the ego asked, in a prelude to another tirade.

I didn't think I wanted to listen, but the searing pain of each step as I walked home seemed to have obliterated the voice for peace.

Not. I am learning that if I am experiencing physical (or psychological) pain and seemingly unable to access my right mind it is *always* because I have chosen to listen to and side with the ego's tale of victimization to preserve my bogus individuality. This need not be. We always have a choice. The pain itself exposes which voice we have chosen and reminds us (if we let it) to choose again for the always available voice of eternal wholeness and comfort. We can always ask for help in looking at the ego's resentful, fearful illusions and seeing past them to a blessedly empty screen.

Whether projecting our denied guilt onto someone else by blaming them for our inner condition or projecting it on the body we identify with and appear to inhabit, our seemingly compromised mood should always raise a red flag that we have chosen wrongly but can choose again. As our kinder and gentler ex-President (reminiscent of Course Collaborator Bill Thetford's original invitation to the scribing of the Course: "There has to be another way") put it in my dream: "There has to be a better way." And there *always* is.

It is possible to feel the body's physical and emotional pain as bodies do while recognizing its guilty motive and withdrawing support for it. *A Course in Miracles* is never asking us to deny the body but to remember its purpose and choose again for the part of our one mind capable of guilt's undoing, a practice that eventually heals all thoughts of pain.

Susan Dugan

The House That Guilt Built

I was walking my dog on another oddly mild December day here in Denver, Colorado, the kind of weather that would have catapulted pre-*A Course in Miracles* Susan into a frenzied contemplation of the inevitability of global warming. But today, in the throes of another imaginary interview with Jesus, the *symbol* of the one mind healed of the thought of separation the Course uses to lead us home to the one love we never left, I wanted to truly understand the allure of my continuing impulse to take this dream and the figures that appear to populate it seriously. Including the figure I still believe I am. I wanted to know how to answer students who constantly wonder aloud how we can possibly live in a world of bodies without believing we're forgiving something real, i.e.; the ostensibly bad behavior of other bodies. How we can possibly swallow that most frequently repeated yet continually startling lesson in the workbook: "I am not a body, I am free," while witnessing the deterioration of the bodies of those we love, let alone our own bodies.

After all, I had dreamt last night of a family member's death, and was now moving like a plant toward the sun, hoping to soak up Vitamin D-infused rays to heal the ribs I had cracked on another walk a few weeks earlier in which I was trying to rid my body of the tension caused by a host of perceived external demands that seemed to have overloaded my vulnerable nervous system. Today, I was also hoping to stave off the effects of winter light deprivation and serotonin impoverishment while spending a little quality time with Jesus, a win-win activity for body, right mind, and canine. The sharp angle of the winter sunlight stained the walls of the brick and stucco homes around me pink. Dry native grasses bent generously in the wind, dead leaves clattered against the bike path pavement winding along the gulch sending Kayleigh spinning Sufi-like in appreciation.

As I paused a moment, gazing at houses "protected" by elaborate alarm systems, surrounded by fences designed to keep the bad behavior of other dream figures at bay, it came to me—our embarrassingly irresolvable predicament—in a way I had never quite considered before. I could *feel* the nothingness of it all; the nothingness within my seeming body and the nothingness without. I could somehow sense the nothingness within the yards and the homes around me, the nothingness in the bodies moving without and within, the nothingness of my little dog now sitting at my feet on the pavement, tilting her head and sniffing as if having caught a whiff of it too, the rare scent of healing.

For a moment I was acutely aware that my body—like the yards and homes and bodies around me—was truly a defense against the truth, my identification with it the major block to real love's awareness the Course speaks of. For a moment, I could see with the Holy (Whole) Spirit's true X-Ray Vision, feel the nothingness of it all, and give thanks for the abstract unity we remain despite all these elaborate shields our belief in the ego's tale of separation from God invented to protect ourselves from our father's impossible retaliation. To keep us so busy defending our doomed fortresses that we forget completely about the real, abstract, *everything* with which we remain universally fused.

The ego has built a shabby and unsheltering home for you, because it cannot build otherwise. Do not try to make this impoverished house stand. Its weakness is your strength. Only God could make a home that is worthy of His creations, who have chosen to leave it empty by their own dispossession. Yet His home will stand forever, and is ready for you when you choose to enter it. Of this you can be wholly certain. God is as incapable of creating the perishable as the ego is of making the eternal. (*A Course in Miracles*, Chapter 4, IV. Right Teaching and Right Learning, paragraph 11)

We spin out our days striving to make our impoverished house stand, an impossible task based on a lie. But when we choose to look with Jesus at all we have created to defend against the love we believe we squandered in our selfishness but have in truth never left, we see beyond form to the content of guilt in the one mind. A content resulting from a perceived violent act against our creator that never happened. Our bodies will come and go within an ego thought system frantically trying to justify its existence at God's expense by keeping our denied guilt over that original belief in separation realized alive, projecting it outward into endless neighborhoods of forms fighting for bogus survival. But when we take responsibility for our perception of vulnerability at the hands of others back to its source in the mind and offer it to true vision, the absurdity of it all can only yield a smile and a deep sigh of relief as the memory of our uninterrupted, all-inclusive innocence returns to our mind. Until we become afraid again.

On the way home, we turned a corner and almost ran smack into a coffin descending the steps of a picture-perfect Anglican Church on the shoulders of grieving parishoners. I caught the tear-stained eyes of a woman about my age following the procession, and wanted to beam her my confidence in what I had felt but moments earlier. But not wishing to intrude, I instead dropped my eyes to the pavement and crossed the street.

"I am not a body, I am free." I repeated, to resurrect my former certainty.

"Easy for you to say," the ego weighed in. He had a point. The truth is, I don't have any idea how I would react if I were facing the death of this body I still think I am. *Except* in the holy instant in which I forgive another form I think has compromised my peace and observe with our inner Jesus my attachment to judgment, attack, defense and, yes, guilt over having taken the tiny, mad idea of separation seriously. Fortunately, looking with my inner, kindly amused Jesus day in and day out at all the external manifestations of an inner condition I would use to hurt me and prove I exist at whole love's expense, interviewing him despite the fact that he—you know, doesn't really talk—is enough.

We cannot possibly fully understand that we are not bodies, we are free as we look at the dream figure we identify with staring back at us in the mirror every morning. But we *can* free ourselves from the body of guilt in the mind by forgiving the walls we have erected to imprison us and choosing to look beyond every single one of them with Jesus as our teacher to our abstract innocence, the uninterrupted *everything* we share and remain.

Susan Dugan

Rocking Around the Christmas Tree

Last week we put up our Christmas tree, strung it with brand new LED lights, adorned it with ornaments, and watched, aghast, as it fell down. The little dog, thankfully spared, spun in mad circles. I stood a moment, stunned, reflecting on the smashed crystal ballerina's final pirouette, and the welcome beheading of the clumsily crafted snowman I had never much liked anyway. We wrestled the fir back into stately position in its plastic stand. My daughter and I steadied it as my husband rushed downstairs to grab a vice-like instrument in an effort to stabilize the base. He got it all cranked in. We stepped away, and ... it fell down again, although we caught it this time mid-swoon.

We tried a length of twine next; attaching it to a nearby door handle but, alas, it fell down, much to the dog's escalating consternation. There was nothing else to do. My husband dashed out the door to purchase a new tree stand before the stores closed, as my daughter and I stood gripping the tipsy Tannenbaum; she texting with her free hand, me bemused by the vintage recording of Brenda Lee singing "Rocking around, the Christmas tree, have a happy holiday" emanating from our stereo and marveling at my apparently unflappable right-mindedness.

Because this little scenario was exactly the sort of thing that might have catapulted pre-*A Course in Miracles* student Susan's ego into a full-blown meltdown, seemingly triggered by the shattering of her persistent perfect family Christmas hallucinations. Instead, I remained pleasantly calm as we waited for my husband's return and then worked together to settle the tree into its new stand where it finally achieved that all too elusive state of equilibrium. I swept up the debris of heirloom ornamental carnage, congratulating myself that all this forgiveness practice really was paying off, just as the Course promises it will.

That night, drifting off to visions of sugarplums doing their blissninny thing in my head, I dreamt that I had murdered someone. I didn't remember the dastardly deed but somehow knew I had done it. I found myself in some kind of camp, unsure about what I was doing there, but certain I needed to escape, and fast, before the weather turned and dashed the possibility of making it over a nearby mountain pass. Still, I didn't want to arouse suspicion and needed to get rid of the weapon—an enormous, gleaming blade with predatory teeth, part sword, part chain saw—first.

I wrapped it in a towel and carried it out of my cabin into some kind of communal center. In the lobby of the rustic building, a man worked at a carpentry table while a woman sat at a desk talking on a phone. I said hello before hurrying past them through an institutional style kitchen and out the screen door to a yard surrounded by pasture, intending to bury the knife behind a barn. But other people kept wandering over and trying to strike up a conversation. They did not ask what was in the towel, but stared at it knowingly, upping the ante on my already escalating anxiety. Furious, I finally stomped off toward the surrounding woods and hurled the weapon, rolled up the towel thinking to stash it in someone else's cabin, and started running, guilt-fueled, faster than I have ever run, conscious I must leave this place before someone discovered what I had done.

I woke enveloped in the cliché of a cold sweat, contemplating the creation myth the Course uses to explain our descent into the darkness of the ego thought system, the one Son of God's refusal to smile at the "tiny, mad idea" that it could separate from its source. The idea involved our desire to experience ourselves as individuals outside the realm of eternally perfect wholeness. As it arose in the one child of God's mind and we *forgot to laugh* at the preposterous nature of fragmenting infinitely indivisible oneness, we imagined ourselves cast into darkness, the light of our source extinguished.

Thinking we had destroyed it, our one mind appeared to split into the ego and the Holy (Whole) Spirit. In our fear over our creator's retribution and continuing selfish desire to sample individuality, we ignored the Holy Spirit's certainty that the separation never happened and instead chose to believe the ego's story that we had murdered our source. Mired in guilt and now perceiving ourselves fugitives from real love, we followed the ego into an entire projected universe of that thought of guilt in the mind, assumed bodies, fell asleep, and set to work projecting that guilt onto other bodies every time it began to rear its ugly head in our psyche. Magically believing the God we murdered would somehow rise again to punish us for our crime, we continue to defend ourselves and condemn others in an effort to establish our relative innocence versus their greater guilt.

Enter forgiveness *A Course in Miracles*-style, our only function here if we hope to begin to heal our minds of the persistent belief we murdered someone and must constantly flee the source of that original thought in the mind to protect ourselves from certain retribution. As workbook lesson 192, "I have a function God would have me fill," tells us:

> ... Forgiveness represents your function here. It is not God's creation, for it is the means by which untruth can be undone. ...Yet on earth, you need the means to let illusions go. (from paragraph 2)

By practicing *A Course in Miracles* unique forgiveness—looking with the Holy (Whole) Spirit/Jesus, that *symbol* of the split mind healed of all impossible thoughts of fracture at our attempts to nurture the guilt in our mind by projecting it outward and then interpreting it as an incoming attack—we begin to change our mind about what's really going on. In the holy instant in which we admit our error and accept what's really happening, we sample the release and completeness permanently available to us once we allow the undoing of all our errors in judgment, return to uninterrupted right-mindedness, and finally awaken to the everlasting wholeness we remain.

But that happens at the very end. On this "journey without distance to a place we never left" we must patiently work with the forgiveness lessons that daily arise in what the Course calls the classroom of our life, that individual curriculum in which we learn from our inner teacher to change our minds about the special relationships we have crafted in which to conceal the proverbial murder weapon we all secretly believe we are toting.

> "Forgiveness gently looks upon all things unknown in Heaven, sees them disappear, and leaves the world a clean and unmarked slate on which the Word of God can now replace the senseless symbols written there before. Forgiveness is the means by which the fear of death is overcome, because it holds no fierce attraction now and guilt is gone. Forgiveness lets the body be perceived as what it is; a simple teaching aid, to be laid by when learning is complete, but hardly changing him who learns at all." (paragraph 4)

The practice of learning the lessons of forgiveness has ancillary benefits. Focusing on forgiving our stories of unfair treatment at the hands of others day in and day out can help us heal our mind about the doomed-from-the-get-go special love bargains we make with others to substitute for the love we believe we destroyed and can never find again. We might even find ourselves this Christmas smiling with our inner amused teacher at the messiness of the ego thought system as it strives to preserve its impossible dream. Until we once again catch ourselves attempting to pin a thought of murder on someone or thing seemingly out there both to exonerate ourselves and to preserve an illusion of individuality that has, in truth, only brought us suffering.

And so, we choose again to accept our only function here and forgive, releasing ourselves from certain imprisonment by releasing our judgments of each other.

> Therefore, hold no one prisoner. Release instead of bind, for thus are you made free. (from paragraph 9)

Susan Dugan

A Meaningless World Engenders Fear

So far this seems to be the winter of dreaming myself closer to waking awareness that I am actually living a dream of my own making, and not even a very entertaining one at that. In the most recent sleeping version, now available on DVD, I found myself in a movie multiplex along with thousands of fellow film buffs apparently attending some kind of marathon festival. Aware I had already seen four disappointing flicks back-to-back, I had just entered another theatre hoping the fifth might prove the charm and was searching for a seat when I spied a good friend sitting toward the front with a couple other people. She invited me to join them and began describing in animated detail several other films I absolutely shouldn't miss for their certain, perfect, "*je ne sais quoi* sensibilities," (I am directly quoting here). A familiar, competitive jolt of adrenaline beckoned me to critique the films I had viewed but I couldn't seem to engage my inner Chatty Cathy before other people chimed in, supporting or arguing the various films' merits with alternating enthusiasm and agitation. I listened politely, overcome with a heavy sense of exhaustion at the very thought of attending all these additional movies.

Finally, the lights dimmed, squelching conversation. The featured film's credits had just begun to roll when the sound and video abruptly died. The audience sat grumbling a few moments before the lights came up and a theatre employee hurried down the long aisle to announce the projector had failed and they would instead show the movie in the theatre next door. Swept up in my friend and her entourage's rush to push ahead of the crowd milling toward the exit door my feet grew heavy. My quads ached and I could barely keep my eyes open. How could I possibly watch another one of these movies, I wondered, when they all seemed the same?

Lately, here in the "waking dream," I have been watching yet another, all-too-familiar movie in which Susan, overwhelmed by the seemingly ceaseless demands of lesser mortals, struggles to create a perfect holiday, a perfect family, a perfect career, a perfect little life; despite overwhelming odds perpetuated by imaginary external forces hell-bent on thwarting her most noble efforts. And really noticing—as I ask for help observing what *A Course in Miracles* refers to as the "hero of the dream" I think I am while largely forgetting I am, in truth, the "dreamer of the dream"— how terribly anxious it makes me to recognize (even momentarily) that I am indeed that dreamer. How ironically helpless I feel when presented with the opportunity to take responsibility for all I experience by claiming authorship for yet another version of the same fictitious script and production that has only brought me suffering and isolation from true love and has begun to feel so painfully clichéd.

"A meaningless world engenders fear," *A Course in Miracles* workbook lesson 13 tells us:

> Recognition of meaninglessness arouses intense anxiety in all the separated ones. It represents a situation in which God and the ego 'challenge' each other as to whose meaning is to be written in the empty space that meaninglessness provides. The ego rushes in frantically to establish its own ideas there, fearful that the void may otherwise be used to demonstrate its own impotence and unreality. And on this alone it is correct. (paragraph 2)

While this should theoretically spell good news for the decision maker I think I am—extinguishing a genre I believe I have outgrown—it doesn't. Because the decision maker that originally sided with the ego in taking the tiny, mad idea of separation from our source seriously while ignoring the right mind's assertion of indivisible oneness, recognizes on some level that it, like the ego, disappears in the light of that same blank page and screen. And it still can't remember a life beyond that choice for a tiny, mad, but thankfully impossible idea. Or a story that does not involve its puny differentiated existence.

It all comes down to this. Without the latest release in the epic story of Susan's victimization and periodic histrionic triumph over ultimately insurmountable odds, who am I? The truth is, as *A Course in Miracles* teaches, I can't see beyond the meaninglessness of the blank screen or page except in the holy instant in which I choose to absolve you from all responsibility for my suffering wherein my vision merges with the right mind's invincible, eternally loved and loving viewpoint and all meaningless questions made to circumvent the real, coherent, all-inclusive answer cease.

Our fear and amnesia notwithstanding, in truth we have not destroyed God who could never compete with us since he cannot recognize illusion. We remain one dreamer dreaming of hideous dissection, which is why the thought of that final fade out to eternally uninterrupted invulnerability still scares the hell out of me. Believing as I do that I must continue to fill the screen with my story, a script that grows harder each day to believe in, articulate, and defend as I observe it in the company of our loving inner teacher whose presence in the theatre of my mind I find harder and harder to ignore.

So here's another story, the story Jesus whispers to us from outside the dream. I am awake in God, dreaming of exile. And if I trust Jesus, our symbolic scout in the vast unknown of the awakened, as I at least claim to want to, and he tells me it's a great place—you'll love it—trust me, then maybe he's right and I have been happily wrong about everything. Just maybe, regardless of the unfair, perilous, elusive details of the film, the conflict and resolution really *are* always the same. I have written, directed, produced, and projected the entire thing simply to convince myself the problem lies on the screen instead of in the mind of the one decision maker that believed it had something to gain from impersonating an individual as well as something enormous to lose.

Or, maybe—the ego has just bent my fingers back and implored me to add—*not*.

Susan Dugan

I Want to Want the Peace of God

As 2010 drew to a close, I found myself once more reviewing past resolutions, those cockeyed optimistic corrections for guilty behavior or the setting of more ambitious goals all based on atoning for the many ways I had fallen short during the prior year as the clock ticked down and the annual opportunity to weave a better dream presented itself. Because, once again; the dream—*A Course in Miracles'* term for our so-called lives in this so-called world—had fallen short of the ego's expectations. Circumstances in the world in general—from the economy to our failure to deal with the health care crisis, to tensions in the Middle East and U.S. House of Representatives, to our continued inability to address and often even acknowledge the reality of climate change—continued to devolve. On a personal level, a number of last year's earnest resolutions lay scattered like ribbons and wrappings from recently opened Christmas gifts, the promise of true fulfillment they concealed once more expired. More importantly, that state of inner peaceful equilibrium to which I will return when all my forgiveness lessons are complete remained elusive. I was still somewhere in the murky middle of this journey home to the one love we never truly left, and judging myself harshly for it.

I had once more retreated with family and friends to Crested Butte, Colorado, a remote idyllic ski town complete with Victorian storefronts, a summit endearingly reminiscent of Mount Crumpet in Dr. Seuss's *The Grinch Who Stole Christmas*, and a comforting blanket of flamboyant drifts of snow. It had been a year of hard work with few immediate rewards, rife with the bittersweet awareness that my in-house parenting days were numbered as my daughter completed her final high school year and applied to colleges, a year of aches and pains echoing past injuries that made it ever harder to deny, as my generation still strives to, the inevitable deterioration of the human body.

A perennial intermediate skier (versus the expert status of the rest of our party) and still not fully recovered from breaking a couple ribs prior to Thanksgiving, I knew I could count on some much needed solitude. In the mad dash to the year's finale I had been postponing the quality time with Jesus (that *symbol* of our one mind healed of the idea of separation from our source) I believed I had earned, knowing I would soon be largely left to my own devices. And yet, the very first morning as I headed for the single line at the base of the Red Lady lift I could not seem to summon his inner presence. As I attempted to ski heretofore easy blue runs, I reverted to amateurish maneuvers in my fear of falling and further injuring my still fragile torso. Preoccupied by self-preservation while frustrated by this latest evidence of investment in the body, I could not seem to summon the inner BFF I had come to count on.

And yet, a part of me simply watched, detached, as the week wound on, a two-day blizzard made skiing for puny Susan impossible, the thermometer plunged and the streets iced up, the pads on the dog's paws nearly froze, and my sinus issues escalated into a full-blown infection, and we cooked and hung out and rang in the new. Although I wasn't experiencing the special relationship with a visualized embodied Jesus my mind-on-ego craved, a part of me knew I remained within the quiet center of that all-encompassing love we shared. Although I kept summoning some kind of prolonged, mystical, holy instant—a kind of end-of-the-year bonus for the hard work of forgiveness—I gradually realized that a personal identity designed to defend against universal love could not really experience anything. And I wondered if "looking with Jesus" really meant merely peering through the ongoing illusion of Susan *and* Jesus to the welcome truth of non-specific, mutual, and gently amused sanity.

In the end I experienced a heretofore unknown confidence that all was well despite the wildly fluctuating dream details and Susan's inability to *feel* the love and peace of God in some

Hallelujah Chorus kind of way. And I realized that nothing in a dream crafted to keep me mindless needs to occur for me to experience myself as the decision maker capable of recognizing the ego for the defense against the truth it is and choosing to want the peace of God even as the ego continues to throw its hissy fit curve balls designed to prove the chaotic dream real.

> … We want the peace of God. This is no idle wish. These words do not request another dream be given us. They do not ask for compromise, nor try to make another bargain in the hope that there may yet be one that can succeed where all the rest have failed. To mean these words acknowledges illusions are in vain, requesting the eternal in the place of shifting dreams which seem to change in what they offer but are one in nothingness. (From *A Course in Miracles* Workbook Lesson 185, paragraph 7)

This year, I just can't take it all—including my own resistance—as seriously. Which is not to say I still don't *want* to take it seriously except in the holy instant in which I actively choose for the right mind, thereby activating the memory that it is all a dream from which I have already wakened, a certainty I will permanently embrace once my belief that specialness has anything left to offer finally dissolves in the light of forgiveness *A Course in Miracles*-style. A vision of Jesus, a conversation with Jesus, a sense of holding my big brother's hand, didn't show up for me during this getaway. But a near constant awareness that I am the decision maker did. My certainty that the ego will appear to do what the ego will appear to do with or without my support did. And the knee-jerk impulse to join with all I would use to hurt my real self? Not so much.

Who knows, maybe I am slowly but surely growing up by doing the work of forgiveness day in and day out, looking with the part of my mind that can truly see at this internal state of fear and guilt I've chosen to see "out there" differently. Rather than asking to see this person's behavior or this situation differently. The person and behavior and situation and body don't, after all, exist, except in the dark recesses of a mind made mad by a thought of guilt over the impossible crime of separation from eternal wholeness.

Moving away from the understanding that I am forgiving what seems to have taken my peace to owning it as my unconscious choice to once more push God's love away changes everything. I honestly have no resolutions to offer this year except that I want to want the peace of God, and to remember that it is always there if I but continue to look with an inner Jesus whose presence I accept more and more as my own. Seriously!

A Course in Miracles: An All-Inclusive Healing of the Heart

I have been teaching the Course now weekly for a year-and-a-half and find myself amusingly challenged at times by really meaty questions that sometimes leave me feeling as if I am entertaining lobbyists for the ego, as if the ego were some embodied reptilian creature much like the snake in the original ego creation myth hell-bent on tripping me up with its forbidden fruit. (No offense to lobbyists, of course.) A while back in my regular *A Course in Miracles* forgiveness class, a flurry of such questions erupted about the exceedingly confusing (to the ego) topic of level confusion.

In an interview I did with Ken Wapnick several years ago I asked him about level confusion and he defined it as "... the misunderstanding of the mind and the body, which in Chapter 2 is called level confusion. All misunderstandings—the role of the Holy Spirit, the purpose of the Course, hearing guidance, hearing a voice—stem from not understanding that there literally is no body, no world. Once you understand that, everything falls nicely into place."

Easy for Ken to say. :)

I could feel judgment slithering into the room from the recesses of our one split mind as we began to discuss examples of level confusion among Course students including asking Jesus to help them solve specific problems in an illusory world or believing that because I am not a body and the world is an illusion (true on Level 1) I don't need to take care of my body, work, pay taxes, obey laws, etc. (false on Level 2).

> I do not foster level confusion but you must choose to correct it. You would not excuse insane behavior on your part by saying you could not help it. Why should you condone insane thinking? (Chapter 2, VI. Fear and Conflict, from paragraph 2)

We condone insane thinking and thereby foster level confusion all the time, mainly because we don't know it's insane, fused with the ego mind as we appear to be. Seemingly immersed in and insanely identified with physical and psychological bodies imagined to distract us with their constant neediness and vulnerability, we have forgotten that the answer to all seeming problems remains in the one mind where the one seeming problem began. The one mind that originally took the "tiny, mad idea" of separation from its source seriously, seemingly catapulting us into an entire universe of forms competing for imaginary survival. Unconscious that the correction for the error of the belief in separation (the right mind/Holy Spirit/our memory of our true, infinitely undifferentiated self) remains unscathed in the mind. The last place any healthy ego (unconsciously invested in preserving its twisted but highly effective thought system) would ever choose to look.

So even as we pick up the big, blue book and sincerely declare ourselves *A Course in Miracles* students, we forget what the Course is telling us: that we exist in truth only on Level 1 but that our guilt and fear over believing we have obliterated our source and our continuing enchantment with the possibility of uniqueness causes us to perceive ourselves exclusively on Level 2. Immersed in a dream of our own making, a world of perception barricaded by our physical senses to block our awareness of our true, uninterrupted union with God, we stagger across the stage, acting out our stories of unfair treatment at the hands of others out to get us, stridently lobbying for our innocence relative to their greater guilt.

Once we find the Course and hear about our true loving nature in Level 1, we often try to prove we have accepted this reality for ourselves. "God is but love," we may quote from the workbook, "and therefore so am I." We may have this really dreamy, stoner look on our face as we repeat this Level 1 statement. But even if we have managed to convince ourselves this is true, we have done nothing to undo the unconscious guilt in the mind the Course clearly states we must allow through the *process* of forgiveness. That daily *work* of looking at our projections—the guilt we prefer to see in others rather than own—with the inner teacher of wholeness in our mind that merely smiles at the preposterous idea of guilt (and levels, for that matter) and teaches us to smile, too.

Level confusion manifests itself in a variety of ways. Course students may hear only the Level 1 statements and cleverly ignore the bulk of the Course's emphasis on exposing the vicious selfishness of the ego thought system. They may seek to engage the Holy Spirit as a kind of personal valet to do their bidding in the world, reinforcing their specialness by believing they have a unique relationship with a voice that gives them specific advice to help themselves and others, even though the right mind has nothing at all to say about a hallucination however vivid except that it's not real. Some students interpret the Course's assertion that the world is an illusion to mean they don't have to do normal things like paying bills or putting gas in their cars here in Level 2.

But while the body's senses may perceive level confusion arising in *A Course in Miracles* students all around us, if we are truly practicing forgiveness and thereby making the healing of our one mind our priority, we need to understand that the level confusion we observe without (and too often react to) is our own. So far in my relatively short experience with the Course, this is one of the most tempting pitfalls, forgetting that the resistance I notice in other Course students who believe they can jump into God's arms (Level 1) for example, without doing the mindful, ongoing *work* of forgiving our impulse to hold others responsible for our compromised peace of mind (Level 2), is my own.

Everyone in a body—the most earnest Course students included—dabbles in level confusion. We all use magic (the Course's term for trying to solve the imaginary problem of guilt in the mind by imaginary physical means, part of the ego's strategy to keep the body and the world of form real) every time we breathe. We all, at times, try to entice God into the world. We all, at times, unwittingly allow the ego to join the journey, believing our latest forgiveness lesson has rendered us especially ego-free. But we are ego-free only in the holy instant outside time in which we see no separate interests and allow the deeply comforting relief and release from all judgment of ourselves and others the choice for forgiveness *A Course in Miracles*-style brings.

If we are sitting in a literal *A Course in Miracles* classroom discussing level confusion and citing its manifestation among *other* Course students rather than witnessing its attraction within our own mind we are firmly, intoxicatingly, once more grounded in the ego thought system. The ego has joined the journey as Jesus repeatedly warns us it will. What to do? Simply recognize it, own it, and release it to a part of our mind that has its number. That knows it for what it is (a defense against the truth) and isn't (an attack on God or anyone else).

When we do this, the certainty of our collective innocence returns and the mind healing we experience automatically includes all those Course students we previously held less advanced or more defended than we are—hilarious, really! Our gentle sense of humor returns and we can laugh at such a thought; restored to the understanding that, in truth there is only one *A Course in Miracles* student sitting in this Level 1 classroom trying to get over the Level 2 idea that there are other Course students studying and practicing in ways that require forgiveness. One Course student trying to learn that, in truth, there is really no Course student, no big, blue book, only one all-inclusive child of God seamlessly fused with our Father in ways impossible to understand here in Level 2.

We, the decision maker, must constantly remind ourselves that the lobbyists for the ego thought system we see everywhere around us as we begin to look at our projections—all too often confusing which teacher we are really looking with—are on our payroll. We sent those persuasive, manipulative, dare I say cunning voices out into the halls of Congress. We all share the same miserable ego thought system and the same memory of invulnerable, eternally innocent unity in our one mind. There is no point to practicing *A Course in Miracles* if we use it to further strengthen the thought system of division.

We need to see the call for love expressed in level confusion of all kinds as our own, reflective of our own deep-seated fear that we will never get home, never be accepted back into the loving fold. We save ourselves and every other seeming self from the overwhelming desolation of guilt in the one mind by refusing to strengthen it in others and ourselves. By simply looking at the ego without judgment which *is* looking with our inner, gently amused Jesus/right mind at the decision maker's fearful choice for the pain and specialness of the ego thought system and choosing again for the memory of abstract wholeness we remain.

A Room of My Own

In the dream I am back in Boston, in college again, about to begin a graduate program. I have rented an apartment in yet another roach-infested tenement and am doing my best to make it livable, scrubbing floors and scary, mysterious residues on kitchen cabinet shelves. Even singing a little tune—the *Working Song* from the Disney film *Enchanted* a la Amy Adams—while making up the bed and congratulating myself on finally nabbing a place of my own. I leave to find a grocery store to procure more cleaning supplies and on my return, am startled to find another woman moving her belongings into *my* apartment. I explain that there must be some mistake because I have signed a lease. She produces an identical document adorned with *her* signature. The landlord is unavailable when I phone. I tell her she has to leave; I was here first, after all. She waves her lease at me. I wave mine back. "Chill out," she says. "We'll just have to share." Share my apartment with this interloper? I don't think so.

I wake up, angry and uncomfortably aware of the self-imposed condition which preceded this dream, a day of internally complaining about—and not so successfully forgiving—seeming external demands over which I feel I have no control and a mounting and all-too familiar suspicion I am just not an organization-friendly type person. I am an introvert, after all, a writer, a loner, just not a team player. Although I have spent a lot of time denying this tendency and feeling inadequate because of it, if I am really honest I have to admit I find the kind of dynamics that inevitably arise in organizations—the abundant discussion and vying opinions that characterize meetings within departments and boards and committees and advisory councils and groups of every kind—taxing at best. Participating in a variety of such associations over the years—regardless of the type of organization or how passionately I may support its mission—often leaves me suppressing an overwhelming urge to bolt, to flee from the

abundant opinions and disagreements and decisions and assignments and barricade myself in a room of my own.

Ironically I had been cruising along for a week or so in a seemingly right-minded, expansive and creative flow following the
flurry of forgiveness opportunities the holidays inevitably bring.
Steeped in blessed hibernation and attending to my own ample
To-Do list when what the Course calls our "concealed desire to
kill" resurfaced in the form of these group dynamics and my
resistance to them. In the past I had often found myself triggered
by individuals within groups and focused on asking our inner
teacher to help me observe without judgment my own wish to
blame my unconscious guilt over the belief in separation from
our source on someone seemingly "out there." But this time, there
was no one in particular to blame. The situation itself seemed
to have assumed a separate identity with which I felt at odds.
Bringing me face to face with that primal desire to slam the door
on perfect oneness and strike off on my own at the bottom of this
aversion to organizations of mine and judging myself harshly for
the apparent absence of the joining gene others seemed to possess.

I wish I could say I was gentle with myself as I looked at this,
that I remembered to call in the inner teacher of gentleness and
unity as I advise my Course study group students to do, but I was
looking with the ego, condemning myself for my essential selfishness and thereby reinforcing the ego's agenda of strengthening
the mad idea of individuation. The more I looked with the inner
teacher of division, the more unstable my mood and the more
self-loathing I experienced. Unable to take it anymore, I finally
stomped up to bed ridiculously early, only to be awakened in the
middle of the night by a nightmare that cut to the core of my
continuing identification with specialness.

And so I finally chose again for the inner voice of wholeness.
In the deep quiet that followed, I could see the same old and only
problem at work in my decision for judgment—leveled at myself
this time. I could see I had once more chosen to reinforce a guilty

thought system created to uphold the seriousness with which we took the "tiny, mad idea" of separation from our indivisible loving source. And I could begin to smile at a transparent sleeping dream that merely exposed the same old concealed desire to protect the specialness each and every one of us—introvert or extravert—seemingly stranded in bodies, seeks to preserve.

Whether we enjoy participating in groups or prefer working by ourselves we are still always unconsciously striving to reinforce the impossible dream of separate interests. We don't need to join with other bodies in form but we do need to lay our belief that our involvement with other bodies could in any way enhance or jeopardize our peace of mind on the desk of our inner teacher who gives everyone willing to hand over that assignment a big fat A.

As I learn to apply forgiveness to everything that arises in the classroom of my life, I am noticing more and more that I rarely need to follow up with action in form. Once I have made the inner decision to listen to the teacher of wholeness, the urge to "do something" often vanishes. If I do act, it comes (thankfully), without my apparent premeditated involvement through honest, direct, sane communication. I am slower these days to act in form when I catch myself holding something external responsible for that same old internal condition, and quicker to act internally. Even though I still may resist for a day or two, I can't really kid myself for long about which teacher I have chosen. If I'm experiencing anything but inner peace, seeing anything but my essential sameness with all characters in my dream, I know I've chosen the ego, even though I may still be reluctant to immediately choose again.

But the decision is always available and never too far from my awareness. As Chapter 5, VII. The Decision for God, paragraph 6, reminds us:

Decision cannot be difficult. This is obvious, if you realize that you must already have decided not to be wholly joyous if that is how you feel. Therefore, the first step in the undoing is to recognize that you actively decided wrongly but can as actively decide otherwise. Be very firm with yourself in this, and keep yourself fully aware that the undoing process, which does not come from you, is nevertheless within you because God placed it there. Your part is merely to return your thinking to the point at which the error was made and give it over to the Atonement in peace. ...

I can do that!

When the Going Gets Tough, the Tough Make Red Beans and Rice

"Well, I've been afraid of changing 'cause I built my life around you." The Stevie Nicks classic song *Landslide* had been stuck in my head for days, accompanying an internal slide show reaching all the way back to adolescence, featuring people I apparently chose to build my life around, including the individual I still think I am when I look in the mirror. As well as people I, for one reason or another—reasons that often seemed as fated and beyond my control as those I chose for—turned my back on along the way. The lost ones haunted my waking and sleeping dreams, sometimes presenting little videos of roads not taken together, sometimes arguing cases from long ago and confronting me in a scolding manner for *my* abandonment, even when it usually felt the other way around at the time.

The ones I chose for haunt and scold, too, reviewing unmet expectations and broken promises until I am filled with fresh guilt and regret. Immersed anew in the quick and dirty sand of the ego thought system's sticky tale of "seek but do not find" and almost convinced I still might have a chance to close this big, blue book for good and instead invest my yet considerable energy in creating a perfect relationship, body, and career for this person I see in the mirror, before time ticks away and the inevitable landslide of my investment in this special identity brings me down for good.

Trouble is, I know too much. I know I am confusing the deep longing for love I feel resurrected in the many guises of this thing we call our personal history with real longing for the one and only love it masks within us all. Longing to be absolved from the crime of separating from perfect love I believe I pulled off before time began and have been robotically projecting onto others ever since in a futile effort to exonerate myself. Or striving to join blissfully with another believing the solution lies in finding the one magic, missing piece of my puzzle perfectly suited to restoring my wholeness.

I know too much. It didn't work then, and it doesn't work now and yet, I find myself lately lamenting all that never was or could be, temporarily seduced into believing that *A Course in Miracles* is asking me to give up something real, instead of offering the everything that awakening to all-inclusive wholeness guarantees. Conscious, as I watch the ego's persuasive performance, that I am not the ego but the one that chose to take the thought of separation seriously at the very beginning, thereby breathing life into the empty husk of the ego thought system but seemingly paralyzed to choose again for the part of my mind that can smile. Why? Because I still want to wake up as Susan; still want to have my Course and wallow in the bittersweet Indie films of my so-called life, too.

As we are reminded in *A Course in Miracles* Manual for Teachers under The Development of Trust, it takes a long time to give up what never was. Our unconscious fear and guilt over believing we pulled off the impossible creates enormous resistance in the myriad expressions of the one split mind. The only existence we know is our identity as the lead in this dream that passes for our reality. We equate giving up that role with the body's death and the even more terrifying prospect of psychological annihilation. At best, we believe the Course is asking us to forfeit our own best interests to a vast unknown.

> ... If this is interpreted as giving up the desirable it will engender enormous conflict. Few teachers of God can escape this distress entirely ... the period of overlap is apt to be one in which the teacher of God feels called upon to sacrifice his own best interests on behalf of truth. He has not realized as yet how wholly impossible such a demand would be. He can learn this only as he actually does give up the valueless. Through this, he learns that where he anticipated grief, he finds a happy lightheartedness instead;

where he thought something was asked of him, he finds a gift bestowed on him. (Manual for Teachers, 4. What Are the Characteristics of God's Teachers? 1. Trust, A. Development of Trust, paragraph 5)

The solution to the one problem, as always, lies in forgiveness *A Course in Miracles*-style. Continuing to watch my wish to blame others for my internal unrest, or to credit them with the magic ability to fill the void created by believing I forever destroyed the one, eternal love we share. Watching the ego at work and my wish to keep it alive and asking for help from my right mind to see its motives clearly. When my fear and resistance subside, the deep comfort of the all-encompassing, invulnerable completion that embraces all things returns to my awareness, obliterating all thoughts of loss, gain, and regret.

But sometimes, a delay appears between choosing for the inner teacher of love and receiving the happy lightheartedness forgiveness brings. When it does, it helps to try to treat ourselves as gently and patiently as Jesus does in *A Course in Miracles*. To recognize that although invented by the ego, we can learn to use time kindly to *reverse* our investment in our projected guilt as we practice forgiveness day in and day out and experience its mind healing. Jesus refers to us frequently in the Course as children (often as infants) but even children get older and, over time, learn to trust that we have nothing to lose and everything to gain by changing our mind about what, where, and why we are.

Still, when I seem to find myself stuck in the time lag between my choice for the right mind and my willingness to accept its loving translation of what's really going on, I sometimes turn to cooking for temporary solace. This past week I defrosted the remnants of the ham bone upon which we feasted Christmas Eve and decided to make red beans and rice, that Mardi Gras favorite my New Orleans-hatched in-laws depend on to celebrate the approach of Lent.

For me, the ham itself—my brother Michael's favorite food when we were kids—has deep links to my personal past. Its heft on a Christmas Eve buffet table, reliable presence among Irish lace linens Easter afternoon, or shocking pink cameo at funerals a reassuring bead on the infinitely hearty thread that still connects all those who seem to come and go in this dream. Something about resurrecting my ham bone from the deep freeze on a cold winter day and stirring up a pot of my own version of spicy Cajun delight brings smiles to others and keeps me distracted from judging myself harshly as I await the return of my right mind my call for help guarantees.

Red Beans and Rice

One large half ham bone, trimmed of fat but still with ample meat
2 medium onions, chopped
1 large bell pepper, chopped
5 stalks of celery, chopped
6 cloves of garlic, minced
3 large bay leaves
1 t thyme
1 ½ t marjoram or oregano
½-1 t cayenne (or more, to taste; I like heat)
1 t smoked paprika
Sea salt and ground black pepper to taste
3 large cans red beans, drained and rinsed
2 T canola oil, divided

In large, deep pot brown ham in one T of canola oil on all sides. Remove. Sauté onion, bell pepper, and celery, until translucent, in remaining canola oil. Add garlic and all spices, stirring, and cook until garlic is just fragrant. Return ham bone to pot and add beans and enough water to just cover. Bring to a boil, cover, and reduce heat to simmer. Cook the heck out of it—3-4 hours or until beans have given up a lot of starch and mixture has thickened. Adjust seasonings to taste.

Cool several hours or overnight in fridge. Remove bone, shred remaining ham, and return shredded ham to pot. Re-warm and serve with white rice, steamed Swiss chard, and corn bread. Pass the hot sauce while observing your projections and awaiting the true comfort of our one right mind.

Susan Dugan

Crusader Rabbit Retires

By far the most popular of the humiliating nicknames I endured in junior high (Susan of Arc, Susan of Troy, etc.) was "Crusader Rabbit," in honor of the TV cartoon character of the same name whose efforts to save the day from his nemesis Dudley Nightshade in constant reruns enthralled my brother Michael and me when we were little. Like Crusader Rabbit, I seemed to have come in with a keen eye for folly and an insatiable appetite for justice that belied mild-mannered first impressions.

I spent my childhood taking on neighborhood bullies and rescuing injured birds and animals. In fifth grade I organized our class to remotely "adopt" a Korean child. By junior high, I attempted to launch Civil Rights and Vietnam War protests within a community then referred to as Nixon's "Silent Majority" for reasons that defied logic given the frequency and volume of their opinions. Although I theoretically had access to persuasion through my role as student council president and newspaper editor, I had yet to learn that no amount of cajoling, educating, or bargaining could necessarily convince someone to change his mind. And I did not yet understand that morality in this world exists only in the eye of the beholder.

I spent another two decades seeking and never really finding justice in one way or another—through political activism, volunteering, and the written word—an exhausting and ultimately isolating experience. I couldn't figure out why people of my generation—even some of my friends—did not share the same perception of the world's troubles, let alone solutions, I did. More importantly, I didn't comprehend why nothing I worked for ever seemed to make a *lasting* difference, or why, even when participating in groups in which members shared a common mission, conflict and divisiveness reigned. It wasn't until I found *A Course in Miracles* seven years ago that I began to realize I had been looking for justice where it can never be found, but with a little willingness to admit it wasn't working, could begin to seek and find a better way.

And yet, here I am again this morning bemoaning injustice; contemplating, for instance, the many ways in which lives appear to be randomly plucked from this world for no apparent reason. And wondering again how to answer the question of *why* when it comes to the subject of physical and emotional suffering. Culminating in death as it inevitably does for every embodied one of us who first get to witness its seeming brutality in those we love and finally confront for ourselves.

I suppose I found myself once more seduced into believing the ego's world could offer any sane answers based, as it is, on the insane idea of fragmenting invulnerable, perfect wholeness. The "tiny, mad idea" *A Course in Miracles* tells us the one child of God took seriously at the very beginning thereby seemingly fracturing invulnerable oneness and propelling itself into an entire hallucinated universe of forms competing for their seeming survival. Programmed to sooner or later self-destruct to prove they existed at God's expense in the first place but completely unconscious of that original belief. I mean, really?

And yet, in grappling with the sudden death of a healthy, young person close to someone I love this past week, struggling to console the seemingly inconsolable, I discovered anew just how invested I still am in what *A Course in Miracles* refers to as "the hierarchy of illusions." The idea we share that some problems are greater or lesser than others. That the injustice of someone cutting in line at the supermarket or on the highway for example pales before the injustice of a terrorist attack; the death of an elderly person in his sleep after a long, full life somehow makes more sense than the loss of an innocent child or an admired, generous person in the prime of her life.

Within the ego thought system, of course, such logic holds, along with the belief that God works in mysterious ways and has his own reasons for calling us home. But the ego's God, like the

thought system that engendered it is—how to put this nicely—
seriously disturbed. Unconsciously informed by and invested in it
as we are, the only solution—regardless how trivial or conversely
painful, unfair, and catastrophic the problem appears—remains
calling on the sane part of our mind for help. Actively engaging
the memory of eternal, perfect, all-inclusive safety and wholeness
that followed us into the dream and patiently awaits our call to
heal our mind in every circumstance.

> It is not difficult to understand the reasons why you do not
> ask the Holy Spirit to solve all problems for you. He has
> not greater difficulty in resolving some than others. Every
> problem is the same to Him, because each one is solved in
> just the same respect and through the same approach. The
> aspects that need solving do not change, whatever form the
> problem seems to take. ... (*A Course in Miracles*, Chapter
> 26, II. Many Forms; One Correction)

And there's the rub, from the ego's point of view. What happens if we begin to depend on the part of our mind that sees
beyond all illusory problems to the same old story of separation
taken seriously at the beginning, and offers us the same deeply
comforting answer: it never happened; we remain awake in God
dreaming of exile? Our blind and deaf allegiance to and belief in
the ego eventually weakens while its frightening story that always
ends the same heart-breaking way disappears into the ether from
which it sprang.

Note to self: Crusader Rabbit needs to retire. He will never
vanquish Dudley Nightshade. But the child within all of us
screaming out for justice in the perceived face of this world's
bitter ways can find true, enduring, inalterable solace where it
always resides. Patiently waiting in our one mind, providing healing instants of relief and release each time the injustice of the
ego thought system in all its guises rears its ugly head and we
remember to ask for help in seeing truly. Until all our confusion

about where all seeming problems lie is healed and we awaken to find ourselves eternally united within the perfect love we never really left. Fused with an infinitely living and loving God (thank God) oblivious to our silly dream of individualized, conflicted, finite banishment.

> This one mistake in any form has one correction. There is no loss; to think there is, is a mistake. You have no problems, though you think you have. And yet you could not think so if you saw them vanish one by one, without regard to size, complexity, or place and time, or any attribute which you perceive that makes each one seem different from the rest. Think not the limits you impose on what you see can limit God in any way. (paragraph 3)

When we look with the part of our mind that can truly see, all problems reveal themselves for the ravings of a terrified mind tortured by guilt over a crime that never occurred. In gently accepting the certainty of shared innocence and protection the Holy Spirit offers for ourselves, we silently comfort others. Without speaking one word about this Course, words filled with compassion for the injustice of the condition all of us in bodies find ourselves in will simply flow as needed from our forever indivisible heart. Finally—internally resolved to awaken through forgiveness by changing our inner teacher again and again until all lingering guilt over the thought of separation dissolves—we will open our eyes together on the true, whole, invulnerable nature we have never really left.

Susan Dugan

Objects of Projection

I suppose the clouds of squelched guilt had been gathering for some time in the dark recesses of my scant gray matter. Following a weekend in which I appeared to have remained remarkably right-minded despite distressing developments in the objects of my projection, I awoke once more mouthing the words of *A Course in Miracles* workbook lesson 185: "I want the peace of God."

"To say these words is nothing," I read. "But to mean these words is everything."

I searched my mind, reviewing recent developments in the dream including the apparent suffering and seeming unfair behavior of certain costars, reminding myself as the Course often does that it was *my* dream, after all. That although I believe in the leading role I am playing, I am no more real than the rest of the cast I assembled to prove the ego's miserable tale of sin, guilt, and fear. That the part of my mind that took the "tiny, mad idea" of separation from invulnerable, all-inclusive oneness seriously at the seeming beginning has a strong investment in keeping that story of individual entities vying for scarce emotional and physical resources in a finite world alive. But another part of my mind survived the insane thought completely unscathed. It knew I remained at home in God dreaming of exile, just like everybody else. I could turn away from the ego's latest sad Indie release this minute by simply wanting the peace of God with all my heart. Well, sort of.

"I want the peace of God." I repeated the words again in my head, striving to mean them, acutely aware even so that I was really asking to forgive with the help of the memory of wholeness in our mind all the seeming external obstacles I still saw to peace and still forgot I had imagined. The following words bobbed to the surface of the little Magic 8 Ball screen behind my forehead: "Help me make learning to practice true forgiveness in every circumstance my only goal." I wrote them down on a yellow sticky note and posted it on the wall behind my desk along with a few *A Course in Miracles* quotes and a photo of a yoga retreat in the mountains I occasionally flee to that helps me remember to, you know, *breathe*. (Because we all know what happens when we forget to do that.)

Within minutes, I found myself dreaming again, frustrated by the fact that my doctor—apparently out of town—would not return my phone calls about a prescription I really needed that had apparently expired. His secretary was less than helpful on the phone, completely unwilling to intervene on my behalf despite the fact that I had known her and her boss for years. After calling the pharmacy again and leaving a message on my doctor's cell phone, I turned back to my morning project and struggled with it for a couple of hours, but the computer database I attempted to interact with had turned—for reasons beyond my comprehension—completely antisocial.

I gazed at my sticky note. I asked for help in seeing these latest hiccups as the same old desire to hold external circumstances responsible for the internal condition of fear and guilt in my mind. Arising from the unconscious belief that I had destroyed perfect, unified love with my wish to experiment with individuality and could never be accepted back into the infinite loving fold. I turned back to the computer, but each time I entered the information required and attempted to submit, it mysteriously vanished. I gazed at the sticky note and decided to walk the dog to clear my head.

Although the sun shone and the temperature had at least inched out of the sub-zero range, the streets remained deeply rutted with ice. (For reasons that continue to defy the understanding of a transplant from the Northeast, Denver does not believe in plowing anything but main thoroughfares.) Bundled in her little parka, Kayleigh, the five-pound wonder dog, and I picked our way along the sidewalks, some relatively clear, those of homeowners who failed to shovel extremely treacherous.

Half way down a westward-bound street I noticed a woman walking a German shepherd approaching a perpendicular street corner from the north. As always acutely aware of my own dog's size, I crossed diagonally to the opposite street and headed south to completely avoid them. About half way down that street I heard a woman's scream and turned to see the German shepherd bounding in our direction. I scooped Kayleigh up and held her to my chest but the dog was already upright and on us.

Fight or flight! the ego chanted, but the ice had halved my options. I kept turning around, trying to keep my back to the dog even as it continued to lunge for Kayleigh, or me, or both. And I screamed at the woman, also slow to approach because of the ice. "Control your dog!" I struggled to keep my balance as the canine's leash wrapped around my ankles.

She finally got hold of the leash and was able to pull the dog off me. I think she said she was sorry; I honestly don't remember. I wish I could say I wanted the peace of God. I wish I could say I defended myself in form but held her harmless in my mind. But I did not. And who in a body could blame me, I reasoned? Buzzed on adrenaline, informed by the ego, intoxicated by the notion of victimization, I continued. "Your dog could have killed my dog!" I shouted, in parting, unable to keep my death-grip on the obvious to myself.

Kayleigh continued to tremble in my arms as I did our Zombie-like ice walk away. At one point I peered around and spied the woman simply standing in the same spot beside her vicious dog as if frozen, reigniting my anger. I can't remember if the words "Go away!" came out of my mouth or merely boomed in my head. It doesn't really matter. A couple blocks later my heartbeat returned to normal and I set Kayleigh down, overwhelmed with regret. What kind of an *A Course in Miracles* student let alone teacher was I? I had awakened wanting the peace of God, after all, and just look what a mess I'd made of it all. We made it home without further incident, still judging myself but at least asking for help to review with my inner Jesus what had just appeared to happen in my forgiveness classroom.

> No one can mean these words and not be healed He cannot play with dreams, nor think he is himself a dream. He cannot make a hell and think it real. He wants the peace of God and it is given him. For that is all he wants and that is all he will receive. Many have said these words. But few indeed have meant them. You have but to look upon the world you see around you to be sure how very few they are. (from paragraph 2)

The trouble is however much I mean these words, my mind is still split. A part of me wants the peace of God and a part of me wants to prove my relative innocence compared with a stranger whose failure to control her dog may (or may not) have actually jeopardized me and my dog. The rapidity with which I choose the ego's interpretation of illusions when the script involves my body or a loved one's is quite literally mind-boggling. I am back in the dream in a nanosecond, swinging at windmills Don Quixote-like.

But the decision maker in my split mind does not require a dramatic ambush by a potentially threatening predator to find myself back in the dream and siding with the ego again. Although it wants the peace of God, it also wants my doctor to call me back and give me the damn prescription already. It wants the peace of God but it wants the hosts of this database to fix the freaking problem even though there is really only one problem. And it doesn't stop there.

I want the peace of God, but I also want a Venti, three-quarter decaf, light-room Americano or a Girl Scout cookie (Tagalongs being my current favorite) or a See's dark chocolate Bordeaux candy from the left-over Valentine's stash. I want the peace of God and money back on my tax returns and a chilled glass of

New Zealand Sauvignon Blanc at the end of a long day. I want the peace of God and the return of warm weather and compliant family members and the pain-free joints and muscles of a 20-something.

Instead I have only this recognition of a denied part of me that just rejoiced in retaliating against a person who, I find it hard to believe, once my cortisol levels have stabilized, actually decided to let her dog have at me. If I had really wanted the peace of God, I could have defended myself without anger or the need to exact revenge. But my mind is split, and until it heals completely I will constantly (albeit unconsciously) seek to find an object of projection for the concealed guilt I would rather die than own.

Fortunately, Jesus knows we have a split mind. He does not expect us to want the peace of God; he knows that's impossible. Instead he wants us to look with him at just how tempting we find it to throw the peace of God away. To look with him at just how irresistible the objects of our projection can seem. How much we want to blame others for our unconscious inner guilt and fear. How invested we are in the very idea of others that at least preserves the idea of me.

And so I sit at my desk once more gazing at my sticky note and recommitting to my real goal: To learn and practice true forgiveness in every circumstance. I do that by seeing how much I don't want to do that. Humbled by the intensity of my own resistance I again turn to Jesus/my right mind for help in forgiving myself. Help in looking at the unreal, seeing its purpose, and accepting its correction, the complete certainty that I am not at odds with the objects of my projection the ego would like me to use to block my awareness of the one love we remain.

… What do you ask for in your heart? Forget the words you use in making your requests. Consider but what you believe will comfort you, and bring you happiness. But be you not dismayed by lingering illusions, for their form is not what matters now. Let not some dreams be more acceptable, reserving shame and secrecy for others. They are one. And being one, one question should be asked of all of them, 'Is this what I would have, in place of Heaven and the peace of God?' (paragraph 8)

If I make learning and practicing true forgiveness in every circumstance my goal, I am learning I feel better when I look with my inner teacher on all I believe is out to get me, change my mind about its origin and purpose, and remember what I truly want. Each time I do, the fissure in my mind mends a little more, until I am healed of the silly idea of a split mind for good.

Hooray for Hollywood Redux

In the middle of a winning performance with one of my costars the other day the ego apparently hacked into the script.

"You always ..."

"I can't believe you ..."

"How could you ..."

Her accusations multiplied exponentially like runaway cancer cells. My improvised responses to this sudden shift in dialogue precipitated by what I considered a legitimate, serenely delivered request were met with unexpected rage. Shrieks and tears followed. I backed out of the room before any heads started spinning around, the dog cowering at my feet. The door—having taken sides—slammed in our faces.

This was the third time in a week that a special relationship (not always the same one) had appeared to go ballistic on me without any seeming provocation, shattering a period of seemingly tranquil right-mindedness during which I had naively begun to believe that my ongoing choice for a better way of living in this world was reaping actual benefits in form. Even though the Course makes no such claims because, after all, there is no form.

"There is no peace except the peace of God," I read the next morning, following this latest opportunity to see things differently.

> Seek you no further. You will not find peace except the peace of God. Accept this fact, and save yourself the agony of yet more bitter disappointments, bleak despair, and sense of icy hopelessness and doubt. Seek you no further. There is nothing else for you to find except the peace of God, unless you seek for misery and pain. (paragraph 1)

(And people say this Course's message is unclear.)

I read *A Course in Miracles* workbook lesson 200 all the way through for what felt like the billionth time. Despite my intimacy with what this lesson was saying—that *nothing* in this world will ever deliver lasting peace and happiness and will, in fact, sooner or later, break my proverbial heart—I was not "glad and thankful" but sad and bitter it was so. I suppose a part of me still clung to the romantic notion that practicing forgiveness *A Course in Miracles*-style would eventually deliver the goods. My career would finally find its destined meteoric trajectory. Financial worries would dissolve. All conflict in my closest relationships would resolve, and I would at last enjoy the calm, grounded, loving, and supported life I had been seeking and never finding for as long as I could remember.

But in the past two weeks the "ego's raucous shrieks" the Course refers to had been escalating to say the least in my apparent forgiveness classroom. My special relationships had been acting out again all over the place like nobody's business, all red-faced and righteously booming my thoughts about them back at me almost faster than I could frame them.

I did my best to remember it was *my* projected guilt I was really looking at, *my* unconscious choice for the ego's dire story of competing interests. I continued to ask my right mind for help in viewing this latest installment in the long-running series of my life as merely another opportunity to choose the inner teacher of peace over the inner teacher of conflict with whom I had obviously aligned. But the explosive drama just kept coming until I couldn't take it anymore. I finally called on Jesus much the way Elizabeth Montgomery used to call on Dr. Bombay in the sitcom *Bewitched* (I still enjoy in reruns) whenever she had problems with her secret powers. "Emergency, emergency, come right away," I cried out to Jesus, doing my best Samantha impression.

And so it was I found myself draped in a girlie black frock, once more magically borne aloft on my broom and coming to rest atop the Hollywood sign, my favorite fantasized venue for observing with an imaginary, embodied Jesus the comings and goings of the actors I commissioned to make this movie of Susan's perilous individuality real in the battleground below.

Jesus seemed to be getting used to this and handed me the popcorn.

I lobbed a kernel down at one of them passing below. From a distance he looked a lot like Brad Pitt. I have never liked that man.

"You know they can't feel that, right?" Jesus said.

"You can't know that for sure," I replied.

"We've talked about this."

"You need to lighten up, mister."

He threw back his head and laughed.

I picked up another kernel, aimed, and fired. I think it was one of those sisters this time, Kourtney, Kim—who really cared? In my peripheral vision I swear I saw Jesus reach for a kernel, too. A girl can dream.

"Please don't make me go back down there," I begged. Because as much fun as I was having, the real targets were not these celebrities I loved to hate but these costars that just wouldn't quit blaming me for what anyone with half a mind could clearly see was happening only inside their twisted little heads.

Jesus smiled. He eavesdrops sometimes; I just know it. I hate it when he does that.

"Did you see that?" I said. "She just slammed the door on me again."

"Beautiful girl, that daughter of yours," he said. "Such an open heart; you must be so proud."

Yeah, right. "I know what you're really thinking," I said.

His brows shot up.

"You're thinking that I called you." I had a point, you had to admit. I usually do. "You're thinking that I keep forgetting this is a path in healing our mind about our relationships and yet I keep trying to avoid them. You're thinking I need to look at them with you so I can see them for the hallucinated barriers against eternally inclusive love they really are, but, you know what? I've been practicing forgiveness like crazy and nothing ever changes down there. I mean, honest to God, did you hear what he just said? Just look at him—right there."

Jesus squinted in the general direction of the perpetrator I was frantically stabbing the air with my finger toward, but shook his head.

"Christ," I said.

"Hey." He smiled.

"Why don't you just come out and say it already," I said.

"What?"

"I'm trying to get you to look with me instead of looking with you. When I'm finally ready to do that, I will truly see. And I'll feel better, too; you know I will. Because right now, in case you haven't noticed, I'm not exactly feeling the peace of God."

His eyes widened.

I studied the scene below. "They're still there; I can see them. And I'm telling you, they *so* do not have my best interests at heart. So, I have a better plan. Let's get rid of this popcorn and find some real ammo. I mean, if it's all an illusion anyway, why not just nuke them?"

"We've talked about this."

I sighed. "Yeah. Don't you have any special glasses you could give me?"

"Sorry."

I tossed another couple kernels of popcorn down into the fray. "I'm never going to have the perfect family, am I?" I said, after a while.

He shook his head. "But look at it this way. You did get the family of your dreams."

"Funny."

"Thanks."

I watched the battleground a while longer. "You know it's not even well written," I said. "The screenplay, I mean."

He nodded.

"No, wait, I think it's getting foggy or something down there because they're all starting to look alike."

"Imagine that."

"Oh, my God, now I can't see anything at all. Nada thing."

He lifted the palm of his hand in the air.

I high-fived him back.

"You planning on sharing that popcorn, or what?" he said.

The Runaway Bunny

"Read it again, Mama," my then two-year-old daughter would chant night after night at bedtime. And regardless of how tired I was, I would start over, vaguely conscious even then that my own little bunny would all too soon be running away as all little bunnies eventually do.

"'Once there was a little bunny who wanted to run away,'" I read.

"So he said to his mother, 'I am running away,'" my daughter would chime in. She loved that part.

"'If you run away,' said his mother," I continued, "'I will run after you. For you are my little bunny.'"

Like most young children, Kara loved this heartfelt tale by Margaret Wise Brown concerning a little bunny's fantasies about striking off on its own, assuming various identities and hell-bent on trading the security of a safe, toasty warren and a parent's adoration for more alluring horizons. Becoming for example a fish in a trout stream that tries to swim away only to have its mother come after him and fish him out with a pole. My daughter would clap her small hands as the little bunny became a rock on a mountain, a crocus in a garden, a circus performer, and a sailboat in its frenzy for freedom, and laugh as the patiently indulgent mother followed in hot pursuit, morphing into a mountain climber, a gardener, a trapeze artist, and a steady wind to blow him back into her loving fold.

"Read it again, Mama," Kara would command each time I attempted to close the book. Because, in truth, she liked the descriptions of the bunny's adventures and the Mama's chase much more than the ending where the bunny gives up and comes home. She has always been like this. In daycare, instead of clinging and pitching fits like normal children, she would wiggle down off my hip and toddle bravely off toward the playroom, calling out names and dispensing hugs like a politician working a fundraiser.

Susan Dugan

I would stand watching as the other parents labored to pry their writhing, wailing spawn from their calves, trying to convince myself this was a good thing. I had raised a confident child. Still, it was all I could do to resist casting a line and reeling her back in.

Fast forward 16 years and my daughter is mentally and emotionally preparing to hop out of the family warren in pursuit of the proverbial dangling carrot without so much as a backward glance, as all brave bunnies eventually will. Chomping at the bit to forge a new, improved, and more exciting life for herself. I am acutely aware—as we begin her final semester in high school and final varsity soccer season; as we start filling out graduation announcements and planning a celebration for family and friends—that my days as a live-in parent are numbered. As she studies for her final IB exams and weighs final college offers, I am also conscious that the story of *The Runaway Bunny* is everyone's tale, a story of taking the "tiny, mad idea" that we could flee our Father's all-encompassing, eternal love and play hide and seek with him in a hallucinated world of which he—remaining thankfully, unalterably sane—knows nothing.

I'm OK with this, I tell myself, as I set about whipping up another nouveau, comfort-food classic—macaroni and cheese and tuna noodle casserole and my famous spicy turkey meatloaf—she is, ironically, rarely around long enough anymore to eat. I know I am really trying to assuage my own persistent sense of loss. A nagging regret that defies my growing faith in what *A Course in Miracles* is saying. Its take on the nature of our closest relationships and the enduring specialness of this specific relationship in particular I still think I want more than the perfect, all-inclusive love all the seeming fragments of the one child of God continue to pretend to push away.

Then, too, I catch myself watching my daughter sometimes with a deep sense of longing, wishing I could impart what I am learning in *A Course in Miracles* about our universal authority problem, the ego's journey into an invented world wherein it continually seeks but never finds itself. A reenactment of the original journey away from the mind we embarked on when we forgot to laugh at the thought of separating from our creator, choosing instead to follow the ego away from the one mind and then forget we ever had a mind. Assuming bodies—intent on competing both for survival and divine attention and approval— and forging deeper and deeper into a dream of self-imposed exile from perfect, eternal, all-inclusive love. Cutting deals with others to get our needs met that never work for long enough while continuing to try to entice the ego's God to follow us into this world and validate our illusions.

But I know we cannot fix or change or spare any of the inhabitants of this world what the Course calls their "curriculum," not even the ones we literally bring into it. This comes as a particular affront to parents and yet, we can only choose love over fear whenever an opportunity to do so presents itself. We can only choose for the inner teacher of love, thereby teaching love, the inner teacher of invulnerable strength, thereby teaching invulnerable strength.

On the level of form, I find myself grieving what still sometimes feels like my daughter's impending defection, even as I recognize the time has come for her to give this world's illusions her best shot. We have outgrown my long fantasized ability to protect and control her and I realize that the faster she experiences all the world has to offer, the more quickly she will learn to resign as her own teacher, as we all eventually must. Still, a part of me wishes I could somehow intervene, somehow spare her the time and disillusionment that eventually propels us to finally plead for a better way.

Sometimes I still wish I could just convince my daughter to accept the ending to *The Runaway Bunny*, wherein the little bunny realizes it might just as well stay put and reap the benefits of maternal nurturing and the mother rewards him with a big, fat carrot. But I know too much about how this dream works now.

Besides, that would require me to accept it myself and I am not quite there yet, still invested in this world at least when it comes to the fate of my little bunny as I swallow another spoon of baked mashed potatoes in her behalf and wait with my little dog for my daughter to come home.

Baked Mashed Potatoes

(Adapted from a similar recipe, instead calling for sage and cheddar that appeared in the November 2003 issue of *Bon Appétit* magazine, these magic mashers are guaranteed to chase away the blues of the ego thought system.)

5 large russet potatoes peeled, cut into chunks, and submerged in a pot of salted water
1/2 cup unsalted butter
1-1 ½ cups fat-free half and half
1 ½ cups grated Fontina cheese
1 T finely minced Italian parsley
1/8 t cayenne, or to taste
Fresh ground pepper to taste

Boil potatoes until very tender. Drain. Mash together with butter and half and half. Add remaining ingredients (reserving ½ cup of cheese). Fold mixture into a buttered or cooking-sprayed casserole dish. Top with additional cheese and sprinkle with paprika (optional) for color. Bake at 375 degrees about 45 minutes or until lightly browned on top. For best results, enjoy while waiting for your children to come home.

Looking with Jesus: Now in 3-D

I knelt on the floor and shot Kayleigh's well-worn cloth piggy down the long hall. "Strike one," I said.

Instead of fetching, my little dog merely blinked. Then she turned her back on me and pretended to scratch her belly.

"We're burning daylight here," I told her, glancing at my watch. I wagered I had exactly 10 minutes to play with the dog like the good pet Mama I strive to be before heading back to my computer.

"Speak for yourself, Mama," I answered for Kayleigh, as I often do, perfectly delivering the little falsetto voice with which she converses with me in my imagination.

I rose, rummaged in her toy box for a more alluring trinket, knelt once more, and hurled the baby blue chick that emitted an irritating peeping noise down the hall. Kayleigh watched it thwack against the hard-wood floor with a shrill hiccup. Then she lay back down with a yawn, stretched out on her side like the world's tiniest horse in a puddle of sunlight, and closed her confounding little eyes.

Jesus, I thought, exasperated; even dogs have authority problems. I had been contemplating that very topic discussed in *A Course in Miracles* Chapter 3, VI. Judgment and the Authority Problem, and apparently running rampant in the objects of my projection for more than a week.

> The issue of authority is really a question of authorship. When you have an authority problem, it is always because you believe you are the author of yourself and project your delusion onto others. You then perceive the situation as one in which others are literally fighting you for your authorship. ... (from paragraph 8)

Just like they think God is. I had practically memorized those words and yet—although frequently and earnestly asking for help from my right mind to see my dog, my daughter, and my husband's refusal to in any way, shape, or form comply with the simplest and most sincere of my requests to deliver on their meager family responsibilities differently—I remained annoyed by their lack of cooperation. Ironically, in another facet of my curriculum, multiple organizations with which I am affiliated vied for my attention, upping the ante in their requests for more of my "voluntary" participation even though I thought I had firmly stated my inability to expand my involvement given my currently overflowing plate.

I squeezed my eyes shut in frustration, mentally rehearsing yet another conversation with one of these apparent adversaries seemingly hell-bent on thwarting me. It was time to head back to the proverbial classroom and present my findings to Jesus. I wanted to get him to look at the authority problem run amuck in all these nut cases "out there" and help me forgive them. I had even designed a special pair of glasses to enable him to discern the bittersweet poignancy of the human condition which—with all due respect—totally seems to elude that man. They were pink, oversized, and studded with little plastic smiley faces.

"What's up with these?" Jesus asked.

"Magic," I said.

He looked puzzled.

"You know, to help you see my 3-D world. You don't usually see it; I know you don't. I can tell by that goofy look you get on your face. Admit it, you're extremely farsighted."

"You think?" He put on the glasses and squeezed into the desk beside mine.

I flipped off the lights, raised the remote, and hit play on the DVD player. "Exhibit A," I said, as the machine whirred to life, featuring a scene of me walking Kayleigh yesterday around our neighborhood. "There," I said, backing up. "Did you see that?"

Jesus tilted his head.

On the screen, I stood at a corner with Kayleigh, ordering her to stay as she yanked on the leash and spun in frantic circles.

"Sit," I commanded, but she stood her ground, peering up at a squirrel scaling a flowering pear tree, its buds raised in tiny fists. "No respect whatsoever," I said, hitting play once more as the film advanced to the next scene.

I stabbed the screen with my little pointer. "Just look at that right there—can you even see the floor in that room?"

Jesus adjusted his glasses.

"Thumbing her nose at me is what she's really doing. And here, allow me to zoom in on that volley of emails right there." I enlarged them and adjusted the focus. "Demand, demand, demand, demand, demand—silent recrimination—demand," I summarized. "It's like they want to consume me, you know? Suck every little drop of lifeblood and sweat right out of me."

"So let me get this straight," Jesus said. "Your dog, your daughter, and your husband blow off your requests while the rest of them won't stop badgering you?"

"You are a quick study."

"Do you think you might be being a tad dramatic?"

I gave him the look.

He covered his mouth and pretended to cough.

"I know what you're thinking," I said. "You actually want me to believe it's *all* just a symptom of their authority problem."

"*Their* authority problem?" he said.

"Exactly. The way she just has to have it all her way all the time. OK, so that's what egos do—especially, young ones. Annoying as it is, I suppose I get that. But what's his excuse? I mean, he still perceives every little request no matter how sweetly delivered as a threat to his precious autonomy. And that group right there?" I tapped each one of them upside the head with my pointer.

"Demand, demand, demand," Jesus said.

"Those glasses really are helping."

"So this whole authority problem they all have, refresh my memory on that?"

I hit the pause button. "Everyone out there has it," I said. "They think they invented themselves."

"Really?"

How many times did I have to go over this with him? I mean, he might as well have written the book. It was a trick, of course; I knew that by now; just another thinly veiled pop quiz. I was so going to ace this class. "OK," I said, "at some point—and please do not even think about asking me why—the one Son of God wondered what it would be like to strike off on his own and forgot to laugh at the tiny, mad idea of it. Suddenly, he perceived himself cast out of Heaven and no longer included in the one loving fold. Overwhelmed with guilt and fearful of God's retribution the one mind seemed to split into the ego—the part of the mind that believed in and cherished the idea of separate identities—and the Holy Spirit—the part of the mind that remembered it never happened."

"Seriously?"

"'Funny.' Anyway, curious to experience specialness while avoiding responsibility for it, the now little 's' son of God followed the ego into an entire projected universe of form to hide out in. The one mind seemed to splinter into a gazillion fragmented forms, assumed bodies, and then started competing for its very survival. Oh, and all the seeming separated ones fell asleep so they would never remember they even had a mind outside the body to which they could return and choose again for truth."

"Yikes," Jesus said.

I nodded. "See, now they believe they exist at God's expense and want to continue doing so. They believe they have to constantly defend themselves to prove their autonomy even though they secretly know on some level that it's all based on a lie. Eternally alive God could not cease to exist, which means that the selves they think they are really don't since they are still a part of God. See, they think their self-worth comes from being better than others, independent from others, proving they can manipulate others into doing what they want, and resisting allowing others to manipulate them all the while forgetting their self-worth still comes from God."

"*They* really do sound like nut cases."

"Right?"

He took off his glasses, carefully blew on each lens, and cleaned them off with a sleeve of whatever you call that draped getup he wears. He did not put them back on. "I know what you're thinking," he said, after a while.

I thought a moment. "And tell me again what their behavior has to do with me?"

"Bingo." He smiled.

I glanced back up at the screen but the images were gone. The DVD player, too, had miraculously vanished. The lights were back on. "I know what *you're* thinking," I said.

"Class dismissed?" Jesus said. "I mean, for now, anyway."

"Hey." I smiled back. You just had to love that guy. "Those glasses didn't really take, did they?"

"Not so much." He put them back on. "They are rather fetching, though."

"Yeah," I said. "They really do make your eyes pop."

Father, Christ's vision is the way to You. What He beholds invites Your memory to be restored to me. And this I choose, to be what I would look upon today. (*A Course in Miracles*, workbook lesson 271, paragraph 2)

I Gotta Be Me! (Well; Maybe Not So Much)

I started writing at a very young age—long before kindergarten—asking adults around me to pen specific words and practicing, practicing, practicing until my wobbly hieroglyphics slowly morphed into reasonable facsimiles of the word in question. Not surprisingly, the first word I asked to learn was my own name. I practiced writing out SUSAN—not SUE or SUZY as some preferred to diminish it—until I had mastered through repetition the intricacies of my unique moniker. Inflated with that sublime accomplishment, I scribbled it everywhere I could think of, a pre-school tagger before the invention of that word.

On a trip to visit my aunt at her summer camp on a lake whose name I can no longer recall, I even etched it—using the side of a dime from my piggy bank—into a shingle on her garage and was busted within minutes by my mother, soon joined by a posse of adult relatives. Ambushed as I spun out of control on a tire swing hitched to the branch of an enormous black walnut tree. Mother hauled me unceremoniously back to the scene of the crime, her similarly outraged tribe in toe, and asked me what I thought I was doing. Terrified, I denied it.

"Who else would write it?" my mother's tight lips somehow managed to inquire. Of course, she had a point. (I couldn't exactly attempt to pin it on my little brother.) Nonetheless I stuck with my story, and was banished to a bedroom for the rest of the day while my brother and cousins—high on my exile—loudly frolicked in the meadow outside the open window. I know I cried a lot for a long time at the unfairness of it all. Eventually, though, I opened my notebook and started writing my evil name all over again, robotically leaving my mark on page after page, somehow soothed by the survival of those five little letters that defined me.

In junior high, my focus shifted to hitching the last name of an unsuspecting boy we'll call Jonathan Brown to my first name, filling notebooks with the signature of Susan Brown, beloved wife.

Each stroke of my pen weaving a web of our idyllic life together in a Cape Cod house overlooking a glossy river wherein a voice was never raised, a Disney score played 24/7, and animated woodland creatures joyfully assisted with household chores.

Fast forward more decades than I care to count and here I am still grappling with that fatal attraction to the power of me. Only it's not bringing me much in the way of pleasure these days. Practicing *A Course in Miracles* has pretty much obliterated my ability to mindlessly self-indulge, the key word here being *mindlessly*. I still self-indulge all the time I am sorry to admit, but my awareness of what I'm doing has taken all the fun out of it. After all, I am studying a big, blue book which tells us repeatedly and in many unique and creative ways that we are not the selves we think we are, these puny little children vying for differentiation and recognition. You'd think I would simply give it up as a result, but the habit is strong, and apparently takes time to completely dismantle. And so I watch as I continue to vacillate between craving attention and abhorring the spotlight certain to illuminate what the Course calls the "secret sins and hidden hates" I have cherished for so long, not nearly as secret and hidden since I've been practicing forgiveness *A Course in Miracles*-style, but still.

The thing is, as Course students it may be relatively easy to wrap our heads around *A Course in Miracles'* creation myth wherein the one child of God forgot to laugh at the "tiny, mad idea" that it could separate from its eternally loving, united source. We can certainly understand how—guilty and terrified by the imaginary crime—it followed the ego's plan for salvation, projecting that shameful thought into an entire universe of unique forms, repressing the memory of that decision, and assuming bodies with which to compete for its survival.

The problem is I don't remember any of this. I have completely identified with the body, brain, and personality of Susan to the point that it is impossible for me to experience myself otherwise, *except* in the holy instant in which I again judge myself victimized or victimizing, better or worse, greater or lesser than others, feel the pain of that same old hallucination, and ask to see things differently. The "I" I still think I am can't pull this off alone. While the decision maker—the part of the split mind that appeared to choose for the ego at the very beginning—can indeed learn to watch the ego, unless it chooses to watch accompanied by the quiet, loving, knowing, smiling right mind/Holy (Whole) Spirit/Jesus, it will not experience the release and relief forgiveness brings.

When the Course tells us in Chapter 18 that "I Need Do Nothing" it means that the "I" I think I am does not forgive. My only job is to recognize in my persecuting and persecuted feelings that I have again mistaken what I really am. That's my cue to join with the part of my mind that knows what I am. The part of our one mind that did not take the tiny, mad idea of separation and specialness seriously from the very beginning merely waits for us to join with it. It will not swoop down and save us from ourselves because it knows with every fiber of its being that nothing real could ever have been threatened because nothing unreal exists, as the Course's preface so poetically reminds us. It knows the peace of God remains intact. And so we must choose for it, over, and over, and over again, gradually experiencing ourselves as the empowered decision maker, until the catnip of unconscious guilt that lures us back to the ego has completely dried up and we find that there never was a split mind to begin with, only uninterrupted, endlessly creative, completed and completely supported, relentless love.

I am learning as I practice *A Course in Miracles* what's really in a name, as Shakespeare so aptly put it. The thought of specialness I once coveted in the name of Susan is losing its luster. The thought of specialness I once coveted in the names of my closest relationships has followed suit. This does not mean I no longer value my family and friends, but that I see their real, infinite, endlessly magnificent value far beyond my petty needs and expectations of them, at least when I so choose. And in that ongoing choice from moment to moment to truly see, I am gradually healed of my investment in a name.

Forgiveness: No Prior Understanding Required

I had been mentally complaining to Jesus (that *symbol* of the one awakened mind we share) about a number of brewing situations in my seemingly cavernous, interactive forgiveness classroom, asking him to help me count like beads on a Montessori chain the many new ways in which I perceived myself vulnerable. I recently had a book published about practicing *A Course in Miracles* forgiveness in my personal life which—even though barely a hiccup on the radar—left the introvert in me feeling wildly exposed and scrambling for cover, a lizard in the desert suddenly sans camo.

In another classroom corner a life-size action figure I've been intimately interacting with and forgiving for years appeared to be breathing fiery accusations again. Some directly aimed at me and some intended for an all-too frequently-absent other he secretly believed had slighted him. At a computer lab I sat opening emails that appeared to contain astonishing, thoroughly unprovoked demands and affronts defended by preachy arguments. At yet another hands-on learning module, I found myself playing the role of a parent listening to an administrative panel from the college to which my daughter had recently committed answer parents' probing and increasingly troubled questions about the school's alcohol and drug culture and incumbent disciplinary protocols.

Once again marveling at the way in which my dream of exile from perfect love can sometimes resemble a Bergman film, complete with grim reaper lurking in the shadows, and sometimes present more akin to *Pee-wee's Playhouse*, I turned to *A Course in Miracles* for help. Hoping to kill two birds with one stone—multi-tasking student that I am—by finding a passage that would not only instantly return me to right-mindedness but also offer perfect fodder for the weekly Thursday night forgiveness class I teach and needed to prepare for. I longed to find the consummate summation of the many ways in which our original albeit unconscious choice for separation and ongoing desire to preserve our "specialness" feeds on perceiving our problems outside the one mind-on-ego that put them there. But someone appeared to have snuck in the back door and rewritten every word of that big, blue book in a foreign language. No matter what section of the Course I turned to, I had no idea what the hell Jesus was talking about.

This fruitless pursuit in attempting to understand with the brain of an individual specifically designed to prevent true understanding went on for the better part of a day—interrupted only by mandatory appearances at various classroom stations wherein situations continued to spiral out of control—leaving the imaginary self I still think I am, needless to say, increasingly anxious. What if I could no longer comprehend let alone attempt to apply *A Course in Miracles*? What if the ego's legendary "hungry dogs of fear" had finally busted through the steel fence of their kennel and picked up my particular scent?

I posed these and other questions to Jesus, of course, but he had apparently taken a sabbatical because the incoming silence was deafening. The more I flipped through the big, blue book's pages, the more obscure it's hieroglyphics. I slept fitfully that night, only to dream of diabolical action figures plotting against me, thoughtlessly fired emails, and my only little girl unleashed in a pit of drug-pushing piranhas a decade before I would ever be ready to let her go. In and out of sleep, I begged my right mind to help me see things differently.

In the morning I arose smiling, seemingly recovered from my ego attack. The action figure had morphed back into work attire and we engaged in a reasonable conversation. The objectionable emails from the previous day appeared to have been replaced overnight with ordinary requests and explanations. In another corner of my classroom I played a parent listening with excitement to the many service and travel-abroad opportunities my daughter could partake of next year, sighing with gratitude that she had received a scholarship that would make it all possible.

Back at my desk with a Venti, three-quarter-decaf, light-room Americano perfectly brewed to my liking by baristas at the nearby Starbucks; I opened *A Course in Miracles* to Chapter 11, VIII. The Problem and the Answer, wherein Jesus gently and humorously leads us to entertain the idea that we understand nothing about what's really going on in our own lives, let alone the greater world. But, like small children suffering from night terrors, can learn to interpret the threatening images bouncing on our bedroom walls differently, with help from an inner teacher capable of translating their meaning for us from monster to curtain shadow.

"You do not know the meaning of anything you perceive," I read in paragraph 3. "Not one thought you hold is wholly true. The recognition of this is your firm beginning. ..."

I could not help but smile, noticing that Jesus did not claim recognizing we do not know was akin to awakening, as I often hear it so interpreted by other dream figures. Instead he referred to it as a "firm beginning." The open, beginner's mind to which we must return again and again, recognizing we have chosen the inner teacher of division and unhappiness but can choose again for the teacher of union and peace.

The key word here is: *choose.* Simply returning to the decision making mind that chose to imagine the experience of separation in the first place is not enough. We must then admit we do not perceive our own best interests. We do not know what this Course is really saying because it can't be understood with an imaginary body's brain. We must actively ask for help from the part of our mind outside this dream of time and space that does know. And then do nothing but wait for the light of our one right mind to shine away our dark hallucinations, the barriers to love's presence we have erected in our guilt and selfishness to push the awareness of eternally present, all-inclusive love away.

You are not misguided; you have accepted no guide at all. Instruction in perception is your great need, for you understand nothing. ... Perceptions are learned, and you are not without a Teacher. Yet your willingness to learn of Him depends on your willingness to question everything you learned of yourself, for you who learned amiss should not be your own teacher. (from paragraph 3)

I realized with growing relief that I had once more convinced myself I knew what and where the problem was. Insisting on seeing it outside myself where it can never be solved. Instead of as the outward picture of the inner, repressed condition of guilt in the mind over believing I had thrown God's love away by indulging my impulse to experience myself as a separate individual competing for survival with other individuals under the influence of the same painful delusion. Completely forgetting that the purpose of transforming my life into a forgiveness classroom was to allow another teacher to show me what's really going on in all my interactions and how to heal my mind of the belief that there is anything but the enduring experience of all-inclusive wholeness.

My sudden-onset Course amnesia had ironically helped me realize once more that I know nothing unless I turn away from the ego's 24/7 broadcast of attack and defense and instead tune in to the silent voice of universal inclusion and common interests. Wherein I admit anew I know nothing and simply listen until I can hear and answer only my own call for love emanating from every nook and cranny of my forgiveness classroom.

... To love yourself is to heal yourself, and you cannot perceive part of you as sick and achieve your goal. Brother, we heal together as we live together and love together. (from paragraph 11)

Amen to that!

Susan Dugan

Wilted Lilies, Growing Up Too Soon, and a Recipe for Forgiveness

It all started benignly enough the Thursday night before Easter with a lovely discussion and meditation in my weekly *A Course in Miracles* class. We considered II. The Gift of Lilies, Chapter 20, wherein we learn that the true meaning of this most sacred of Christian holiday turns out to be not unlike the true meaning of Christmas, Groundhog Day, April Fools' Day, Halloween, or any other day of the year—learning to take back responsibility for our own peace of mind. You know, rather than attributing it to everyone and everything seemingly "out there" on which we project our guilt over secretly believing we succeeded in separating from the forever-loving fold of our one eternal wholeness. Yes, I'm talking once more about forgiveness *A Course in Miracles*-style. Learning to identify our choice for the ego's bizarre story of original separation realized in the form of our condemning judgments and needy expectations of others. And then choose again for a different inner teacher capable of seeing beyond our dualistic projections to the uninterrupted unity we continue to share.

> Would you not have your holy brother lead you there? His innocence will light your way, offering you its guiding light and sure protection, and shining from the holy altar within him where you laid the lilies of forgiveness. Let him be to you the savior from illusions, and look on him with the new vision that looks upon the lilies and brings you joy. (from paragraph 9)

Nonetheless, although I thought I had been laying lilies of forgiveness on the holy altar of the mind all week they appeared to have succumbed on the vine to unknown blight. My dream of exile from perfect wholeness once more seemed all too convincing, my costars throwing little prima donna hissy fits until I once more completely forgot I was not the forsaken heroine of the dream, but its dreamer. Then, too, the body I think I inhabit appeared to be turning once again on the self I still think I am. Creating four suspicious looking moles my dermatologist was all too happy to scrape off and biopsy a couple of days earlier. I had committed to helping prepare the pre-dinner for my daughter's senior prom—another culminating event in Part I of our journey together—scheduled to take place the night before we hosted 18 friends for Easter at home, a meal I couldn't seem to help from seeing as a kind of Last Supper for our live-in family unit.

Seemingly driven to distraction fielding the requests of imaginary dream figures and situations, I again reached for my newly sculpted muscle of forgiveness only to find it oddly disabled even as the muscle of condemnation and neediness pulsed with new-found vigor. And so, I decided to take a time out from forgiveness and turn my attention instead to finally succeeding at another elusive task: making the perfect potato gratin, my daughter's favorite holiday food. A dish I have never quite mastered to my satisfaction but was determined to conquer this final Easter before she headed off to college in the fall.

I had called Jesus (that *symbol* of the awakened mind) in for a consult earlier that day before withdrawing my request to look at the ego's dream figures with him in favor of looking with you know who. But he was still hanging around, dangling his legs from the counter where he sat hunched over—the discarded mandolin package in his hands—studying those confounding directions as if trying to decipher a foreign language. I had ordered it on Amazon hoping it might help me create the completely uniform, sheer slices I had partaken of years ago at a little restaurant in the Saint-Germain-des-Prés in Paris where my husband and I celebrated the specialness of our engagement, or the "finalizing of negotiations," as we referred to it. Unable to figure out how to run the big fat potato in my hand through the blade without slicing off a finger in the process, I had already abandoned the perilous device.

One damn thing after another, I thought, banging around the kitchen reviewing the ghosts of potato gratins past and realizing that my relationship with everyone and thing in this world was not unlike those potatoes—always something lacking. Too mushy one year, not tender enough the next. Too runny, too dry. I flipped through the recipes I had downloaded from the Internet in a futile effort to find some common theme I might adopt to ensure success, to no avail. Some called for half-and-half, some for milk, and some for cream. Some instructed you to par-boil the potatoes in the cream mixture, others did not. Some insisted on slicing potatoes extremely thin, others had no opinion on heft. Recommended oven temperatures and cooking times varied wildly as did the addition or omission of ingredients such as cayenne, nutmeg, rosemary, and cheese. My anxiety levels rose with every piece of advice touted. In mounting distress, I pressed my ring fingers into the dike of my tear ducts.

Jesus cleared his throat in case I had forgotten he was still there, as I am apt to do.

"I know what you're thinking," I told him.

"You always do."

"This is not about perfect potatoes."

"You think?"

"This is about those dream figures isn't it? The ones I can't stop hating, and the ones I can't stop loving. The ones I think will give me what I want and need if only I deliver the goods."

Jesus picked up the timer and set it at just under an hour. "Go on," he said.

"Funny."

"Thank you."

This was about magically thinking I could hold on to the form of a child's love by mastering her favorite dish, for God's sake. That if I just got that perfect ratio of creamy goodness to crunchy topping, maybe she wouldn't leave me behind.

I shut my eyes and continued to press at those tear ducts with my fingers. Jesus patted my arm.

"There's just no way out, is there? In the dream I mean. There is no perfect recipe. Loving is not something we do, it's something we are." I opened my eyes. "What are you still doing here?"

Jesus smiled. He was humming a song—*Ob-La-Di, Ob-La-Da* by the Beatles.

I had to smile, too. We sang together for a while. He has a very good voice, actually.

I tossed the recipes in the trash, picked up my chef's knife, and started slicing potatoes.

Potato Gratin

Do it any way you want or peel a bunch of russet potatoes, slice as thinly as you can without losing a finger, and evenly layer to cover the bottom of a lasagna-type pan sprayed with cooking spray and rubbed with smashed garlic. Generously pour half-and-half over the potato layer, sprinkle with coarsely ground black pepper, nutmeg, and cayenne, if desired. Repeat until you've used up all the potatoes. Top with grated gruyere cheese and bake at 350 degrees for one hour and 15 minutes. Allow to rest covered with foil for 15-20 minutes and prepare to forgive.

Susan Dugan

The Egg That Cracked

When my daughter was in kindergarten she won an award in our school district's "Young Authors" competition for a picture book she wrote and illustrated entitled *The Egg That Cracked*. The story involved an egg fearful of cracking, of giving up its shell to the life within. One day the long stationary egg found itself rolling down a big hill, terrified. At the bottom it hit a rock, cracked open, and discovered it was not the shell after all, but the baby bird within. In the nostalgic frenzy I currently find myself in preceding my daughter's impending high school graduation I have been frantically searching for that book, along with a number of other missing talismans of our early life together, including a diary she kept during a family visit to Paris at around the same age (but that's another story).

The book about the egg came to mind last week when I awoke to a shocking ambush of emotion over the encroaching transformation of our relationship from live-in parent/child to the maturing long-distance variety. I had just been congratulating myself and bragging to a friend about my ability to embrace this perfectly normal passage calmly and philosophically, knowing the time had more than arrived for my daughter to test her own already vigorously flapping wings. And then, without warning, I found myself plunged into this darkest of places, grieving and consumed with regret over how quickly it all had passed, how elusive so many of my perfect parent/child fantasies had proven, much like the photos and mementos I couldn't seem to locate now.

As I sat with Jesus (that *symbol* of the awakened mind used in *A Course in Miracles*) and a box of tissues watching Susan rummaging in yet another file cabinet for documentation of her parenting role, all the special roles I seemed to have played in this lifetime bobbed to the Magic-8-Ball screen of my puny little brain for review. Can I survive the relinquishment of these roles,

I wondered aloud, to you know who. Because releasing them felt like death to the self I still think I am.

Jesus just shook his head and smiled.

Even though I was in no mood for reality, I already knew the answer. My *identification* with the self I think I am would eventually have to go, along with the roles I created for Susan to play and then forget she was only playing. I would have to release my investment in these roles, and costars, sets and costumes. Not in the scary, obliterating, cataclysmic manner the ego keeps describing in gory detail but gently, gradually, kindly with a proverbial Jesus at my proverbial side. I would need to turn my fear of cracking the self I still think I am over to the part of my mind that knows no fissures. And then wait for these blocks to the awareness of love's presence crafted from the secret fear I destroyed eternal love with my desire to experience individuality to pass. I would have to quit resisting the inevitable ride down that big hill, to trust that facing my fear of cracking wide open would finally reveal my true identity instead of the bleak emptiness a part of my mind could not stop picturing.

Jesus was getting on my nerves again with that little knowing smile of his so I took a break in my wallowing to open the big, blue book to a random page for a second opinion—a practice I refer to as *A Course in Miracles* as Ouija Board—and had to laugh. In Chapter 15, V. The Holy Instant and Special Relationships, paragraph 3, I read:

> You cannot love parts of reality and understand what love means. If you would love unlike to God who knows no special love, how can you understand it? To believe that *special* relationships with *special love,* can offer you salvation is the belief that separation is salvation. For it is the complete equality of the Atonement in which salvation lies. How can you decide that special aspects of the Sonship can give you more than others? The past has taught you this. Yet the holy instant teaches you it is not so.

196

I was sitting beside Jesus again, acutely aware of all the highs and lows my special relationship with my daughter has offered as well as the roller coaster ride of all the other special loves I had turned to for salvation in this personal past. Acutely aware that—conceived from a finite thought system that seeks to mete out the punishment it thinks we deserve over that original belief in separation from our source realized—so-called love in all its seeming forms here in the dream can't help but constantly morph into different forms and cannot, by its very nature, stay.

> Because of guilt, all special relationships have elements of fear in them. This is why they shift and change so frequently. They are not based on changeless love alone. And love, where fear has entered, cannot be depended on because it is not perfect. (from paragraph 4)

Fortunately, we can transform our special relationships to holy (whole) relationships by taking responsibility for the belief that we exist separately back to the part of our mind that knows only the whole love we are and have always been. In the holy (whole) instant outside this tale of time in which we accept the right mind's uninterrupted, benevolently amused certainty that the separation from perfect oneness was just a tiny, mad, idea completely void of consequences, we discover the one life within that has been waiting for us all along. In so doing, our mind is healed of the need to find its identity outside itself. We crack wide open to embrace the eternal, joyful present in which our attachment to the form of our special relationships dissolves, leaving behind only the infinitely loving content we continue to share and can always count on.

A Course in Miracles is not telling us to get rid of our special relationships but to change our mind about their purpose. To recognize the many ways in which we use them to reinforce a bogus belief in dueling interests, how we employ them as human shields to defend against our awareness of the only real relationship we have: our one relationship with our one creator with whom we are seamlessly fused in our one mind in ways beyond the comprehension of non-existent brains specifically invented by a guilty ego to accept only dualistic lies. We need to recognize what our clinging to specialness and exclusion has cost us with our inner teacher and choose again for the part of our mind that remains happily unaffected by our hallucinations and continues to smile the gentle, knowing smile of the eternally present.

> God knows you *now.* The holy instant reflects His knowing by bringing all perception out of the past, thus removing the frame of reference you have built by which to judge your brothers. Once this is gone, the Holy Spirit substitutes His frame of reference for it. His frame of reference is simply God. For in the holy instant, free of the past, you see that love is in you, and you have no need to look without and snatch love guiltily from where you thought it was. (paragraph 9)

Even though I am not yet ready to let go of this shell called Susan completely, in honestly recognizing and forgiving the fear underlying that reluctance with Jesus/Holy (Whole) Spirit/right mind I can—for a moment—step out of time and allow the egg of false identity to crack. Thereby admitting a little more of the light in our one, united mind to shine away the dark idea that love has or ever could vacate the premises.

I Need Do Nothing

It was that kind of day in the dream. I awoke to NPR interviewing a few believers in the rapture (apparently scheduled to arrive May 21, 2011) awaiting the descent of Jesus from the heavens to gather them up into the loving fold while the rest of us ... Well, let's just put it this way, as one pastor did (although I *am* paraphrasing): "If I'm still here on May 22, I'm in deep dog you know what." (And since I have to hang around for the graduation party we're throwing for my daughter that day I guess I know where that leaves me.)

This illuminating discussion, sandwiched in between the latest on genocide in Libya and the ongoing debate about the significance of the body of Osama Bin Laden, was soon followed by a forwarded email filled with dazzling photographs of resort areas in South Africa, Egypt, and other irrelevant tourist destinations imploring readers to consider this provocative question in regard to the continent of Africa: *why aren't their rich helping their poor, instead of us!*

Perhaps inspired by sudden-onset spring weather—a harbinger of impending outdoor family celebrations—people were flipping each other off en masse in the parking lot at Costco, as if responding to an invisible choreographer, as we ventured in to order a graduation cake. Clinging to our over-sized, bumper car-like cart as we navigated the crowded warehouse aisles, my daughter burst into tears over a classmate's apparent texted attempt to deliberately exclude her. *Again.*

On the way home, the anti-abortion protestors were out in full force at the intersection in our university neighborhood, waving their graphic dismembered fetus signs at passing infidels—Praise the Lord! Am I the luckiest *A Course in Miracles* student on the planet or what, I thought. Because it was going to be one of those days in the classroom where I could learn I need do nothing but forgive, a process that in truth has nothing to do with the me I think I am, or the me I think they are, or with actually "doing" anything at all on the level of form.

Allow me to review. According to the creation myth *A Course in Miracles* uses to explain the hateful ego dynamics that drive *all* human interaction here in this dream of exile from perfect love, in the beginning we (the individual physical/psychological bodies we independently identify with) were one with our source (still are, actually). Seamlessly, eternally, peacefully fused to our creator in a manner that defies understanding in the condition we mistakenly believe we now find ourselves in. At some point—for reasons that also defy the oxymoron of the term "ego understanding"—we wondered if there could be something more than perfect wholeness and desired to experience it. Although our belief in this "tiny, mad idea" didn't in reality alter anything, believing we had pulled it off, we now experienced ourselves plunged into metaphorical darkness, blinded to our own infinitely shared light.

Our guilt over believing we had destroyed eternal life/God and deserved to be punished for it was so crushing that the one mind appeared to split into the ego—the part of the mind that believed in the "sin" of separation and continued to reinforce that belief—and the Holy (Whole) Spirit, the part of the one mind that could only gently smile at the impossibility of fragmenting perfect oneness.

Like the nut cases we secretly think we are, instead of siding with the Holy Spirit, the one Son of God (now referred to as the decision maker) chose in his fear and morbid curiosity to side with the ego's delusion. He then projected his guilt over this unfortunate move into an entire universe of independent forms projecting their "individual" guilt onto each other to prove their greater innocence to a vengeful, ego-invented God. Figuratively fell asleep, and forgot he even had a mind that can always choose again to smile gently with an inner teacher completely confident we remain one, awake in God, merely dreaming of exile.

A Course in Miracles teaches us we are not these separate selves by learning to recognize our ongoing impulse to blame others for the excruciating, unconscious guilt in our mind or exempt ourselves from the hatred of the "human condition" playing out in our dream. Rather than aggressively charging back into the dream to attack or defend other dream figures, we learn to catch ourselves in the act of projecting and instead join with the part of our mind that knows we're only dreaming because it makes us feel a whole (pun intended) lot better.

Through this process of changing our mind about all we experience, our dream becomes a classroom in which we learn to forgive ourselves for our terrifying projections of the original guilt in the mind. We begin to understand that we all share the same shameful, conniving, selfish, terrorized, and terrorizing ego and the same memory of uninterrupted, all-inclusive, eternal wholeness. Our desire to judge others may imprison us in a hell of our own making, but we can experience heaven in any moment by choosing a different inner teacher. Truth can only come from a part of our mind we deliberately pushed away but now deliberately turn to for a second opinion that always starts with a reminder that this is *my* mind-on-ego I'm watching in all these clever disguises that have no effect whatsoever on the one love we share.

As *A Course in Miracles* chapter 18, VII. I Need Do Nothing, paragraph 5, reminds us:

> ... One instant spent together with your brother restores the universe to both of you. You are prepared. Now you need but to remember you need do nothing. It would be far more profitable now merely to concentrate on this than to consider what you should do. When peace comes at last to those who wrestle with temptation and fight against the giving in to sin; when the light comes at last into the mind given to contemplation; or when the goal is finally achieved

by anyone, it always comes with just one happy realization;
"I need do nothing."

Even though there is (in reality) no individual "I," *A Course in Miracles* meets us where we think we are in the condition we think we're in. So this is a path in healing our mind about our *seeming* relationships—the ones on the radio and TV, the ones in our emails, the ones in our parking lots, the ones in our living rooms, the ones on our street corners, and the one we see when we look in the mirror. Every day I have numerous chances to remember I am the dreamer of this dream, not the hero. The hatred I perceive around me is just a mistaken belief in the "sin" of separation and the desire to get rid of it by picturing it in another dream figure. Presenting my illusions to the part of my mind that can see them as the imagined defenses against the truth they really are, I return to the quiet center in the one mind wherein the split mind we share begins to heal. I need do nothing but recognize in my impulse to blame or credit you for how I feel my own desire to get rid of concealed guilt over believing I exist at God's expense and ask the part of my mind that knows better what's really going on. The final step—the release of my victimized or victimizing thoughts—is done for me.

> Yet there will always be this place of rest to which you can return. And you will be more aware of this quiet center of the storm than all its raging activity. This quiet center, in which you do nothing, will remain with you, giving you rest in the midst of every busy doing on which you are sent. (from paragraph 8)

On this particular Saturday, in response to the seeming antics of my fellow dream figures and the strong pull of my rush to judgment, the choice to do nothing but accept the inner teacher of peace's assurance that all was well for once seemed a no brainer and I found myself flooded with gratitude for the practical, transformative power of this path home. Deeply grateful to each of these dream figures for helping me remember there is really no me or you to forgive, thereby undoing a little more of the unconscious guilt that must all (eventually) go to awaken from this dream. Until my secret fear came boomeranging back the next morning in the form of tree pollen on steroids partnered with a mighty wind intent on interfering with *my* plan for the perfect Mothers' Day hike and I again forgot I need do nothing but forgive.

Just a Little Willingness

Through the mottled glass of the window on the office door I could see Jesus bent over his desk, grading papers, no doubt. You'd think he would keep the door open, being Jesus and all, I thought, before remembering that someone might have accidentally slammed it on her way out the other day. I drew a ragged breath cut short by this damn choking cough that wouldn't quit despite my pleas to you know who to see things differently.

"Come in," Jesus called, before I even lifted my fist to knock. He was always doing things like that.

I carried my notebook over to the chair beside his desk and sat down. He wasn't grading papers after all, even though I had given him a stash of new red pencils all sharpened and ready to go on more than one occasion. No, he was playing with those finger puppets he had fancied and apparently pinched from my collection several weeks ago—George Bush and Mother Goose appeared to be engaging in a kind of mimed conversation to which I was not privy. Jesus looked on, seemingly amused.

I took out my pen, opened my notebook, scribbled out the situation I found myself in, and pushed it toward him.

"You mean you can't speak?" He had raised his voice—as if he suspected I had lost my sense of hearing, as well—and seemed annoyingly on the verge of bursting into song from sheer delight.

I shook my head.

"Tell me more," he said.

I grabbed back the notebook and picked up my pen. The sickness had commenced ironically enough after a hike I took with my daughter and husband Mother's Day, a sentimental journey to an Open Space park in the foothills we used to frequent all the time when our child was little. Swinging her between us on a wide footpath that climbed after a while toward the ruins of a castle constructed in the early 20th century by a millionaire with big dreams for a wife he adored.

An unseasonably warm, gusting wind coated us with dust and pollen as we re-read the ruins' story before moving on to retrace our steps along the rest of the winding trails, our little dog's feet turning green and rusty brown from pine pollen and parched earth. As we recounted the various times we had come here together, Kara tried her best to humor our memories although they had clearly long faded for her, as early *happy* childhood memories will. By the time we returned to the car I was wheezing. My eyes burned, my head and muscles ached, and my plan to spend the remaining afternoon cooking a fabulous and instructive meal with my college-bound daughter as obedient sous chef had pretty much bitten the dust.

By Monday morning, although barely able to swallow, I steeled myself to complete my writing assignments, work out, and show up to lead an *A Course in Miracles* class I had committed to that evening, but by the following day a full-blown case of laryngitis had set in. Still, even though swallowing brought tears to my eyes, I continued working, prepped for my regular Thursday ACIM class, and kept a lunch engagement I'd been looking forward to.

That afternoon, the last of my voice spent, I cursed my fate and called my acupuncturist for Chinese herbal remedies to treat an infection that had spread to my sinuses and lungs. I had so much to complete this week before the festivities around my daughter's graduation commenced next week and out-of-town family descended for the celebrations. I had no time for sickness, no time for these nagging feelings of inadequacy. Let's face it; I could barely keep up with my current schedule while *well.* I had so wanted everything to be magical next week, perhaps hoping that an idyllic ending might somehow mitigate our less than exemplary, all-too-complicated, eighteen-year journey together. I put down my pen, drew another ragged breath, and again pressed my index fingers to those all-too-leaky-lately tear ducts.

Jesus pushed the box of tissues toward me with his palms. George Bush and Mother Goose stood at attention.

"I know what you're thinking," I wrote.

George and Mother Goose nodded from their perch on Jesus' fingers.

I had just been re-reading *A Course in Miracles* Chapter 18, IV. The Little Willingness, paragraph 4, wherein Jesus explains just how small our contribution to the Course's mind-healing forgiveness really is:

> The holy instant does not come from your little willingness alone. It is always the result of your small willingness combined with the unlimited power of God's Will. You have been wrong in thinking that it is needful to prepare yourself for Him. It is impossible to make arrogant preparations for holiness, and not believe that it is up to you to establish the conditions for peace. God has established them. They do not wait upon your willingness for what they are. Your willingness is needed only to make it possible to teach you what they are. If you maintain you are unworthy of learning this, you are interfering with the lesson by believing that you must make the learner different. You did not make the learner, nor can you make him different. Would you first make a miracle yourself, and then expect one to be made *for* you?

I sighed. All my life I had been trying to make the learner different. Struggling to prepare myself for wholeness, believing that if I could just complete my To-Do list, meet all my obligations, still my thoughts, clear my desk and mind, I could somehow perfect myself enough to receive the light of our creator's forgiveness. If I just worked a few more hours, learned a little more, shed a few more layers, concentrated a little harder, I would be ready to receive the love that has seemed so elusive here in the dream, a love I keep trying to resurrect in an imaginary past or seek in a future that never comes. But love is right here, right now, always has been, always will be, completely unaffected by the constantly morphing conditions of the dream and dream figures I think I need to personally purify and steady to enable peace to arrive.

In a welcome flash I realized my efforts to create the perfect day in which to engage with my daughter, the perfect week in which to celebrate her coming of age, the perfect health in which to enjoy the perfect festivities, were no different than my efforts to become the perfect *A Course in Miracles* student. As if my contribution as a body created like all bodies from a faulty belief that we could (or would want to) exist separately from our eternally loving source had anything at all to offer truth.

"Damn," I wrote, smacking myself upside the head.

Jesus nodded. George Bush and Mother Goose did a happy little dance.

I blew my nose and coughed and did my best to swallow. A lot of things might not get done and I still might be sick when graduation came but love was still here. Imagine that.

"This Course is getting really redundant," I wrote, and pushed my notebook toward Jesus.

Downright gleeful, he grabbed one of those perfectly sharpened red pencils and—as God is my witness—gave me a big, fat A+!

Choose Once Again

I'm not gonna lie to you. There are times with this Course when I seriously doubt I will *ever* make it home. Times when I wax insanely nostalgic over those pre-ACIM days filled with the temporary relief of oblivious projection, much like a certain demographic continues to romanticize World War II and the 1950s, its cold wars raging in cabinet rooms and kitchens. But a couple of days into the two-week marathon of festivities and ceremonies surrounding my daughter's recent graduation from high school, I found myself in just that sort of space, staring down at the big, blue book entertaining various fantasies involving its imminent and brutal demise along with a similar fate for several costars in my personal dream of exile from all-inclusive, eternal love.

I had not bounced back from more than a week of respiratory flu that left me short of breath, wheezing, coughing, and generally stumbling around annoying anyone foolish enough to stray into my wobbly orbit. My parents, who had elected to travel from upstate New York to Denver by train rather than plane, had been delayed more than 24 hours by a washed-out bridge, thunderstorms, and tornadoes and now might not make it to the actual ceremony. My pushing-90 in-laws were literally about to descend and I kept wracking my brain to figure out how to make our three-level home more elder-friendly.

I had lasagna to assemble, food to stock in, beds to make up, errands to run, and multiple Chinese herbal tea pills to pop. The dog, sensing impending upheaval (pun intended) had already hurled on the rug in solidarity with my plight. Worst of all, instead of feeling jubilant during the most recent school awards ceremony last night I felt consumed by unrelenting judgment and regret, picturing myself at an internal awards ceremony accepting a certificate from Jesus for least valuable *A Course in Miracles* player of the year.

I dragged my weary body about craving elusive rest, fretting about how to meet looming obligations, and, yes, secretly resenting a lack of support from those others seemingly "out there," as reruns of the sad and perilous adventures of Susan's entire pitiful life spun out in back-to-back episodes in my twisted little head. Even when I managed to cross a task off my To-Do list, several more—scrawled in an increasingly illegible and disturbed hand—immediately replaced it, the lists cloning themselves and scattering about the house like ransom notes. I had been kidnapped by the ego, the growing conviction that I (the decision maker that chose for the ego in the first place) could choose peace instead of this but a dim, seemingly inaccessible memory.

"Choose once again if you would take your place among the saviors of the world, or would remain in hell, and hold your brothers there." The quote from the beginning of Chapter 31, VIII. Choose Once Again, echoed in my head. Savior, smavior, I thought. The little dog staggered over to the corner and threw up again.

Please help me see things differently, I silently whispered, staring out the window at sheets of rain, this seventh day of a stalled storm that had settled along with a cold front and nearly washed away plans for an outdoor graduation. In which case, the ceremony would have to move inside, leaving us to figure out how to stretch five tickets to accommodate six immediate family members and planting fantasies of counterfeiting additional tickets in my husband's "can-do" brain.

Although I thought I wanted to see things differently, I knew my continuing discontent with and seeming inability to release my death grip on the objects of my projections testified to the choice for another inner teacher, the teacher of separation realized, that dizzyingly popular professor of the ego's sneaky ways. Kneeling on the floor dabbing at the dog's latest mess I couldn't stand it anymore and headed back into the classroom to review the dream's ugly status with Jesus.

He did not even look up as I slipped into the desk beside him.

"This Course is *so* not working for me," I said.

"*Déjà vu*," he said, smiling.

"Funny."

He pushed the box of tissues my way.

"No, no, I mean, think about it. Am I any happier today than I was seven years ago when I first picked up that big, blue book? I don't *think* so! And I'm not the only one. As you may have noticed a couple of other people in my life have been all too willing to point that out along the way."

His brows shot up in mock surprise.

He had to agree I had a point. Although I had become, over time—*an awful lot of time*—increasingly right-minded practicing forgiveness, admittedly able to identify my mind under the influence of ego quicker and generally choose again for peace, I still sometimes found myself hopelessly lost in the ego's mosh pit. Hemmed in by a throng of illusions too numerous and hideous to combat. And it had *all* started to feel hideous; a spill on the rug as upsetting as the jolts of grief that ambushed me now and then around my daughter heading off to college. Then, too, the same old faces appeared reel after derivative reel to occasionally delight, but more frequently torment me.

"I mean, think about it," I continued. "I keep forgiving the same people and situations over and over and over again."

He nodded.

"I know what you're thinking," I said. "It's true; I do have that holy instant of release. But next thing you know they're back in my face again. I mean, *Jesus*, when is this Course going to be over?" I couldn't seem to help quoting my husband who had asked that now seemingly prescient question early on in my study.

Jesus appeared to be doodling, scribbling hearts and flowers no doubt in that notebook of his. Annoying little roses and happy faces like those animated icons in Internet chat rooms.

(Not that I'd be caught dead in one of those.) He pushed his notebook toward me.

"Trials are but lessons that you failed to learn presented once again," I read, from Choose Once Again, paragraph 3:

> so where you made a faulty choice before you now can make a better one, and thus escape all pain that what you chose before has brought to you. In every difficulty, all distress, and each perplexity Christ calls to you and gently says, 'My brother, choose again.'...

Leave it to Jesus to have memorized the whole damn book. "Show off," I said.

He smiled that knowing smile of his.

> The images you make cannot prevail against what God Himself would have you be," I read. "Be never fearful of temptation then, but see it as it is; another chance to choose again, and let Christ's strength prevail in every circumstance and every place you raised an image of yourself before. (from paragraph 4)

"Christ's strength," I repeated.

He nodded.

"You mean yours," I said.

He continued to smile.

"You mean theirs? And...mine?"

He shut his notebook.

"Class dismissed?" I asked.

"Break a leg, kid," he said.

"Ha!"

"Knock 'em dead."

"Cute," I said. "Not exactly ready for SNL, but."

He just continued to crack himself up.

And I was back at the window again, staring at the rain, holding my peaked-looking little dog, Jesus' gentle laughter fading slowly and merging with my own. I patted the dog and put her back down, finished assembling the lasagna, and headed upstairs to make up some beds.

Susan Dugan

Let All Things Be Exactly As They Are

How I longed to breathe a complete sigh of relief as we touched down on the runway in Puerto Vallarta. But I knew the trouble I had expelling all air from my lungs had less to do with the lingering respiratory infection I had not yet vanquished than with the apprehension I couldn't shake over my ability to endure another vacation. After all, in recent years—the more deeply I delved into understanding and practicing *A Course in Miracles*—my vacations had morphed from mindless romps in the ego's various theme parks to mindful field trips in exposing the pain of the ego thought system. Accompanied by my special relationships and unfettered by the distractions of everyday life.

It was on vacation in another part of Mexico just two years ago, for example, that I came face-to-face with my inner ego toddler in full-tantrum mode for days over external conditions falling short of its expectations. Even though that led to an elongated moment of knowing completion, release, and relief—a welcome transcendence of all personal desire—it was only a moment after all, a piddling instant wedged between days of inner strife. (In the corner of my eye I caught Jesus winking at that thought.)

Oddly enough, though, as my husband and I waited in line and filled out forms at the high-end, all-inclusive resort along with my daughter, her boyfriend, and his family, I felt enveloped by an odd calm, caught myself smiling a strangely familiar smile, beaming out at the world despite the sweltering afternoon humidity that had already annihilated my ridiculously fine, ever problematic locks. Although I could feel my IQ plummeting, I willingly extended my wrist as a woman behind the big desk fastened the bracelet that would enable me to gorge and anesthetize myself at the various buffets, restaurants, and bars scattered about the secured, tropical compound. Unpacking in our spacious room I couldn't help but marvel at the expansive view of bay and breakers and the kinds of sunsets that attract couples ready to tie the knot (as they frequently did, all week, right there before our very eyes).

The calm followed me to dinner that night, yoga the next morning, and the breakfast buffet where I gratefully consumed eggs and goat cheese and sunset colored fruits, nodding sympathetically as my husband grew increasingly and understandably agitated by continuous emailed notifications from American Express. The card we had checked in with just hours earlier seemed to have been somehow hijacked; bogus charges multiplying like some runaway, global retrovirus. I was not upset by the high pressure tactics of the representative of our travel agency at our "mandatory" meeting in which he tried to sell us various excursion packages. After all, he was just trying to make a living, feed a family in a harsh environment, fighting the same hard battle as everyone else here in this dream of exile from all-inclusive, enduring love.

The "unusually aggressive" sting rays that prevented us from swimming for days did not trouble me. The fumes in the back seat of the sans air conditioning taxi my husband, daughter, her boyfriend, and I took into Puerto Vallarta the next morning stung my nose and throat and still infected lungs but did nothing to alter my smile. The drone from the massive construction project on the corner below the balcony where we lunched on grilled fish had no effect on my peace of mind, even as I raised my voice to be heard and leaned forward to hear. I was not upset by the proprietors in the shops on the boardwalk where we purchased gifts and a Day-of-the-Dead figure for our collection, as they tried to pedal yet another property that was "*definitely not* a time share, senor and senora," although I was happy to end the afternoon with a ride back to the hotel in an air-conditioned van.

It did not even occur to me to question this new and improved state of mind as I sat quietly on the balcony watching a yellow bird catch an exuberant breeze, the big, blue book open on my lap to workbook lesson 268: "Let all things be exactly as they are."

I was somehow inexplicably and magically able on this trip to let things be exactly that. Conscious that peace of mind has nothing to do with the way things are in the dream. Peace of mind just *is*, completely independent of seemingly external conditions. It springs not from what happens in a dream of having our own way over God's—our stupendously demented attempts to impersonate God instead of accepting ourselves as part of God—but from what we are. Why would I want to argue with that? Besides, things are exactly as they are because nothing ever happened as a result of our failure to smile at our declaration of independence from all-inclusive, eternal love. The error was corrected the moment it arose in the one mind of the one child of God we are and remain.

I was downright giddy with peace as I headed down to the pool to find Jesus where I thought I'd last spotted him from a distance by the swim-up bar, raising a glass of fluorescent turquoise liquid and taking in a water polo game. He was not in the breakfast buffet either. I could not find him at water aerobics or Bingo or anywhere on the premises. And then it dawned on me that maybe I didn't really need him at the moment, much as I'd love to see him in a sombrero or trailing along in a Conga line. In my right mind, I had merged with his as we all do and (at least for now) no longer required an imaginary, embodied big brother to lean on.

Practicing forgiveness day in and day out had resulted in an extended period of right-mindedness, just as *A Course in Miracles* promises us it will. After months—OK *years*—of changing my mind about what appears to be happening to me in my so-called life and looking at my illusions with Jesus as my teacher I had received these days wherein I resided in the quiet center Jesus talks about, invulnerable to the seeming waves crashing around me "out there."

Not even occasional meltdowns among my closest costars disturbed me. Not even this pushing six-week infection, awareness of my aging body heightened by scant clothing, or the often less than attractive behavior of my fellow Americans on holiday. Admittedly, one morning, I watched myself veer into wrong-mindedness over an encounter at the hotel. But as I began to recount the seeming injustice to my husband as we strolled along the beach, I caught a glimpse of Jesus riding a boogie board in my peripheral vision, immediately let my grievance go, and remained largely right-minded the rest of the trip for reasons that happily defy logical understanding.

There were so many opportunities for judgment and self-judgment on a vacation like this but each time I reached for the muscle of condemnation I found it happily disabled by the work of forgiveness in my daily classroom. Although the ego continually tried to worm its way in, its various antics culminating in multiple jelly fish stings during a snorkeling excursion that left me with an extreme case of vertigo, I was somehow able to withstand the ego thought system's venom. Although, like the jelly fish, it seeks to paralyze and disorient us we are never truly prey.

It is possible to experience even physical paralysis without joining it. I held my husband's hand and leaned on railings and walls as we headed for dinner. Stepped carefully and reneged on the Sake in favor of Ibuprofen and sleep but had no desire to allow fear over my physical condition to send me into panic or unnecessarily involve my costars. Should more threatening symptoms arise I would certainly consult the hotel physician but, until then, I just rode it out. What, after all, did it have to do with what I really am? (Feel free to quote me on that, big guy. :))

At the end of our week, I returned to Denver still un-invested in the dream I seem to be dreaming or the dream figure I seem to inhabit. Still peaceful, the respiratory crud still doing its number, the work I'd struggled and failed to finish before leaving still patiently waiting along with new requests and expectations. I am still willing as I write these words—at least until my secret fear of separation realized and special interests threatened returns—to let all things be exactly as they are. A lot more certain that all I really want is what I really am as one with you.

Let me not be Your critic, Lord, today, and judge against You. Let me not attempt to interfere with Your creation, and distort it into sickly forms. Let me be willing to withdraw my wishes from its unity, and thus to let it be as you created it. For thus will I be able, too, to recognize my Self as You created me. In love was I created, and in love will I remain forever. What can frighten me, when I let all things be exactly as they are? (from workbook lesson 268)

Objects in Mirror Are Closer Than They Appear

A couple years ago I had an epiphany of sorts while contemplating the recurring, ever-strengthening urge to begin formally teaching *A Course in Miracles* classes versus my colossal resistance to that preposterous idea. Since adolescence I had been seemingly crippled with a debilitating fear not only of speaking in public but of claiming center stage in any way. I had forfeited grades in college by refusing to orally present and been dinged for avoiding to do so on job evaluations. A simple request to introduce myself in groups sent me into full fight-or-flight mode, followed by a complete adrenaline meltdown and terror so intense I literally doubted I could physically survive it. Even walking down the aisle as a maid of honor at friends' weddings required bouquets stashed with smelling salts. The only thing worse than the thought of addressing a group of strangers was the nauseating prospect of addressing a group of peers even more intimately acquainted with my many perceived foibles.

As I sat reviewing the legacy of my nonexistent presentation skills, stomach churning, pulse quickening, palms blooming with sweat, I opened the big, blue book craving solace, if not answers to my "special" fragility, and read: "I am so close to you we cannot fail."

It was one of the first times I truly felt the presence of Jesus—that *symbol* of the forever kind, sane, awakened, gently smiling mind *A Course in Miracles* teaches us to call on—within. One of the first times in my life I felt truly and completely loved, loving, supported, innocent, and beyond all external need. And although I knew the Course in its infinite wisdom could not possibly be offering *specific* answers to questions about what to do in an *illusory* world, I felt I had my answer to the question of whether or not to teach. Fear would not plague me provided I turned away from the ego's terrified tales about "Susan's" condition and leaned instead on the strength in my mind that would never fail me, patiently waiting closer than my next breath. Our one inner teacher would always be there for me if I sincerely chose to use this body as a "communication device" (the Course's term for demonstrating compassionate, right-mindedness in our relationships) for the healing of our one mind.

I bring this up because following a couple of weeks of seeming right-mindedness I must have once again become afraid of losing my identity as a separate personality, once again seduced into believing there was something real to lose. Another birthday loomed, ego "evidence" that the expiration date on the seemingly separate self I identify with had inched another year closer. And I had a couple requests for signings and talks about my recently published book coming in, reigniting the story of Susan's terror of public speaking.

In kneejerk defense of my bogus identity I had also once again begun noticing and attempting to interpret the many differences among my fellow dream figures illuminated by the ego in a steady stream that even followed me as I drove around with my daughter to post fliers she had made to advertise her services for babysitting and other odd jobs this summer. As she dashed in and out of community centers and cafes, I held on to our frantic little dog, asking to see things differently but apparently resisting. I could literally see the faces of the many objects of my projection reflected in my rear-view and side mirrors. The ego's taut little PowerPoint presentation featuring the ones I loved to judge, including the one I think I am.

As my daughter climbed back into the car, I handed her the dog and pulled back into the street, glancing once more in my rearview mirror only to spy the face of Jesus wearing those fetching hot pink shades he'd been favoring so far this season and grinning his knowing grin. Changing lanes, I glanced in my side mirror and saw the words etched there as if for the first time:

Objects in mirror are closer than they appear.

Fortunately, I, too, was wearing shades preventing my daughter from noticing the tears welling up as I pulled into the parking lot of her next destination. Despite my attempts to substitute a plethora of individual, imperfect, often problematic faces for that symbol of our perfect, shared oneness, Jesus remained "So close to you we cannot fail." I hugged my dog awash in gratitude for the reminder, watching his nodding image slowly fade.

The words in the mirror haunted me all weekend, each time I found myself judging one of my costars or guest costars in this dream of exile from the all-inclusive love we have never left. Each time I caught myself siding with the ego in registering differences among the faces in the mirror or tempted to tally my progress with this Course versus the seeming progress of others in the dream—as if there really was a separate self engaging in a separate journey home—the words in the mirror came back to me, along with Jesus' smiling face.

Objects in the mirror are closer than they appear.

If Jesus is as close as my next breath he is as close as yours despite every difference in form. It's OK to notice individual differences but not OK to think they mean anything. As Ken Wapnick often says (largely attributed to Plato although there is some disagreement on this) "Be kind, for everyone you meet is fighting a hard battle." We may seem to be at different points in our journey from unconsciously fearful mindlessness to consciously knowing mindfulness, but everyone in a body shares the same split mind. When my unconscious guilt arises and I project it on you, I strive to judge you to prove my greater innocence. But when I turn to my right mind for a second opinion about that, I see that despite our differences in form, we are completely supported in our journey home together and, in truth, already home. We need only look beyond the illusion of our differences (defenses to our awareness of our true nature) to the content of our sameness until we no longer see any differences and awaken as the one child of God we are.

Objects in the mirror are (thankfully) closer than they appear!

... The Father and the Son, Whose holy Will created all that is can fail in nothing. In this certainty, we undertake these last few steps to You, and rest in confidence upon Your Love, which will not fail the Son who calls to You. (from *A Course in Miracles* workbook, Part II Introduction, paragraph 7)

Forget This Book: Well, Maybe Tomorrow

As I sat at my desk carefully cutting out strips of duct tape to suture the frayed spine of my *A Course in Miracles* book the other morning, I became aware of my imaginary Jesus quietly sitting beside me. I did not remember calling on him but his presence indicated otherwise.

"I know what you're thinking," I said.

"You usually do."

"OK, so, I may have become a tad too attached to this book. But honestly, I *know* it's not the form, but the content that's important. It's just that I really like *this* book, you know?" I rubbed it with my hand as if petting a dog. "I mean, it's *mine*."

"I see. A security book."

"Exactly." I folded a strip of duct tape to overlap one side of the broken binding and pressed down hard. "It's just that I started with this book, you know, seven-and-a-half years ago."

"Oh, my," Jesus said.

"I know. It has sentimental value. Not to mention many—if I do say so myself—insightful annotations."

"Like those ones that made it almost impossible for you to read that section you were studying with your class last week?"

"Hey," I said, although, as usual, he was right. My wild, exuberant hieroglyphics coupled with effusive highlighting had all but rendered nearly every page indecipherable, leading well-meaning fellow Course students to wonder aloud why I bothered to highlight in the first place.

"I know what you're thinking," I said. "I am still convinced my understanding is a powerful contribution to the truth. But it's not like that. It's just that this book is evidence of my journey, you know? Evidence of my progress, my desire, my commitment."

"Ah. So, you're saying this particular book belongs to a particular Course student named Susan having the experience of a particular journey home to perfect, undifferentiated oneness?"

"Well, when you put it like that, it sounds a bit precious but, essentially, yes."

"Far out."

I sighed. "Also, this book first belonged to a good friend who died before she ever got around to it. So you can see how I need to honor her memory."

"Go on," he said.

But I knew only too well where we were really going with this.

Ultimately, there's nothing special about this book. It is merely a symbol of the one, awakened mind from which it sprang; the articulated memory of wholeness that followed us into this dream of exile from all-inclusive, ever-lasting love. Just a little treasure map back to our one right mind.

Even this Course can become a defense against the truth if we begin to depend on it for solace and support and forget that it's only a tool to help us become mindful. The answer never lies in form, but always only in the mind wherein the question of our mistaken identity first arose. All we need really do from moment to moment is catch ourselves investing in the dream again through our attachment to our special identities, with their special stories of suffering, triumph, and betrayal, their special talents and disabilities, cravings and preferences.

As workbook lesson 189, "I feel the Love of God within me now," paragraph 7, reminds us:

> Simply do this: Be still, and lay aside all thoughts of what you are and what God is; all concepts you have learned about the world; all images you hold about yourself. Empty your mind of everything it thinks is either true or false, or good or bad, of every thought it judges worthy, and all the ideas of which it is ashamed. Hold onto nothing. Do not bring with you one thought the past has taught, nor one belief you ever learned before from anything. Forget this world, forget this course, and come with wholly empty hands unto your God.

Easy for Jesus to say but I'm just not there yet. I am still attached to many things. The comforting ritual of rising to work and write at dawn, the worn fleece "softie" I don on chilly mornings as I make my way with my three-quarter-decaf light room Americano to my computer, my pink crocs, my battered *A Course in Miracles* book, my amazing daughter I realize will vacate the premises in less than two months with or without my willingness to see her go. I still value my husband, my dog, my home, my cookbook and finger puppet collections, and certain particularly juicy chapters in the bittersweet Indie film of my so-called life.

All these nouns preceded by that pesky little, possessive adjective "my," that bogus stamp of ownership by an imaginary self. Although I believe everything the Course is telling me with all my conscious heart and have experienced the release, relief, and absolute, joyful completeness practicing its forgiveness brings, I still am not entirely convinced that God has a welcome mat waiting for me at the other end of the rainbow, still not one-hundred percent sure losing this special self with its many attachments offers the real freedom and eternal comfort I have been seeking all my life.

And so, even as I celebrate another birthday vowing to make wanting the peace of God once and for always my only goal, I feel the need to hold on to this book a little longer. I do so fully aware it is not the form but the content I really crave. Even as I continue to find its ragged heft on my desk and nightstand, it's liberally tattooed pages, the rainbow of tattered sticky notes protruding lace-like from its edges ear-marking something *really important* to remember deeply comforting.

For a while longer (years, decades, multiple lifetimes?), until my unconscious fear subsides for good, I may still fall asleep with it sprawled open beside me—the light on, reading glasses tangled in my hair—because I want the peace of God and still, often, find it right here between these pages on my way to finding it where it really resides. At the end of this journey to the place we never left. The reality I will awaken to when all my "secret sins and hidden hates" are undone through the practice of forgiveness in my daily classroom, choosing from moment to moment the inner teacher of enduring love over the inner teacher of separation, exile, and fear.

I am still afraid enough of the real love we are to approach it directly. I don't find it a lot easier to remember the lesson for the day in the second part of the workbook (wherein we open our mind to direct experience of God) a whole lot easier than I did five years ago. Still, I am often able to call on Jesus so automatically now that he is simply there when I need a reminder that the time to put away my toys and grow up draws nearer within this illusion of linear time and space. It is almost time to wean myself from my dependency on this big, blue, broken book held lovingly together with duct tape. Not that I would ever stop reading, studying, teaching, or rejoicing in it. But that its specialness related to the imaginary specialness of Susan's fantasized journey home would eventually fade into the welcome nothingness from which it came.

Declaration of Dependence

My husband and daughter had taken off for the mountains to attend the annual celebration of the final day of the last Colorado ski resort (Arapahoe Basin) still open for the season, leaving me to my own devices. It had been a whirlwind of a summer so far—the ego seemingly firing distractions like an alien ship in a video game hell-bent on conquering my serenity—and I welcomed a morning of solitude. Before setting off on my bike to the local farmers' market, I again read *A Course in Miracles* workbook lesson 290: "My present happiness is all I see." Right.

I'd struggled to allow the lesson to have its way with me for several days, but could only seem to notice how difficult (OK, *impossible*) I found staying present to where happiness really lies, far beyond this body and dreamy dream of exile from perfect love. How spectacularly alluring all seemingly external some-things seemed compared with the quiet, assured nothing of our one right mind. Try as I might, the ego's 24/7 static seemed to render the lesson's deeper truth elusive. But this morning my renegade thoughts ground to a welcome halt as I wound through the neighborhoods in the dewy, early-morning breeze and secured my bike in the parking lot racks where the market had just opened, vendors putting the finishing touches on colorful fare, parked trucks already dishing up artery-busting comfort food and ethnic delights.

The recently hosed-down asphalt glistened beneath a benevolent sun high and hopeful in the sky as I perused the still largely deserted stalls fingering bouquets of just-picked Swiss chard and spinach, and followed a perfumed trail to a booth offering just-roasted green chilies. I nabbed a nosegay of the breathtaking, peppery cinnamon-capped mushrooms I had snagged a few weeks ago and successfully married with butter, white wine, Papparadelle, and Romano cheese, and munched on a breakfast burrito as I headed back to my bike. Petting dogs and nodding at the smiling, accumulating passersby and thinking that—dream or no dream—it didn't get much better than this.

I relished that thought (no pun intended) along with new recipes born of the ingredients in my backpack all the way home. But by the time I unpacked and headed out to walk my dog these bountiful, benevolent thoughts, too—like all things seemingly good or bad in this so-called world—had changed. As the sun climbed in the sky toward its scorching apex, I found myself thinking instead about the nature of suffering, how everyone secretly believed they carried its guilty seed buried within, and would literally rather die than own up to its fantasized origins.

As I passed the park—signs of the impending Fourth of July celebration already manifesting—I couldn't help but recall the many Independence Day galas I had attended over the years to commemorate our collective emancipation from a controlling parent. How everyone here (in this seeming dream of exile from eternal wholeness) clung to stories of personal and collective suffering at the hands of a controlling parent to hide the real, unexcavated story within. That heady tale of the one and only child of God deciding to strike off on her own—believing she could, and had, and would possibly want to—and literally disintegrating from the guilty, terrifying pleasure of it all into a gazillion forms vying for survival/exoneration. Spinning declarations of independence old and new in an effort to prevent them from ever finding the dusty scroll of that original tale carefully hidden within the one mind, recalling its fictional nature, and smiling at the frivolity of it all.

Everywhere I looked I could suddenly read the stories of differentiated forms in progress. My contemplative mood must have been contagious because my little dog, Kayleigh, seemed likewise uncharacteristically subdued. We passed greedy squirrels, noisy ravens, and graceful butterflies touting transcendence without incident, a weary wolf hound, an exuberant black lab, a brooding German shepherd, an incensed pug, and two irritated white toy poodles that looked exactly like their owner. And still Kayleigh—an ability to play well with others of her species never among her strong suits—walked obediently at my feet, without once lapsing into so much as a low growl or aggressive twirl.

The Jehovah's Witnesses poured out of their little, shuttered building along the gully in their freshly pressed shirts and skirts, cooing over Kayleigh's effortless adorability. The Quakers smiled and bent to pat her head on their way into Saturday meeting, climbing the stairs beside a sign that read: *War Is Not the Answer,* that left me silently humming and finishing that Marvin Gaye-sentiment: *for only love can conquer hate.* "My present happiness is all I see," I thought, realizing it *was* possible to walk this world of seeming fragmentation from perfect, all-inclusive love. To fully participate while witnessing its endlessly creative pleas (and those would be mine) for separate interests, for duality taken seriously, without once lapsing into as much as a low growl or aggressive twirl.

All weekend long I watched the ego's ingenious performance without feeling the need to react, somehow poignantly aware that our original declaration of independence—thank God—had no effect, rendering everything that seemed to happen subsequently blessedly null and void. I could see our one present happiness even as I looked on my impulse to join with its imaginary detractors. Even as the self I still think I am once more occupied a camp chair and cozied up to my fellow Americans on a field just south of the city. Following a concert by the '60s and '70s Canadian band The Guess Who to watch a stunning display of pyrotechnics accompanied by blaring patriotic music applauding our nation's seemingly exclusive characteristics. All rendered innocent by the rockets' red glare of our one right mind.

And in a burst of clarity, I remembered this: No matter what the body's eyes report, no matter how glorious, gory, or gruesome our "particular" stories, we did not create ourselves. And we are all the same. Nothing happened because of a "tiny, mad idea" that we could strike off on our own, or would want to. We remain seamlessly fused with our creator. Undifferentiated, eternally sane, and thrilled to be so. We are not God! We are part of God. This is great news! This is a huge relief. I have no worries as a part of God. This is the happy truth of what we are.

Unless I look upon what is not there, my present happiness is all I see. Eyes that begin to open see at last. And I would have Christ's vision come to me this very day. What I perceive without God's Own Correction for the sight I made is frightening and painful to behold. Yet I could not allow my mind to be deceived by the belief the dream I made is real an instant longer. This the day I seek my present happiness, and look on nothing else except the thing I seek. (from workbook lesson 290)

Lean on Me

"So self-reliant," they would say. Parents, aunts, uncles, neighbors, and teachers, referring to the way I seemed to have entered this world so assured and independent, preferring to take charge of myself and those around me rather than lean on others. How they would marvel at the way I took care of myself and also pitched in to care for and educate brothers, cousins, playmates, and pets, while freely dispensing cooking, parenting, and organizational advice to my bemused elders.

"Self-reliant." I remember repeating the term silently in my head instead of counting sheep as I tried to fall asleep. Spelling it out, letter by letter—a kind of personal mantra—taking great pride in its constant repetition among those I hoped most to impress. It would take many years to recognize that my greatest strength had also proved my greatest weakness, a barrier to truly opening myself to receiving love and support from others. And many more to understand that my robotic reliance on the self I think I am had literally cost me the "everything" of remembering our true shared and single identity beyond this dream of exile from all-inclusive love.

I bring this up because I've been watching the self I still largely think I am become fearful again about certain situations in the dream with which it has unresolved ego issues. My daughter is away this week providing my dejected dog and me a little preview of what our lives will be like on a day-to-day basis once she leaves for college at the end of August. Then, too, I'm teaching a class and preparing for a talk at a book signing later this week that threatens to expose self-reliant Susan as a sniveling, cowering imposter. And yet a part of me knows there is a strength in me beyond this personal, lower case s self that remains forever invulnerable and always truly helpful. I need only lean on this always available part of my mind to look gently and compassionately at Susan's ego antics—or the seeming meltdowns of any other dream figure—without joining with them. Still, I am not, you know, a natural leaner.

I know this personal self I've identified with for so many years is really nothing but "a defense against the truth" of our one, real capital S Self; the one child of God we remain that could never be divided. Our one identity seamlessly and eternally fused with our one creator upon which no hallucination of separation and differentiation had any effect. But because we believe it did, we rely on the special interests of our special selves, believing these physical fences erected of bone, blood, and sinew we spin out our days attempting to strengthen and protect, will somehow keep us safe. Somehow allow us to prove our innocence versus the greater guilt of those others seemingly "out there" while keeping us so busy defending our territory and viewpoints we continue to forget we have a mind that chose to believe in an idle fantasy to begin with but could, at any moment, choose again to smile, heal, and awaken. If only we surrender our self-reliance and lean on our right mind.

Trouble is the ego in its perpetual sneakiness still sometimes (OK, *often*) convinces me I should be further along with this Course by now, able to simply remain right-minded regardless of the dream's twists and turns, beyond the personal interests my mind-on-ego uses to try to keep real capital L Love away. This ego in spirit's clothing would have me believe I've already healed my mind of personal interests rather than allow me to honestly look with my right mind at my lingering attraction to false self-reliance. That way, I forget to do the work of forgiveness that actually mends my split mind and allows me to awaken to my true nature once all my illusions of special interests have dissolved.

To say we have no personal interests regardless of how "far along" we seem to be on the journey home to the wholeness we in truth never left is a lie, born of the original lie of separation. Recognizing this causes much denial, resistance, and disappointment in the individual self I still think I am. Nevertheless, the ego hangs in until the very end of the journey—feeding us sensory data designed to keep us invested in protecting and relying on these seemingly separate selves—and ups the ante as we age. Attempting to perpetuate its case for separation realized through fear as children move away, relationships end, our roles in the world change, our own bodies deteriorate, and the "other" bodies we have leaned on begin to disappear.

As I learn to lean on my right mind for translation about what's really happening in this dream, my reaction and attachment to what Susan does or doesn't do, has or hasn't, fears or envies, does begin to fade. The muscle of special self-preservation and judgment gradually begins to atrophy from neglect as I exercise the muscle of forgiveness more and more. That means, of course, that I learn to rely on the part of our shared split mind that sees only our sameness. That recognizes that nothing real was ever threatened by the myriad, bombastic scripts we wrote to prove otherwise and keeps no score about how far along anyone has come on our journey home. But my mind is still split. I still have an ego, and still need a second inner opinion about what seems to be happening to me whenever I'm confused, worried, or upset.

Today, in this moment, I'm willing—for a little while anyway—to tear up my story of self-reliant Susan and recognize that only changing my mind about you will lead me home. Leaning on my right mind means I must see you (and me) differently, and truly. I must release you from the prison of my personal opinions and wishes if I ever hope to find my one, true Self. As I do this one person and situation at a time, the muscle of the ego thought system continues to weaken as the muscle of my right mind grows, well, buff. And I understand—more gradually than I care to admit, but still—that all I really want to do is lean.

Susan Dugan

Be You In Charge

I sat at my desk reviewing the latest tips for stage fright I had downloaded off the Internet.

"Visualize a past success," I read. What were these people smoking? "Just be yourself." Really? Now which self would that be? My little-s-ego self had gotten me into this mess to begin with. And if I could just *be* my capital S Self—the one, eternally loving child of God we are in truth and in truth remain—I wouldn't even be here. "Jesus!" I said. "Houston, we have a problem. Come in Houston." I folded my arms on my desk and nestled my face down against them as if preparing for a crash landing.

"Turbulence?" my imaginary Jesus said, appearing beside me.

I raised my head and let out an exasperated gasp. "Nice to see you, too."

He plucked a yellow sticky note—this one a reminder to calm my nerves by visualizing Jesus beside me during the impending book signing—from the patchwork of others stuck around my desk, and studied it.

"I just can't do this anymore," I said.

He nodded.

"I am so *not* giving this talk. Be you in charge, you understand what I'm saying?"

He was wearing those wacky pink shades, always a hit with the ladies. The beard, the sandals, the simple, nubby robe; you get the picture. He could *so* pull this off.

"You understand I'm not talking about some kind of stinking duet here? I mean, I don't even want to be in the house, you know what I'm saying? I'll just go hit a pool or something. This has got to be entirely your gig or we're screwed."

He jabbed his thumb in the air in a gesture of agreement.

"You're the best," I said. "Now, I've announced it on Facebook. Twice in the last few days; don't like to overdo it. And I've emailed it to a couple of spiritually minded friends and members of my *A*

233

Course in Miracles group. Only to people I'm sure won't be critical or think I've gone round the bend with this book."

"A pretty short list," he said.

"You know it."

"A kind of hierarchy of email lists you've got going?"

"Don't push your luck," I said.

"What about Twitter?" he asked.

"What are you, crazy? I don't even know who most of those people are."

He smiled. "I see."

"Look," I said. "It'll be fine. You're a lot funnier than I am, really."

"Not to mention younger," he said, smiling.

"Hey. Here's the thing, though. If you crash and burn, you're dead meat."

"Crash and burn?" he said. "Seriously?"

I nodded. "Dead meat."

"Whoa," he said, widening his eyes.

"I know. Also, there are a couple things you need to remember. Make sure you mention Helen and Bill. This Course came in answer to a troubled relationship. That's important. And it has nothing to do with bodies, OK? Even when you're talking about God's hands and feet and tears they're only symbols, you know? Meeting us here in the condition we think we're in—blah, blah, blah."

Jesus saluted.

I handed him the little grounding stone someone had given me.

He peered down at it resting in his open palm.

"I'm told it can be very helpful. Keeps you connected with the earth. You feel nervous, just give a little squeeze."

"Magic," he said.

"Only if all else fails, of course."

"'So close to you we cannot fail,' remember?"

"I know, but just in case."

"Plan B," he said.

I nodded, and lowered my voice to a whisper. "And try not to mention how we secretly believe we murdered God, OK? Beginners find that really hard to take."

"Wow," Jesus said. "I hadn't thought of that."

"I know. Exhausting, isn't it?"

"Usurped authority?"

"I like that. See, you're a natural!"

Jesus smiled and adjusted his shades. "It's nothing, really."

"Ha, and funny, too. Just remember, Stevie Wonder, 'you are as God created you.'"

"I know you are but what am I?" Jesus said.

"Cute."

"Can't help it, really."

"And if you get nervous just try to turn it over again. Remember, you're not in charge. I am always with you:

> And if I need a word to help me, He will give it to me. If I need a thought, that will He also give. And if I need but stillness and a tranquil, open mind, these are the gifts I will receive of Him. He is in charge by my request. And He will hear and answer me, because He speaks for God my Father and His holy Son. (from workbook lessons 361-365)

"Well said." He followed me out to my car.

"Break a leg, J." I opened the door and slid the chart I was all too ready to surrender into the back seat. I handed him the keys. "No joyriding, OK?"

"You're funny," he said.

"No you are."

Jesus smiled. "Right."

Shark Week

"You always. You never. Why can't you just? Do you realize you?"

I stood in my kitchen, futilely swatting at fruit flies with a potholder, again replaying the recent accusations of a special relationship like a favorite song stuck in my head. Vaguely, increasingly, and uncomfortably aware that a part of me actually enjoyed the volleyed, verbal return of my silent recriminations, relished the proof that I didn't deserve to awaken from this dream given my many less than admirable qualities and undeniably hateful nature.

It had been that kind of week in the dream; the lid on my personal Pandora's Box of un-forgiven ego issues inexplicably blown wide open. The moods of the dream figure I still sometimes completely forget I am not vacillated as wildly as the disingenuous accusations of the buffoons in Congress I so wanted to blame for the downward trajectory of the country I still sometimes completely forget has nothing to do with what we are.

Then, too, I was recovering from yet another sinus infection, the miserably ironic result of allergies to an explosion of breathtaking wildflowers during a visit to the idyllic mountain town of Crested Butte, Colorado, to attend a wedding. A trip during which a blister resulting from a pair of brand new hiking boots derailed further mountain forays, and an ill-fated attempt to act my daughter's age on the dance floor resulted in a pinched nerve in my hip that has left me hobbling around in battered flip flops since.

Meanwhile, on the home front, a battalion of fruit flies having hitched a ride on a bag of produce were breeding like bunnies in our kitchen, despite the little bowls of apple cider vinegar laced with dish detergent recommended on the Internet, strips of fly paper dangling above the sink (which doesn't work on fruit flies, by the way), and my vigorous attempts to annihilate them with said potholder. On the TV, The Discovery Channel's annual *Shark*

Week—that peculiar, addictive celebration of all things good, bad, and horrific about that most feared of oceanic creatures—had just commenced, spewing spine-tingling footage of sharks in all shapes, sizes, and varieties insatiably hunting their prey.

Whack! Another fly met its maker while my little dog cowered in the corner and the TV narrator at last revealed the venue of the most shark attacks ever recorded in the world (The U.S. House of Representatives, notwithstanding): Florida.

"I knew it," I thought, my mind-on-ego suddenly reviewing a more-than-decade-old video involving the highly suspect shenanigans of another set of politicians in that great Southern state. Until the lyrics of my special relationship misery came boomeranging back again and I found myself once more in that rawest of places, begging for help from you know who to see things differently even as a part of me secretly reveled in the personal feeding frenzy born of a drop of human blood a shark can smell a quarter mile away.

"Jesus," I said, and presto, there he was again—my imaginary friend—in full fantasized regalia. In honor of Shark Week, he had donned a wetsuit and flippers, but had not given up those wacky pink shades I had so come to envy these past few months. He stared down at a bowl of vinegar wherein a dozen fruit fly corpses lay perpetually suspended.

"I did try catching them in a Dixie Cup and taking them outside," I said, understandably growing defensive under his knowing gaze. "Have you ever tried to catch a fruit fly? It doesn't work. I just can't let them take over in here. I mean, they carry disease."

He nodded.

"I know what you're thinking," I said.

"You usually do."

"A minor twinge of annoyance conceals the thought of murder. There's no hierarchy of illusions, blah, blah, blah."

"An illusion is an illusion is an illusion."

"Easy for you to say."

He smiled, adjusting his glasses.

I lowered my voice. "The thing is, there are still sharks every-where you look in this dream."

"You think they can hear us?" He was whispering, too, just in case.

"Let's get real, J. I've been practicing this Course for a pretty long time now. God knows how earnest I've been."

His brows shot up above the frames of his shades.

"OK … maybe not so much with the God part. But I'm here to tell you I honestly don't think." My hip throbbed. Fruit flies swarmed around my head, evoking thoughts of another "F" word if only for the sake of alliteration. I grabbed his arm. "Come on," I said.

We sat on the leather couch in the living room. I turned down the volume, but allowed the TV to continue zooming in on the seductive image of a Great White feeding off an Australian reef, revealing a close-up of its jagged grin and serial-killer eyes. I sighed. "The thing is, I must still feel so guilty, you know? I mean, I go along all right-minded and peaceful for a while and then— bam! I can't seem to stop judging, the incoming attacks begin, and all hell breaks loose."

He handed me a tissue from his infinite, invisible supply.

"You want to know the truth?" I asked.

He nodded.

I leaned toward him, and lowered my voice some more. "I can't stand any of them, sometimes. Not him, not her, not those Bozos in Washington, not *me*. And don't even get me started on the fruit flies."

On the screen a shark opened its cavernous mouth and lunged toward a cage containing an evidently lobotomized photographer in a wetsuit. And I found myself secretly rooting for the shark. I dabbed at my eyes. "I just can't wake up, J!" I said. "It's never going to happen."

Jesus took my hand. On the screen, a person stood on a surfboard off the coast of South Africa, paddling through translucent, turquoise waters above the shadow of a long, fluid, strikingly beautiful shark. My shoulders relaxed.

"I know what you're thinking," I said, recalling a section from that morning's *A Course in Miracles* workbook lesson 181:

> A major hazard to success has been involvement with your past and future goals. You have been quite preoccupied with how extremely different the goals this course is advocating are from those you held before. And you have also been dismayed by your depressing and restricting thought that, even if you should succeed, you will inevitably lose your way again. ...These concerns are but defenses against present change of focus in perception. Nothing more. (from paragraphs 4 and 5)

"Jesus," I said, smacking myself upside the head.

"Hey." He smiled.

"It's only about now, isn't it? What I choose now, in this moment. Not what happened last week or this morning. Not where I'm going. Just right now. That's where my mind is, has always been, and will always be. That's the only place I can go to choose again. The only place I can go to be with you. The only place I could ever be to see things differently. I am so going to ace this course!"

Jesus had his feet up on the coffee table and was fiddling with the volume on the remote. "Now that we got that straightened out, do we get popcorn?" he asked.

Should Healing Be Repeated?

I had just discovered my little dog's "accident" on the upstairs carpet and knelt on the floor with the stain remover and a damp cloth rubbing away. Kayleigh gazed on from a distance, hanging her guilty little head. I didn't have to say anything. We had been here before and she knew only too well I was not pleased. But I wasn't really angry, either. I suspected she had gotten into something at the dinner party we'd hosted the other night and perhaps wanted to signal me to keep an eye on her for the intestinal distress to which she was chronically predisposed. Nevertheless, she cowered in shame, and my heart opened. After all, I knew that look in her eyes all too well, the look we all share over our repressed belief in a secret sin of separation from our source that keeps repeating itself over and over and over again—ad nauseam, no pun intended—here in this dreamy dream of exile from eternal, all-inclusive love.

Downstairs, Kayleigh sprinted across the room—skidding on the hardwood floors in that endearing, cartoonish way of hers—and grabbed the baby chick toy she had pilfered from an Easter basket last Spring and added to her stash. Then she sat on the rug by the door, the chick in her teeth, ferociously shaking it and whacking it against the floor to the tune of its pathetic, mechanical peeping noises. And I suppose she felt better—temporarily anyway—taking her shame out on the chick like that. Projecting her guilt over and over and over on her toys in an effort to exonerate her from the "accidents" to which her nervous system seemed prone.

This got me to thinking about the way in which certain forgiveness scenarios seem to repeat themselves in the classroom of my life over and over and over again. How certain dream figures appear to attack in the same manner, using the same dialogue and body language, over the same issues. Although I apply forgiveness *A Course in Miracles*-style—asking the sane teacher in our one mind for a different interpretation of what's really going on—and receive the comforting assurance that all is well despite the current, repetitive movie of my so-called life's twists and turns; a few days or weeks later I find myself watching—and all too often reacting to—the same scene. Once more in need of help from my right mind and once more doubting this Course will ever heal my perception of my most painful projections.

Asking for help from the loving inner teacher in our one mind with this, led me back to *A Course in Miracles* Manual for Teachers, Section 7, Should Healing Be Repeated, paragraph 5, wherein we learn that doubt is the ego thought system's linchpin, arising from the original belief that we effectively created false selves to defend against the one Self we believe we destroyed.

> The real basis for doubt about the outcome of any problem that has been given to God's Teacher for resolution is always self-doubt. And that necessarily implies that trust has been placed in an illusory self, for only such a self can be doubted. …

The thing is, I *want* to doubt my true capital S Self. That was our wish at the seeming beginning and we believe we got what we wished for; forcing us to project the guilty thought of it into an entire universe of fragmented forms, find one of them to hang out in, and begin reenacting the original projection all over whenever the guilt that never goes away once more surfaces in the back of our mind. Of course we doubt ourselves here in the condition we think we're in, inhabiting separate bodies vying for survival and constantly striving to prove our greater innocence at another's expense. Of course we are secretly invested in keeping the dream intact, its characters and scripts persistent and impenetrable, its stories invincible. But that doesn't mean our mind is not healing each time we choose again.

> … For a teacher of God to remain concerned about the result of healing is to limit the healing. It is now the teacher

of God himself whose mind needs to be healed. (from paragraph 1)

If I find myself doubting that mind-healing has occurred because of circumstances in the plot of my dream, I need to offer my doubt to the part of my mind that remains unwaveringly sure of what I am and what you are. But my mind is split; and although my faith in the stable peace of my right mind is growing every day as I practice the Course's forgiveness, I still believe this personal identity offers me something. I still want to awaken as Susan, to have my Course and my specialness, too, to preserve that original idea of differentiation no matter the cost.

One of the most difficult temptations to recognize is that to doubt a healing because of the appearance of continuing symptoms is a mistake in the form of lack of trust. As such it is an attack. (from paragraph 4)

Although we've repressed the original, hallucinated "attack" on our eternally, whole source, its guilty residue keeps bubbling to the surface again and again and again until our split mind is completely healed and only the invulnerable, undifferentiated love of our true nature remains. Until then, we don't need to worry about the mechanics of our healing or the symptoms of our seeming dis-ease. There are only two choices to make from moment to moment in the dream if we ever hope to awaken: fear/hate or love; only two teachers to learn from: the ego, or the Holy (Whole) Spirit/right mind. Until our split mind is completely healed and we open our eyes, we remain the decision maker, learning to catch ourselves secretly siding with the ego and bringing our guilty choice back to our right mind for translation, the assurance that "not one note in Heaven's song was missed" regardless of what the body's senses tell us.

But even though I know all this and believe it, I can only sing along with that tune in the holy instant, the eternal present in which I join with the right mind's faith that all is well. Even as the movie of my special relationships rewinds and begins again, I must turn over my doubt that this Course is working to the part of my mind that gently smiles at that question, the part of my mind that knows it has nothing to fear, the part of my mind that knows only love. That is the practice, and practice, and practice this path calls for. I must learn to side with the part of my mind that can never fail and knows beyond all shadows of ego doubt that love forever prevails in me and you regardless of the details of the dream. And that recognizing my call for love in your seeming behavior and answering that call with a loving refusal to join with it will bring us all home and remove all doubt for good.

What Is Forgiveness?

An unforgiving thought does many things. In frantic action it pursues its goal, twisting and overturning what it sees as interfering with its chosen path. Distortion is its purpose, and the means by which it would accomplish it as well. It sets about its furious attempts to smash reality without concern for anything that would appear to pose a contradiction to its point of view. (From *A Course in Miracles* Workbook Part II, 1. What Is Forgiveness?, paragraph 2)

A sudden death in the family, moving my daughter to college for the first time, becoming an empty nester while relocating my father-in-law to a retirement home in Denver. Lately, my dream has been filled with complicated endings and beginnings, unexpected forks in the road, and 180-degree shifts in plot and direction so distracting I am often seduced into forgetting I am the dreamer of this dream of so-called life rather than beleaguered protagonist. That—for better or worse—this is *my* dream. I am dreaming it precisely (albeit unconsciously) to prevent me from remembering I collaborated with the ego in crafting and projecting every detail of its production, but can always hire a new, lucid director.

Forgiveness *A Course in Miracles*-style means taking responsibility for my experience back to the mind that made it up in the first place and looking at its concealed purpose with a different collaborator, the Holy (Whole) Spirit or right mind, the part of our one mind that remembered to smile at the "tiny, mad idea" of separation from our one, eternally loving, unified source. The part of our mind that continues to know that nothing that happens in a dream of exile from perfect love—based on repressed guilt over the false idea that we pulled off celestial homicide—could possibly threaten our awakened reality; just as nothing here in our seeming sleeping dreams affects our reality upon awakening.

I have been acutely aware lately of just how much my decision-making mind would like to make the dream real, would like to get lost in the ego's script in which no one could possibly blame Susan for feeling victimized by forces completely beyond her fragile control. But as I have said in these pages before and will likely say again: I know too much. Having asked for a better way of living in this world and made awakening through forgiveness my primary goal, there is really no going back. Having experienced (however intermittently and briefly) the deep release and relief from the crushing bondage of guilt in the mind we all secretly share by choosing the Holy Spirit's vision, I can no longer *completely* deceive myself that the dream is happening *to* me. Even given the current, rapid-fire scenario of seeming loss and complexity I can't quite swallow it all for long without remembering that peace of mind is only a decision away despite the conflicted images on the screen.

I need to remind myself that this world we made—a literal projection of the guilt in the mind over believing we traded eternal oneness for individuality and could never be accepted back into the loving fold—could not possibly hold any lasting comfort. It appeared to arise from a finite lie, and will never ultimately offer us anything we truly want. But unwavering solace and a gentle, knowing smile is only a change of mind away. As we are further reminded in the beautiful description of forgiveness in the second half of *A Course in Miracles'* workbook:

Forgiveness... is still, and quietly does nothing.

Forgiveness, for example, does not curse out Jesus or the big, blue book for failing to deliver when shit happens as it inevitably will. It does not quote *A Course in Miracles* workbook lesson titles to the objects of its projection that appear to be going ballistic. It does not berate the decision maker on having chosen for the ego *again* or indulge in senseless musings about how much time this

Course seems to be taking or why the one Son of God wanted to separate from its source in the first place if he had it so good.

It offends no aspect of reality, nor seeks to twist it to appearances it likes. It merely looks, and waits, and judges not.

Forgiveness does not argue with reality, jump in and try to fix it, or dig in its heels to resist it. Forgiveness takes Jesus' figurative hand and looks straight on, but without judgment, at just what a sneaky little bastard the ego can be. How it will use anything and anyone to improve its ratings with the decision maker. How no story on a micro or macro level is too bizarre, brutal, or fantastic for its purpose. How brilliantly it has mastered its special effects to persuade us to suspend our disbelief and enter and invest in its smarmy world. And how funny that is, really, given the fact that—you know—it doesn't actually exist.

It merely looks, and waits, and judges not.

Forgiveness—unlike the decision maker's mind-on-ego—is patient. It does not measure the success of its ability to forgive and eventually awaken by plot twists and turns in the movie. Its peace does not depend on the behavior or fate of costars, or the fate of its own role. It merely looks compassionately on the decision maker's continuing identification with fear over real love—aware of its insane confusion of fiction and reality—while patiently awaiting the inevitable return to sanity.

But he who would forgive himself must learn to welcome truth exactly as it is.

Forgiveness reminds us that we are always forgiving only ourselves because there is—in truth—only one self, always forgiving what never was because nothing ever happened as a result of the "tiny, mad idea" that we could differentiate ourselves from the indivisible or would possibly want to. When I, the decision maker, choose to join with the ever-available and patiently waiting one right mind within, my perception of what seems to be happening to me or you heals. And I recognize it is all but a movie of my own making. And that after the credits roll—only the love that is all I've ever wanted, the one love we share—remains.

Do nothing, then, and let forgiveness show you what to do, through Him Who is your Guide, your Savior, and Protector, strong in hope, and certain of your ultimate success.

Okey, dokey—I'll have what he's having, please.

You Gotta Wear Shades

"I would just—for once in my life—like to have a little direct experience of God, is that too much to ask? A little preview of our Father's capital L Love, my real, capital S Self, eternal wholeness, boundless, all-inclusive creativity and all that …" I hesitated, considering my present company. "Jazz," I said.

My imaginary Jesus continued walking beside me in Washington Park, taking long, swift strides and swinging his arms to keep up with me. Kayleigh, the microscopic wonder dog, enthusiastically trotted between us, occasionally executing an exuberant twirl among a crowd thankfully thinned by the long Labor Day holiday weekend that had enticed much of Denver's population to the mountains. After two months of dizzying heat, a welcome whiff of fall rode the breeze. The sky shone the vivid blue of medieval Italian paintings, and an embarrassment of green, courtesy of unusual, abundant rain—the dubious up side of climate change—engulfed us.

"I know what you're thinking," I said.

"You usually do."

"What about all those holy instants of release I've had as the results of forgiving? But just for once a direct experience of our true grandeur would be nice, you know? An uninvited recognition that, 'Not one note in Heaven's song was missed.' I mean, *Jesus*, how does that song go? Could you hum a few bars?"

He adjusted his wacky pink shades, and smiled.

"OK, listen. You and I have gotten pretty close, right? How about you put in a good word for me?"

He threw back his head and laughed.

I sighed. Time to get down to what was really bugging me. "See those fields right there?" I said, pointing. "That's where she learned to play soccer. Before the drought came and they closed the fields for good."

Last weekend my husband and I had driven our daughter to college for the first time following a week in which the little scenario I had crafted involving how we would spend our "final days" together had pretty much—like most of my doomed, meteoric fantasies over the many decades I have inhabited this planet—crashed and burned. I had planned to spend quality time together, to do some of those mother-daughter things in the coupon book I had made her a couple years ago for Christmas the extreme busyness of her final two years of high school had prevented her from cashing in. Vouchers for activities such as seeing movies, shopping, getting our nails done, taking day hikes and yes, even baking my famous chocolate chip cookie bars together. *I know.* I had even booked us for an overnight trip to the yoga sanctuary I occasionally flee to in the mountains, hoping to commune together in the idyllic setting and indulge in the fabulous classes, hiking trails, and inexplicably delicious, vegetarian cuisine. But a horrible cold prevented her from taking full advantage of most of the ashram's offerings. Undeterred, I vowed to at least make the whole moving-her-to-college weekend memorable.

We had planned to go down Friday night before the dorms opened for a celebratory dinner at a restaurant I had heard good things about, over which I would deliver some stellar, parting, pearls of wisdom, but a variety of daunting issues prevented it. Instead we rose at dawn and arrived in time to move her into the dorms that opened at 8 a.m.

In case you haven't done this before, let me just say that there is nothing quite like moving your child into college to help you get in touch with your much denied albeit actually quite glaring to the rest of the world, middle-aged geekdom. As the temperature skyrocketed toward its record-breaking 98-degree apex, we attempted to stuff far too many irrelevant belongings into a double room converted by necessity to a triple, ran additional errands to pick up the many items not on our list that now seemed essential, and make nice with other sets of equally apprehensive, emotionally challenged parents and students.

Late that afternoon, the heat at its most life-threatening, we entered the historic, un-air-conditioned college chapel for the president's opening remarks, and returned a couple hours later for an evening program in which a faculty panel downloaded the fear of God into gathered parents and spawn. They explained the rigors of the special program, the minimum six hours of daily homework required, and the extreme competition that would likely cause our children's grades to plummet in the next few weeks to heretofore unknown depths.

After leaving our daughter to fend for herself in the dorms that night for the first time, my husband and I headed to the nearest liquor store to pick up a bottle of wine to bring back to our hotel and wash down the unwelcome news that we had made a terrible mistake. A stampede of like-minded parents—nametags still swinging like ours from their lanyards—had also stormed the premises, providing us with a welcome moment of comic relief in a long, hot, emotionally charged blur of a weekend.

As for the week that followed? Suffice it to say I had never been more aware of the elusive, ephemeral nature of the dream we call life, as I moved about the house and city we'd shared all these years. Try as I might, I couldn't seem to wrap my head around the reality that this long, vivid, engrossing journey of up-close-and-personal parenting had come to such a pedestrian end.

I let out a ragged breath.

Beside me, Jesus still smiled.

Below me, Kayleigh forged on.

"Oh, look, there's the boathouse," I said. "It's under construction right now but we used to stand right there and watch the geese and ducks. They didn't have paddleboats back then; they added those a few years ago. We always talked about renting one, but now ..."

Jesus tilted his head, as if to take it all in. A pelican from mysterious, far-off shores spiraled downward, puncturing the white-capped water.

"And right across the lake there's this Wynken', Blynken', and Nod statue. Every time we passed it I would help her climb up and recite the poem. She would finish each sentence." I swallowed hard.

"It's just that it's been really hard to process, you know? Maybe I've just been too busy dealing with everybody else's emotions. Trying to steel myself against them or comfort them to the point that I have no idea anymore how *I'm* really feeling. But I know what you're thinking. If there is only one self and I am responsible for what I see then these are my emotions merely disguised as coming from another dream figure. Designed to reinforce my belief in other dream figures preventing me from knowing what Susan is feeling, as if Susan is any different from any other dream figure, you know what I'm saying?"

Jesus' brows shot up and down like the late John Belushi's behind the rims of his glasses.

"As a baby she had colic; did I ever mention that? I thought it was probably from all the spicy food I ate while I was pregnant, who knows. But she would cry every day from three in the afternoon until ten at night like clockwork. I would strap her in her snuggly and button her into my jacket and walk around and around this very park in the freezing cold, singing to her and telling her stories. People would give us a wide birth and avert their eyes from the fat, crazy lady crying and singing and talking to herself."

"Ha!"

"I know. We're always talking to ourselves really—who else is there?—but still."

He shook his head to realign his sunglasses on the bridge of his nose without missing a stride.

And then it suddenly came back to me, the whole "seeing differently" thing, I mean. "Hey, could I borrow those glasses?"

To my astonishment Jesus pulled another pair exactly sized for my face out of his pocket and handed them to me. That's just the kind of imaginary action savior he is.

I put them on. "Ah," I said, and couldn't help but smile.

At my feet the dog still twirled. Above my head, the pelicans still banked. Inside my head, my daughter had still gone off to college. Nonetheless, my breaking heart returned to its true default position: eternally open and intact.

"I see," I said. "Maybe I should try these more often."

Jesus just continued to smile. You know how he is.

The End

Well, except that … "This course is a beginning, not an end." (*A Course in Miracles* workbook, Epilogue, paragraph 1, line 1) Hmmm … I think I feel a sequel coming on.